T0109013

Elections and Voters

Also by Martin Harrop

Comparative Government: An Introduction
(with Rod Hague)

Also by William L. Miller

Electoral Dynamics
The End of British Politics?
The Survey Method

Elections and Voters

A comparative introduction

Martin Harrop

and

William L. Miller

NEW AMSTERDAM BOOKS
New York

First published in the United
States of America 1987
NEW AMSTERDAM BOOKS
by arrangement with
Macmillan Education Ltd

0-941533-11-5 (cloth)
0-941533-84-0 (paper)

New Amsterdam Books
171 Madison Avenue, New York, N.Y. 10016

Contents

Preface

When Steven Kennedy of Macmillan suggested we write a textbook on voting behaviour we readily agreed. There clearly was a need for such a book and we felt familiar enough with the literature. We thought it would not take very long to write.

Several years and as many drafts later the manuscript is now complete, but it is no longer restricted to electoral behaviour. To understand voters, we had to understand elections. To understand competitive elections, we had to understand non-competitive elections. And so the book's scope expanded into its present form. To teachers, students (and publishers!) who would have preferred a shorter text restricted to the findings of voting surveys, we can only say that it makes more sense to look at both elections and voters together.

As the book's range has extended, we have drawn more and more on the expertise of our colleagues. We would like to thank Hugh Berrington, Richard Crook, Rod Hague, Stephen White and John Wiseman for their help. We are also grateful to Macmillan's academic readers for their constructive (if occasionally conflicting) advice. The errors and omissions remain our own.

On one point we have not wavered. A textbook written *for* students must be comprehensible *by* students. We are grateful to undergraduates at Glasgow, Newcastle and Strathclyde Universities for ruthlessly expunging any unnecessary jargon from earlier drafts – and for persuading us that most of the jargon *was* unnecessary.

Joint authors often indicate which author wrote which chapters. We began by drafting out half a book each. But as the text evolved we edited each other's drafts with vigour, shifted material between chapters, and recast the structure of the book. A few single-authored paragraphs may have survived, but we take joint responsibility for all the chapters.

MARTIN HARROP
WILLIAM L. MILLER

Preface

1

Introduction

Control and Choice in Elections

Elections concern voters; they also concern governments. Elections are about freedom and choice; they are also about control and constraint. So while this book is primarily about free, competitive elections in Western liberal democracies, it is *not* just about voters freely choosing their governments.

In the first part of the book we look at how the voters' choice is conditioned and restricted by governments and, in particular, by the way governments design electoral systems and organise the conduct of elections. But it would be a mistake to suppose that all constraints and restrictions are imposed on voters by governments and institutions: in a sense voters themselves also restrict their own choice. So in the second part of the book we look at the constraints imposed on the voters by the logic of their own ideologies and belief systems; by their psychological attachments to politicians and parties – their political loyalties; and by their location in a social and spatial environment. Even a book about free elections turns out to be about constraint as much as about freedom. Finally, in the concluding part of the book we look at the functions of elections – at what elections do – in order to see how these elements of electoral freedom and constraint relate to political freedom and control in a wider sense.

We begin, in the next chapter, with a discussion of elections where choice is extremely limited or even non-existent. This serves to highlight some of the functions and characteristics of free elections which are often overlooked. We seek *not* to draw a contrast between free elections and these 'elections without choice' as they are sometimes called: the contrast is obvious even to those who are not students of politics. Instead, we seek to point out the similarities; so that we see free, democratic and competitive elections in a new light – so that we are alert to the ways in which *all* elections can be used for political control, even when they also offer a real element of choice.

But this is a book without a moral. We seek neither to defend competitive elections nor to criticise them unduly. We leave the moral judgements to our readers. Our purpose is to present as comprehensive a picture of elections and voters as is possible within the compass of a short, introductory text. We hope that the picture is complex enough to do justice to the topic without being so technical or qualified as to frustrate our readers.

What do we Mean by a Competitive Election?

Our focus is on *competitive elections for national governments*: if we discuss anything else it is only to provide further perspectives on national competitive elections.

Short definitions will not prove very helpful. The whole book may be taken as an extended definition of competitive elections – a definition grounded on realities, 'warts and all'. Still, a short, theoretical definition may make a useful starting point for discussion. So let us begin by defining an election as a formal expression of preferences by the governed, which are then aggregated and transformed into a collective decision about who will govern – who should stay in office, who should be thrown out, who should replace those who have been thrown out.

Elections can be classified in many different ways but one of the most fundamental is based on the degree of choice offered to the voters. First and foremost this depends upon whether the voter has a choice between parties. Elections and parties are intimately linked. Modern, organised parties are a response to the emergence of a mass electorate which cannot know the candidates for office personally, and a response also to the complexity of modern government which makes it difficult to be aware of all important public issues, still less understand their details. Parties have both clarified and limited the choices available to the voter. To a large extent, it is parties that have made electoral choice meaningful. So the primary question to ask about elections is whether they provide voters with a free choice, a limited choice, or no choice at all *between parties*.

A secondary consideration is whether electors can select from a list of *candidates* for the party they prefer. Many voters do not express a preference for specific candidates from their favourite party even when the electoral system allows them to do so. For most voters the party, its programme and its national leaders are the most significant bases for choice. None the less, the ability to discriminate between candidates from the same party is an important, if secondary aspect of choice. And if the system prevents the voter choosing between parties, the question of whether it allows a choice between candidates becomes much more important.

These criteria – choice of parties and choice of candidates within a party – yield the fourfold classification shown in Table 1.1. In this table, we distinguish between (1) competitive, (2) dominant-party, (3) candidate-choice, and (4) acclamatory elections.

In *competitive elections* the outcome is not predetermined and the result influences the party composition of the next government. Voters are given a clear choice between parties. They may or may not be given the opportunity to state a preference for specific candidates within parties; but that is not the most important aspect of choice. Competitive elections are our main concern in this book,

Table 1.1 *A classification of elections*

		Choice between candidates?	
		Yes	*No*
Choice between parties?	*Yes*	Competitive (e.g. Belgium)	Competitive (e.g. Britain)
	Limited	Candidate-choice/ dominant-party (e.g. Poland*)	Dominant-party (e.g. Mexico)
	None	Candidate-choice (e.g. Kenya)	Acclamatory (e.g. USSR)

NOTE: * In Poland the communist party is very dominant and the degree of party choice extremely limited; so we emphasise the candidate-choice classification for Poland.

but they are the exception in the contemporary world: most elections fall into our other categories.

In *dominant-party elections* voters have a theoretical right to choose between parties but, in practice, the dominant party uses the resources of government to bribe and/or intimidate the voters into supporting it; and it resorts to electoral fraud whenever the voters show excessive support for the minor parties which provide a window dressing of competition. Although dominant-party elections carry the germ of competition, they are a surprisingly common and resilient type of election in the third world – Mexico, the Philippines under President Marcos, Singapore provide examples. East European states provide a modicum of party competition though the grip of the communist party remains tighter than that of dominant parties in the developing world.

By *candidate-choice elections* we mean those where there is little or no choice between parties but voters are allowed a choice between candidates standing under the same party label. Competition over national policy is eliminated but elections can still provide a check on the personal performance of elected officials, and especially on their record as representatives of constituency interests. This strengthens the position of the ruling elites at the centre. China introduced such candidate-choice elections at county level in 1981, but the major examples of this type of election are found in non-communist, one-party states in Africa, such as Kenya.

In *acclamatory elections* voters have no choice at all, whether of candidate, party or policy. From a democratic perspective, elections by acclamation are a sham and a fraud. Mackenzie (1958) says that despite having many of the trappings of a competitive election, they 'belong in substance to the category, not of elections, but of public demonstrations such as May Day processions and Nuremberg rallies'. Acclamatory elections are surprisingly rare: the Soviet Union is the major contemporary example.

There are, of course, other ways of classifying elections. For example, Mackenzie himself distinguishes between *made* and *stolen* elections, according to whether a dominant party rigs the rules to make elections or breaks the rules to steal them. He also has a category of *muddled* elections in which there is plenty of free choice but, in the absence of national parties with competing platforms, not a clear meaningful choice. In the 1960s and 1970s, muddle – in Mackenzie's sense – became the outstanding characteristic of elections in the United States as parties grew weaker and policy platforms less distinct: competition and choice require more than freedom. We shall make use of Mackenzie's terminology from time to time, as well as our own. At the very least, his additional categories show that there is no single 'correct' scheme for classifying elections.

It is easier to spot controlled elections than democratic elections. Bribery, intimidation, maladministration – all are obvious deviations from democratic ideals. But can a democratic election be defined positively as something more than an election lacking obvious flaws? The problems here are considerable. When for example, does a manifesto promise become a bribe? As Dahl (1956, p. 68) has remarked, somewhat sceptically:

> The essence of all competitive politics is bribery of the electorate by politicians. How then shall we distinguish the vote of the Soviet peasant or the bribed stumble-bum from the farmer who supports a candidate committed to high support prices?

One approach to a positive definition of free and democratic elections is to ask how elections would function in an ideal, perfectly democratic society. This is Dahl's approach (1956, pp. 67–71). He suggests the following criteria:

During the voting period

1. All electors vote.
2. All votes carry equal weight.
3. The choice with most votes wins.

But that is not enough. The periods before and after the election also matter. So there are further criteria.

Before the voting period

4. All electors can insert their preferred choice among the scheduled alternatives.
5. All electors have the same information about the choices.

After the voting period

6. Winning choices are implemented.
7. All other decisions are subordinate to those arrived at by voting.

Although there are good theoretical reasons for each of these conditions, the fact is that no society has ever met them. Such criteria provide a democratic *ideal* to which reality can only approximate. A more practical, and less idealistic way of defining free and democratic elections is to list the main concrete characteristics of those elections we recognise as free and competitive. This pragmatic approach is taken by a group of scholars (Butler *et al*., 1981, p. 4) who suggest the following, more mundane, requirements for a democratic election:

1. All adults have the right to vote.
2. Regular elections occur within prescribed time limits.
3. All the seats in the legislature are subject to election and are usually contested.
4. No substantial group is denied the opportunity of forming a party and putting forward candidates.
5. The electoral administration must be 'reasonably fair': neither law, nor violence, nor intimidation should bar candidates from presenting views or voters from discussing them.
6. Votes should be cast freely and secretly, counted and reported honestly, and converted into legislative seats as prescribed by law.
7. Those elected should be installed in office and remain in office until their terms expire or a new election is held.

At least with a list like this we could describe an election as more or less democratic even if we should hesitate to categorise it into an ideal category of totally democratic or undemocratic elections.

But even this list is incomplete. In particular, a democratic election should place some limits on the inequalities in media coverage of the main contenders as well as limiting differences in campaign spending between them.

To sustain free and democratic elections, the wider political environment must also meet certain conditions. Political democracy no less than economic development needs some infrastructure. Mackenzie (1958, p. 4) lists four such conditions:

1. An independent judiciary to interpret electoral law.
2. An honest, competent and non-partisan administration to run elections.
3. A developed system of political parties, well-enough organised to put their policies and leaders before the electors as alternatives between which to choose.
4. An acceptance throughout the political community of certain rules of the game which structure and limit the struggle for power.

These requirements are a good deal less severe than Dahl's theory-based list, but in a world of over 160 states there are only about 30 democracies where the government stands a real chance of being replaced through the ballot box. If there are no countries which satisfy Dahl's democratic *ideal*, the more important point is that most countries do not come anywhere near meeting even a *pragmatic* list of requirements for democracy.

National elections based on a mass suffrage are a modern phenomenon, largely inspired by the American and French Revolutions. The United States was the first Western country to develop a mass electorate and a national party system. Voting turn-out reached 80 per cent among white adult males in the 1840 presidential election. Intense competition between Whigs and Democrats was fuelled by a popular press – and by the absence of alternative entertainments! (See Burnham, 1965; also Chambers and Burnham, 1966)

In Western Europe, by contrast, mass suffrage was achieved later and with more difficulty, in response to the political demands of industrial workers. The first modern election in Europe took place in France after the revolution of 1848. Although the reforms of 1848 were soon rescinded, the French example launched waves of pressure for democratisation throughout Europe. A lengthy struggle eventually led to the mass electorates of today.

Representative institutions and concepts of constitutional government came *before* mass elections in Western Europe. Their origin lay in medieval notions about corporations and estates. The nobility, the clergy and in some countries the corporations of merchants and artisans, and freehold peasants, were all represented in the capital. The churches, both Catholic and Protestant, also developed their own systems of internal representation and elections. Remnants of medieval tradition survive in Britain's House of Lords. Other countries generally replaced their old estates with new, normally two-chambered assemblies. But whether pre-reform institutions survived or not, the history of modern elections in Western Europe is the story of how political rights were extended from the members of these corporations to virtually the whole adult population.

The development of mass elections was fundamentally different in Eastern Europe and the Third World. These contrasts explain why competitive elections are so rare outside the West. In Russia and most of Eastern Europe there is no historical tradition of restraint on state power. There is no parallel to the long process by which the British House of Commons acquired the political initiative from the Monarchy. There was no popular control over the power of rulers to tax and coerce their mainly peasant populations. Long before communist rule, dominant bureaucracies were untrammelled by ideas of parliamentary sovereignty. As White, Gardner and Schöpflin (1982, p. 44) point out in their discussion of the history of communist states:

> The discretionary power of the state inherently excluded the doctrine of parliamentary sovereignty and resulted in the transformation of legislatures into facades. In the entire pre-communist period there was only one instance of a ruling government losing power through elections (Bulgaria, 1931); rather, a new prime minister would be appointed by the managers from the power elite and he would 'make elections' by using the coercive power of the state.

This history of the supremacy of state over society was reflected in, and sustained by, communist rule.

In the Third World, elections based on a mass suffrage were introduced during the late colonial period or immediately after decolonisation. Their purpose was to ensure a government was in place once the colonial power had left. But there was even less of a tradition of free elections in the developing world than in Eastern

Europe. Colonialism, after all, is inherently undemocratic. Hurriedly erected institutions to which elections were held in the former colonies also lacked the support of tradition. Parliaments had not evolved from traditional institutions in the manner of Britain's House of Commons. Elections survived but competition did not. Elections became entangled in the social networks linking rich, powerful 'patrons' to their less fortunate 'clients'. Whereas in the communist world prospects for truly democratic elections were dimmed by the dominance of the state over society, in the developing countries the problem was that the state itself was too weak to withstand the power of traditional social elites or military adventurers.

Why Study Elections?

This book examines elections to government office, focusing on national elections in free societies. Why is this a worthwhile subject? After all, various critical studies have suggested that the electorate is incapable of making rational decisions about policy, that electoral systems are incapable of transforming votes into parliaments which truly reflect the electors' views, that parliaments cannot control governments, and that governments cannot alter the march of events.

One reason for studying elections is simply to see whether this pessimism is justified. Do elections make a difference? What do they influence? Under what conditions do they exert more or less influence? What kind of influence do they have? Do they help the weak or the strong? Are they instruments of popular control or the tools of government? Do they stabilise society or do they disrupt it? We need to study elections to find out what they do.

Another good reason for studying elections is to find out about society and politics in general. Elections provide a major test of the political system: 'in these moments of decision, with argument at its height and parties at their most active much of the essential nature of a country's politics can be revealed' (Butler, 1981, p. 9). A close look at a nation's electoral system and electoral behaviour reveals the extent to which elites dominate society and whether they do it by coercion or manipulation, by intention or by default.

It reveals how open that society is to new people and new ideas, how far it is willing to tolerate disagreement and dissent. Electoral patterns show how different social groups interact with each other, how individuals interact with their families and friends, how they respond to the actions of political elites or the content of the mass media.

Asking why people vote the way they do also takes us into the study of political attitudes and ideologies. Do people have strong views about political issues? Or do they see politics more in terms of leaders? Do they have coherent ideologies? Or do they simplify the political world by viewing it in terms of party rather than ideology? How stable are people's political attitudes over time? Are people willing to defer to leaders on policy? Studying voting behaviour, therefore, tells us something about mass political psychology.

Elections also provide valuable indicators of social and political change. Is class voting declining, or are social classes changing so much that they need redefinition? Are ethnic and regional divisions fading or intensifying? Are people becoming more or less interested in politics? Are they becoming more or less ideological, more or less attached to the political system, mor or less disillusioned with party politics, more or less influenced by the mass media? Studying elections through time may reveal not just trends in the elections themselves but also trends in underlying social, economic and political processes.

If the study of elections can help to answer this range of questions it will need no further justification.

Further Reading

On the definition of an election, and the development of modern elections in the West, see Rokkan (1970). Butler *et al.* (1981) is another useful guide. For the distinctive history of elections in the United States, see Chambers and Burnham (1967). Dahl (1956) is an influential analysis of the concept of a democratic election. Mackenzie's (1958) discussion of free elections is more practical; it reflects his experience with elections in Commonwealth countries two decades ago, but is none the less still worth reading.

References

BURNHAM, W. (1965) 'The Changing Shape of the American Political Universe', *American Political Science Review*, vol. 59, pp. 7–28.

BUTLER, D. (1981) 'Electoral Systems', in D. Butler *et al*. (eds) *Democracy at the Polls* (Washington, DC: American Enterprise Institute).

CHAMBERS, W. and BURNHAM, W. (eds) (1966) *The American Party Systems* (New York: Oxford University Press).

DAHL, R. (1956) *A Preface to Democratic Theory* (Chicago: Chicago University Press).

MACKENZIE, W. J. M. (1958) *Free Elections* (London: Allen & Unwin).

ROKKAN, S. (1970) *Citizens, Elections, Parties* (New York: McKay).

WHITE, S., GARDNER, J. and SCHÖPFLIN, G. (1982) *Communist Political Systems: an Introduction* (London: Macmillan).

Part I

Elections: Control Versus Choice

First of all, we look at elections from an institutional perspective. How are elections organised and controlled? How do they contribute towards the more general political control of society? Conversely, what institutional arrangements allow or even encourage freedom of choice and expression? How effectively do they send a message from the governed to the governors? Or from the government to the people?

The restraints and controls that we discuss in this section are primarily external to the voter: they are imposed by 'the system', by the constitution or by those in power. In the second part of the book we shall turn to the restraints and controls that are imposed upon the voters by themselves.

We begin with a chapter on elections in communist states and in the Third World, that is in areas where elections are more about control than about choice. But there is not a simple, clear cut, absolute difference between these elections and elections in the West. Voters in communist and Third World states do have some influence on their rulers. And our next chapter, on Western-style electoral systems, shows how often Western governments try to control those elections which do emphasise choice.

Finally, we look at competitive elections as a communications device: how well do they 'send a message' from the voters? Does freedom of expression for the individual voter lead to freedom of expression for the electorate, or just an uninterpretable cacophony? Do elections convey a meaning, a mandate, or a message?

2

Political Control: Non-competitive Elections

Elections are common but choice is rare. Only a handful of states dispense with elections altogether but only a quarter hold competitive free elections (Taylor and Jodice, 1983, citing 1979 data). Most contests are either a one-horse race or a competition in which only one horse is given a clear run. Although elections without choice are important in their own right they also provide an instructive comparison with competitive elections. This is a matter of similarities as well as differences. By considering the functions common to competitive and non-competitive elections, a deeper understanding emerges of the role played by the electoral process in Western democracies.

Our introduction distinguished three sorts of non-competitive elections. These were *acclamatory* elections, which allow no choice at all; *candidate-choice* elections, which allow some choice of candidates but none of party; and *dominant-party* elections, which permit a degree of party competition as long as it does not threaten the pre-eminent position of the major party. This chapter considers examples of all three types.

We begin by looking at elections under communism, using the Soviet Union (elections by acclamation) and Poland (candidate-choice elections) as case-studies before discussing the question 'what do communist elections do?'. Then we turn to the developing world, taking Mexico (dominant-party elections) and Kenya (candidate-choice elections again) as case studies. Comparison of Poland with Kenya will show that communist rule dramatically weakens the role of elections in comparison with non-communist one-party states.

Elections Under Communism

Many discussions of communist elections concentrate on showing how the reality of communist party rule makes a mockery of their own ostensibly democratic constitutions. There is an implied contrast with an idealised image of competitive elections in Western democracies. Of course it is indeed a central feature of communist elections that they must not threaten the dominant position of the communist party. In that sense they are 'elections without choice' (the evocative title of Hermet, Rose and Rouquie's (1978) book). But this is a starting point, not a conclusion. It raises questions about why the political systems of the Soviet Union and Eastern Europe are not election-centred; about the distinctions which can and should be made between different communist elections; and about the functions of elections in communist societies.

The non-competitive nature of communist elections reflects the historical experience of communist states, which generally lack a liberal and democratic tradition. (Czechoslovakia and East Germany are partial, but only partial, exceptions). In general, communist rule did not replace competitive elections but provided a new justification of autocracy. Under Marxism-Leninism, the leading role of the party is justified by its ability to lead society towards communism. The party's objective is to transform society so that communist self-government becomes possible; power must be centralised before central authority dissolves. It is no part of the party's task to support representative political institutions which would merely mirror the imperfections of present-day society. On the other hand, as part of the supposed transition to communist direct democracy, communist parties *do* encourage direct citizen involvement in *administration*, albeit guided by the party itself. The result is that competitive elections are squeezed out between these two elements of centralisation and participation.

Ideological scepticism and the reality of party rule mean that elections in communist states are less significant than in the West. Campaigns are frequent but ritualistic. Once over, they are soon forgotten. No one would write the political history of Soviet politics in terms of Soviet elections. This is in contrast to Communisty Party Congresses, the pronouncements of which serve as points of reference for years to come (Friedgut, 1979). This position is now changing somewhat, as ruling communist parties become more concerned with maintaining the *status quo* than with transforming society, though even today communist states are not election-centred.

However elections in communist states do vary significantly within the framework of one-party rule (Pravda, 1978, 1986). There are essentially two types of election in communist countries: *elections by acclamation* and *candidate-choice elections* (see Table 2.1). In terms of Mackenzie's somewhat different classification, the two types of communist elections are *elections by acclamation* and *made elections*. (*Made* rather than *stolen* because communist hegemony is so great that there is no longer any need

Table 2.1 *Elections in communist states*

Type	*Acclamation*	*Candidate-choice*
Candidates/seats	One	More candidates than seats
Policy programme	One	One, but candidates interpret it differently
Candidate selection	By executive decision	More influence exerted by voters' meetings
Consequences for tenure	None	None for party, some for individual incumbents
Consequences for national policy	None	Minimal
Consequences for local policy	Minimal	Some
Current examples	USSR Czechoslovakia Bulgaria Albania	(Less choice) East Germany Poland (More choice) Yugoslavia Hungary Romania

SOURCE: Adapted from Pravda (1986).

to stoop to corruption, stuffed ballot boxes or crude personal intimidation in order to secure communist victory.)

The crucial point of contrast lies in the number of candidates per seat. In acclamatory elections, there is only one candidate per seat. The choice of candidate is firmly controlled by the party; all candidates fight on the same platform; there is pressure to achieve a virtually complete turn-out; and the election has virtually no effect upon public policy. The Soviet Union under Stalin was the prime example of *acclamatory* elections under communist rule. Contemporary elections in the Soviet Union, Albania, Czechoslovakia and Bulgaria still fit squarely into this category through the latter two countries do permit some non-communist parties to participate in elections through a communist-dominated front.

Elsewhere in Eastern Europe, in Poland, East Germany, Romania, Hungary, Yugoslavia – and even in China as well, there has been some movement towards *candidate-choice* elections. These allow more candidates than seats, particularly at local level; candidates sometimes differ in their interpretations of the national election platform; voters have some say in the selection of candidates; and the results can influence policy, especially at local level. Broadly, there are two main routes through which limited choice has been offered to voters in communist states. The first, favoured by Poland and East Germany, is to have more candidates than seats but to rig the rules so that official party candidates are strongly advantaged. In Poland, this is done by placing official candidates at the top of the ballot paper, and deeming an unmarked ballot to be a vote for the top candidates. As it is easiest, and politically safest, for voters to place their ballots directly in the box without entering the booth to alter the ranking on the ballot, top candidates have a large advantage.

The second route to choice is taken in Romania, Yugoslavia and (until 1983) Hungary. This avoids in-built bias but ensures that in practice the senior communist party candidates, and the most important posts, are elected unopposed. Steps are also taken to avoid contests between communist candidates and those from satellite parties; choice is between individuals of similar rank, not between parties or national policies. More choice – and more real choice – is also provided at local level. Hungary and Yugoslavia also employed an element of indirect election to provide further insurance against electoral risks.

Candidate-choice elections are becoming more common in communist states. Within the last thirty years they have replaced elections by acclamation in Hungary, Romania and East Germany. Even China has begun to place more weight on its electoral process. With the exception of a major campaign in 1953, China has long preferred indirect elections above the local level. However, direct elections were introduced at county level in 1980/1. Voters were given a choice of candidates in what officially became a secret ballot. This reform was initiated by the centre as a way of monitoring local officials, most of whom opposed this threat to their position. This 'oversight' function is common in elections in communist states.

The Hungarians introduced more radical reforms in their 1983 electoral law. Some seats in parliament were reserved for the unopposed 'national list', but most Hungarian MPs were elected from territorial constituencies as in Britain. The 1983 law *required* contested elections in these constituencies. An absolute majority, that is 50 per cent of the vote, was needed for election – otherwise a run-off was held later, not necessarily with the same candidates. Only 98 of the 172 incumbents who stood in these constituencies at the 1985 election were re-elected on the first ballot; 54 lost outright, and another 20 had to face a run-off. All candidates had to subscribe to the party programme; so we should not overstate the amount of choice offered in this election, but voters clearly acquired the ability to throw (some) incumbent politicians out, even if they could not overturn the government or its policies. In the context of elections in communist states, this was a substantial development.

Toleration of non-communist candidates in several East European countries reflects a small but growing degree of political pluralism. Lacking the power, and perhaps the desire, to hold Soviet-style plebiscites, ruling parties in the more liberal communist states take a small risk that elections will not fuel opposition to their own supremacy. As we will see, this is a problem which has often confronted the Polish party. Its grip on power is not so firm as to allow complete control of elections, at least in times of political crisis. Because *made* elections are easily *unmade* when the opportunity arises, they can rapidly become an arena of political conflict.

Acclamatory Elections: The USSR

Soviet elections involve more participation by more citizens than in the West. Emphasis on mass involvement in the electoral process is characteristic of plebiscites; but the participation is of course carefully controlled. The Soviet Union has over 50 000 units of government, more than 2.2 million elected deputies, holds local elections every two and a half years, and uses reputable citizens rather than paid bureaucrats to administer elections – over 9 million of them for the 1975 elections. While all of these participants in the electoral process must operate under the general control of the party, it is none the less true that citizen involvement in Soviet elections is much greater than in the West.

In acclamatory elections, which give no choice to the voters, nomination is the crucial and most interesting phase of the electoral process. The actual voting is of no importance, said one communist official: 'It has all the inevitability of a marriage ceremony. The courting of the bride has been done.' The nomination process in the Soviet Union typifies the general character of their elections: it involves more people than in the West but real power is concentrated in even fewer hands. Deputies are nominated for local Soviets at work-place meetings. These gatherings confirm the candidates proposed by an authorised organisation, such as a trade union, which has itself often been prompted by the party. Once nominated, a candidate stands as a representative of the 'Bloc of Communist and Non-Party People'. This symbolises the 'unity' of party and people.

The degree of control exerted by the local party over nominations is seen in the success with which deputies are distributed by age, sex and occupation in accordance with quotas laid down by Moscow. However, party control does mean that workers and women are more strongly represented on elected bodies than in the West. Above the local level many deputies are elected *ex officio*; these form a majority of representatives at national level. Thus, even the formal involvement of ordinary voters in the nomination process is concentrated on elections to *local* Soviets.

The local campaign is led by 'agitators' who lecture the public on the virtues of the Soviet Union and its electoral system. Canvassers visit electors to up-date the electoral list and listen to complaints. It all happens under strict party control though neither the agitators nor the canvassers need be party members themselves.

On election day, the activists are out in force doing their bit to raise turn-out to the high levels demanded in acclamatory elections. Efforts to maximise turn-out go far beyond those attempted in the West and are particularly striking when compared with the relaxed approach of Anglo-American regimes. Elections are held on a Sunday which is declared a public holiday. Polling stations are set up in hospitals, on ships and at railway terminuses. Turn-out *statistics* are also boosted by more dubious means. Electors for example can easily obtain a 'Certificate of Right to Vote Elsewhere', which removes them from the register in their home constituency but does not automatically add their name to another register – a traditional way of withholding support for the regime without incurring its wrath. By such fair means and foul, turn-outs of 99.99 per cent (the level achieved in 1984) are regularly reported in Soviet elections. In 1975, for example, only 65 out of 1.5 million people reportedly failed to vote in Tadzhikistan! But the real turn-out – votes cast as a proportion of the adult population – is probably closer to 75 per cent, similar to that in many Western democracies (Friedgut, 1979; White, 1985).

Elections by acclamation necessarily produce an overwhelming vote for the official candidate. The Soviet Union is no exception. To be elected, candidates must receive over half the votes cast; normally they receive almost unanimous votes – 99.94 per cent and 99.95 per cent in elections for the two chambers of the Supreme Soviet in 1984. Defeats occur only at local level, mostly at village level, and these are followed by a second election. The number of defeats fell from 249 in 1961 to sixty-eight in 1975 – about one in 30 000 (Friedgut, 1979, p. 130). There is no doubt that most Soviet citizens who vote do in fact vote for the official candidate; false counting is not the explanation. Nor is the procedure for casting ballots a major biasing factor in the contemporary Soviet Union. To vote for the candidate, the ballot can be placed directly in the box; to vote against, or to consider the matter in depth, electors enter a private booth. But there no longer seems to be much risk attached to entering the booth. The real reason why candidates obtain massive majorities is that Soviet citizens fully understand the first law of survival in totalitarian states: don't make waves.

Were party control ever to relax, elections in the Soviet Union could become more fully democratic than those in the West. There is no *constitutional* restriction on contested elections, for example, though since the revolution the strictly maintained *tradition* has been one candidate per seat. The massive number of elected bodies, the extent of citizen involvement in election administration, the widespread consultation over nominations, the broad spread of people elected to the Soviets, the enormous efforts of the agitators and the ease of turn-out combine to produce a network of institutions which has enormous democratic potential. In addition, deputies in the Soviet Union can be recalled for unsatisfactory behaviour; about 600–700 are recalled each year, rather more than are defeated at the election. There is also a system of 'imperative mandates' whereby voters' meetings held during a campaign can *require* a local deputy to consider implementing its requests for community improvements once the election is over. In 1980 over 16 000 mandates were adopted by deputies, the majority of which were reported to have been fulfilled – a claim that echoes the findings of Rose and Pomper on British and American elections (White, 1985). Apart from California and a few populist states nearby, both the recall and the imperative mandate are almost unknown in the West. But these institutions, along with the entire electoral process in the Soviet Union, are overseen by the party to ensure that democratic potential does *not* become democratic reality. In particular as long as there is only one candidate per seat, Soviet electors will be denied a real choice.

Candidate-choice Elections: Poland

Poland is an interesting example of candidate-choice elections under communism. Its addition of a modicum of competition to what is still fundamentally a one-party state is more typical of communist states than the monolithic elections of the Soviet Union. But even the small amount of competition permitted in Poland has created periodic problems for the Polish communist party, which has never been as secure as ruling parties elsewhere in Eastern Europe.

There are three parties in Poland. These are the ruling communist party (officially the Polish United Workers Party) and two separate Socialist parties – the Peasant Party and the Democratic Party. At elections these organisations form a national front – 'The Patriotic Movement of National Rebirth' – which has a single programme. The result is to eliminate competition over policy.

Elections to the national Assembly (*Sejm*) are from multi-member constituencies which aim for, but in the past did not always achieve, half as many candidates again as seats. New laws in 1984 *required* twice as many candidates as seats. (A similar change took place in Hungary at about the same time.) Even competition reflects the dictat of the centre! As in the Soviet Union, however, the process of nomination is firmly guided by the communist party. This ensures that communist candidates predominate. In contrast to the USSR, there is also a solid sprinkling of nominees from the minor parties, but communist control means that official candidates normally occupy the favoured top positions on the ballot paper.

A single national platform, control over nominations, and control over the order of candidates on the ballot – these are the direct mechanisms by which the Polish communist party 'makes' elections. But indirectly the party can also make elections by its monopoly of government and of patronage. Because there is no alternative government, the party can cajole the electorate into a 'correct' vote by threatening to raise food prices or lengthen working hours if the voters misbehave. As individuals, electors may feel they will lose a high position on the housing list, or a university place for their child, if they do not turn out to vote on election day.

The famous election of January 1957 illustrates the capacity of ruling parties to 'make' elections. This was the first communist election to take place in the relatively liberal reformist atmosphere produced by the death of Stalin and the relaxation of Soviet influence. But electoral reform is a delicate task: popular expectations ran ahead of reality and the communist party feared many voters would use the ballot to express their opposition to the leading role of the party in society. So the popular leader Wladyslaw Gomulka, himself a former victim of Stalinism, was forced to turn the election into a plebiscite on his programme of political liberalisation. In a crucial radio broadcast on the eve of the poll he played his last card – the threat of a Soviet clamp-down, and an end to the reforms, if the election result revealed strong anti-communist feelings: the electorate, not the government, was on trial, he declared. The gamble paid off: in the event only one in ten voters crossed any of the officially favoured candidates off the ballot.

Polish elections also illustrate how important the question of turn-out becomes when there is limited electoral competition. The legitimising power of high turn-out is particular vital when the authority of a regime is already under attack. Consider for example the local elections of 1984. Normally a routine affair, these elections were held against the back-drop of a floundering economy, a hostile church, and a dramatic loss of authority to the free trade union movement, Solidarity. Solidarity called for an election boycott and the church, which had urged its members to turn-out and vote in Gomulka's hour of need, refused to help Jaruzelski by doing so again in 1984. (In passing, we should note that principled abstention has been a recurrent tactic of the disaffected Catholic community in Northern Ireland; it is not limited to communist regimes.)

So the 1984 local elections became a crucial public test of whether the party could control events. It fought a clever campaign, deflating rather than inflating expectations by announcing that even a 70 per cent turn-out would be satisfactory. (Presidential hopefuls use the same tactic in United States nomination campaigns, see Chapter 4.) The authorities again provided the incentives to vote which are available to a party with a monopoly of government. At a collective level, they hinted that political prisoners would be released if the boycott failed; on an individual level considerable pressure was applied to electors in rural areas where the electoral commissioner might also be responsible for such crucial matters as the distribution of fertiliser. Simple coercion was also used to a limited extent: people who produced pro-boycott leaflets were arrested. And behind the Polish government stood the threat of Soviet intervention. As in 1957, the 1984 election was a test of the electorate as much as of the government, and the External Examiner had the ultimate power of decision.

In the event the government claimed a 75 per cent turn-out though Solidarity's monitoring exercise indicated only 60 per cent. But either way, that was a substantial government success and an election which might have further weakened the party's authority ended up by strengthening it, internally and externally.

What Do Communist Elections Do?

The question is, why bother? Why invest time, effort and organisation in holding elections which offer so little choice to the electorate? It used to be fashionable to dismiss all elections that fail to approximate the liberal-democratic norm as non-events with no purpose, no consequence, no function. We do not take that moralistic view. Instead we ask 'what do communist elections do?', 'what functions do they serve?' There are a number of answers, which we list below (see White, 1985 and Pravda, 1986 for a fuller discussion). But there is no escape from the fact that communist elections allow little or no choice by the voters. Indeed it is very important to realise that *voting* is *not* the central feature of communist elections either in theory or in practice. There has been a trend to more choice between personalities in parts of Eastern Europe, but in all communist elections the central features of elections are *consultation*, *nomination*, and *campaign*, not *voting*. Their functions (intended and unintended) include the following list, which is expanded below:

1. Formal reassertion of the doctrine of popular sovereignty.
2. Legitimation.
3. Mobilisation and popular education.
4. Feedback and consultation.
5. Representation.
6. Control through co-option and co-responsibility.
7. Control through affirmation of inequality.
8. National integration.

Formal reassertion of the doctrine of popular sovereignty

Although this claim rests either on convoluted logic or simple hypocrisy it does transmit the notion of bottom-up control to future generations and keeps alive the prospect of elections with real choice.

Legitimation

'The outcome of the elections shows that the people see the regime as legitimate, except for an infinitessimal section' – that was government spokesman, Imre Pozsgay's, claim after the 1985 Hungarian elections. Communist leaders protest too much about the legitimising effects of their elections. Where elections really do legitimise the regime there is far less talk about that aspect of elections.

There have been a few occasions – Poland in 1957 and 1984, Hungary in 1958, and Czechoslovakia in 1971 – when elections may have had some effect in legitimising the regime in the eyes of its subjects. Significantly these were all elections that followed a severe crisis, and usually a military clampdown.

In general, however, we do not believe that communist elections legitimate regimes by winning the hearts and minds of the voters. What little evidence is available suggests that the attitudes of Soviet citizens to their elections vary 'from tolerance and indifference to cynicism and contempt'. Most vote for the official candidate, but surveys show that many electors have no idea who they are voting for. This is not to say that communist states lack legitimacy in the eyes of their subjects; it is to say that such legitimacy as they possess is based on success in war and industrialisation, on socio-economic *performance* in matters like the provision of a health service and maintenance of full employment, not on support for communist *procedures* and certainly not on elections. When economic performance falters, the regime may try to buy some popularity by liberalising its electoral system as Hungary did recently. But it is the *change* in the system, the new concession to pluralism, not the new system as such, that wins support.

No, the reason why communist regimes stress the legitimising effects of their elections, is that elections legitimise the regimes *in their own eyes*. Additionally, the Soviet satellites, particularly Poland use elections to legitimise themselves *in Soviet eyes*. The classic example is Gomulka's use of the 1957 Polish election to stave off a Soviet invasion.

Mobilisation and popular education

Communist elections are used to express the party's programme and priorities, to educate and inform citizens about current problems, and furthermore, to educate and inform the citizens about the communist system of government. Campaign themes are taken from Party Congresses and include details of the latest economic plan – though it seems most people do not listen.

Similarly, the criteria used to select deputies represent another public statement of party priorities. Choosing deputies with a good production record indicates the party's continuing emphasis on economic performance. 'Heroes of Socialist Labour' are rewarded with a spell on a village soviet.

Feedback and consultation

Even in the Soviet Union elections provide an enormous amount of feedback information for the party leaders and a lot of genuine consultation does go on. Individual party leaders can rate their personal standing, not by the number of votes they receive in their constituency, but by the number of constituencies in which they are nominated. (The record is held by Leonid Brezhnev who received 138 nominations in 1970.) Modestly, they withdraw their candidature in all but one.

Elections test the quality of local organisation. They enable the central party to ask: why is turn-out low in this area, and why were there so many spoilt ballots in that village? Elections enable the centre to monitor the performance of local officials, which is one reason why the party has resisted occasional calls to abolish the secret ballot.

Mandates given at local nomination meetings are important in Soviet elections even if candidate selection is not. Along with the complaints made to canvassers and the comments written by voters on ballot slips, mandates are carefully monitored and considered, if not obeyed. Soviet politicians are responsible to their superiors, not their electors, but they are expected to keep the electorate as happy as possible within the constraints imposed by party policy. Complaints at Soviet election meetings get leaky roofs fixed and potholes mended just as they do in the West.

Representation

Soviet elections do not provide representation by party competition but they do provide representation by *quota* and *rota*. First, the centre decrees the quotas of men and women, old and young, bosses and workers, ethnic groups and so on, who are to be elected. Next it insists on a high turnover. So in addition to the fact that about two million people sit as elected members of Soviets at any one time, turnover ensures that many more have had, or soon will have, some experience in government and administration.

Control through co-option and co-responsibility

These millions of Soviet deputies and ex-deputies 'stand shoulder to shoulder' with the party in helping to administer the country.

Deputies and commissioners may have some sense of co-responsibility instilled into them by their participation even if ordinary voters remain cynical. None the less, the party rather than the Soviet remains the key channel of political recruitment in Russia and Soviet deputies are even more powerless than British local government councillors.

Control through affirmation of inequality

The fundamental function of acclamatory elections is to affirm political inequality. They are a device by which the party says to the people, 'We are still in charge! See how we persuade you to vote for us!' Whatever voters may think about the elections, their participation in it is an *act of compliance*. For many authoritarian regimes compliance is the most that can be hoped for – or even the most that is sought, though communist regimes are sufficiently ideological to hope for more than passive acquiescence. Yet for all the stress on participation in Marxism-Leninism, Russian elections are devoid of spontaneity and initiative. Quality of participation is sacrificed to quantity. As Zaslavsky and Brym (1978, p. 371) note, legitimacy comes second to obedience:

> Elections encourage citizens to demonstrate that they have adjusted to the fiction of democracy in the Soviet Union. Elections buttress the regime – not by legitimising it, but by prompting the population to show that the *illegitimacy* of its 'democratic' practice has been accepted and that no action to undermine it will be forthcoming.

National integration

Finally, communist leaders try to use elections to integrate the various regions, ethnic groups, and interests in the nation. Party and non-party (but not anti-party) people are both complimented on their valiant efforts to create a better world. It has all the flavour of an Annual Company Dinner with a vote of thanks to all concerned and workday tensions concealed behind the smiles. Whether it produces more good feeling than cynicism we do not know.

Elections in the Third World

> Chief, I have done everything as you asked me to. Now I would like to know who I voted for.
>
> (Brazilian voter)

> Now son, never ask me that kind of question and above all do not forget that the vote is secret.
>
> ('Colonel' Chico Heraclio, quoted in Rouquie, 1978, p. 19)

Elections in the Third World are as diverse as the countries in which they occur – from the grotesque parodies staged by bloody dictators to relatively free and democratic elections.

Latin American governments seem to be thrown out of office by military coups as much as by elections. Yet when they are not being governed by juntas, and especially during the transitions from military to civilian rule, Latin American nations have had relatively democratic elections. Ghana and Nigeria similarly enjoyed particularly open electoral competition during their transitions from military to civilian rule in 1969 and 1979.

None the less, Third World elections rarely produce alternation in office between parties representing different ideologies. Post-colonial states in which the opposition has taken control of central government after a contested election are few and far between: Barbados (1976), India (1977, 1980), Jamaica (1972, 1980), Mauritius (1982, 1983) and Sri Lanka (1977). It has yet to happen at all in Africa (Clapham, 1985, p. 67): even the relatively competitive systems of Senegal, Botswana and Gambia have not yet passed the fiery test of an opposition victory at the polls. Latin America (for example, Colombia) and the Caribbean (Jamaica) do yield some instances of election-led changes in the party forming the government. Yet even there parties compete over the particular rewards they can offer to specific groups of supporters rather than over general policy issues.

So a single question underlies the diversity of elections in the Third World: why is policy competition between parties so rare? The answer lies in the limited extent of *political* development. In the Western world, competitive elections fought on a mass suffrage only emerged after central government had established its authority over society. But in the developing world, national government is still weak. The state lacks the political strength and autonomy needed to sustain competitive elections even though it has a dominant role in economic affairs. So it is simply a profitable mine to be exploited by powerful groups and individuals for their own benefit. Like a lion with a kill in a drought, those who control the state in a poor country are extremely reluctant to share their prize. Further, politicians and people both regard *economic* development as a more crucial priority than establishing competitive elections. Economic development requires mobilising resources in order to change society rather than sharing resources in order to reflect it. Thus, no powerful group in society has a strong interest in competitive elections; even the voters are oriented to local rather than national politics. Third World governments must acquire power before they can share it through competitive elections. James Madison, one of the architects of the American constitution, put the point well: 'You must first enable the government to control the governed; and in the next place oblige it to control itself.'

When Third World elections are competitive, the object of competition is specific rewards rather than policy choices: votes are exchanged for particular benefits accruing to individuals, ethnic groups or communities. In contrast to class-based parties in the West which use ideology to justify their promise of an improved standard of living for all their members and supporters, the exchange in Third World countries usually lacks an ideological overlay and takes place via a highly personalised hierarchy of patron-client relationships. (For an extended discussion of the patron-client concept see Eisenstadt and Lemarchand, 1981.) Through economic power or communal loyalties, local leaders (*patrons*) often control blocs of voters (*clients*) in their constituencies. A skilful leader then plays the political field to ensure that the best economic return is obtained from this political capital. This return might take the form of control over government jobs or, most useful of all, access to cabinet ministers or the president himself. In addition, the local leader may succeed in attracting development projects to his area, thus strengthening his own position in the community.

In extreme cases, the clients simply hand over signed ballots for the patron to complete. The patron then withdraws the capital provided by these 'vote banks' at the most propitious time. One example of this occurred in the Colombian town of Juanito at the turn of the century. It so happened that the blank votes given by the townspeople to the city boss, General Iquaron, equalled the margin of victory in the national presidential election and this led to an official investigation. When the commissioners arrived in town, Iquaron had the bright idea of shooting out the lanterns in their hotel rooms. They left town the next morning and declared the votes legal (Schmidt, 1980, p. 270).

For the ordinary voter at the base of a patron-client pyramid, the return is often unspecific. He hopes that by supporting the patron's candidate, he will be offered some protection. A classic example of electoral competition reaching the base of the political pyramid is the Philippines under President Marcos. Here 10–20 per cent of the electorate literally sold their votes. Labourers often received the equivalent of a month's wages for their support. Firms gave money to parties to bribe voters so that pro-business parties were returned to office, thus enabling the firms to continue making a profit – and offering bribe money. This cycle made the Philippines a perfect model of electoral corruption (Scott, 1972, p. 97) until the brazen fraud and corruption in the 1986 election (along with Marcos' age and infirmity) led to Aquino's successful revolution.

While patron-client networks are generally strongest in traditional rural areas (though they have also flourished in many African cities, where they are based on ethnic ties and contacts), the *party machine* is the classic mechanism for distributing rewards to voters in urban areas. Party machines flourish in towns where new immigrants from the countryside, or from abroad, lack the skills needed to cope with a modern urban society. Local party bosses provide the link with the wider society, offering counselling, welfare and employment services in return for votes. In Argentine's capital city of Buenos Aires at the turn of the century, district chiefs of the Radical Party provided help, charity and credit for votes. The party even provided low-priced food – 'radical bread' and 'radical milk'. The purest examples of party machines were found in the United States at the turn of the century. By 1900, for example, the Martin machine in Philadelphia had placed 15 000 people in public-sector jobs, all selected because they could deliver the votes of organisations, localities or families (Scott, 1972, p. 119). Sometimes the machines were based upon ethnic solidarity and personal loyalties so that the distinction between patron-client networks and party-machines might not always be clear.

The United States case suggests that personalised patron-client networks and party-patronage machines may be a transitory form of electoral organisation. Patron-client networks rely on strong interpersonal ties of dependence; party-patronage machines develop as voters lose or escape these traditional ties but still lack the resources to cope as independent citizens without support. As populations become more affluent and better educated, as class loyalties deepen, as the state extends its own provision of welfare services, the party machine has less and less to offer. (Readers who are surprised to find references to the United States in a discussion about Third World countries should reflect on the title of Ira Sharkansky's (1975) book, *The United States – A Study of a Developing Country*.)

The rest of this chapter examines elections in two developing countries – Mexico and Kenya. Mexico is a relatively affluent Third World country in which a dominant party has long used patron-client networks to maintain its position in a formally competitive party system. In Mackenzie's terms its elections are sometimes *made* and sometimes (especially recently) *stolen*. Kenya is an example of candidate-choice elections in a non-communist setting. It is a poorer country in which candidates from a single party compete against each other to provide services for local elites and local areas.

Dominant-party Elections: Mexico

Mexico's *Partido Revolucionaria Institucional* (PRI) is the most successful dominant party in the Third World. Since its founding in 1929, no other party (and there are several) has won the presidency, a governorship or a senate seat. In presidential elections the PRI has won between 72–98 per cent of the votes cast. In the Chamber of Deputies, the main legislative assembly, the PRI has received 68–90 per cent of the vote, sufficient to provide an overwhelming majority of seats. How does the PRI do it?

Several factors are involved, most of which are typical of dominant parties throughout the non-communist developing world, though the PRI has exploited them more effectively than most.

First, the PRI has proved adept at exploiting patron-client networks in the countryside where local leaders known as caciques hold sway. The *cacique* and his henchmen are often co-opted into the party, irrespective of ideology. Secondly, many Mexicans are directly represented in one of the PRI's three sectors representing peasants, unionised workers, and the middle class. Members of these sectors benefit from the PRI's monopoly of government: they receive jobs, pay rises, contracts and influence. Thirdly, the PRI is willing to *steal* as well as *make* elections: opposition parties only prosper if they accept their role as a loyal opposition. 'Opposition is support' said a former leader of the National Action Party (PAN), the main opposition group. Finally, since Mexican presidents cannot be re-elected on completion of their six-year term, there is a massive turnover of officials every six years which gives the PRI a dynamism and flexibility which is unusual for dominant parties.

Even so there must be a serious question mark over whether this strategy of electoral domination can survive modernisation. As electorates become more sophisticated and societies more complicated, dominant parties face new problems. In contrast to communist states with acclamatory elections a 'loyal' opposition lies in wait, keen to serve as a focus of discontent. As one of the most industrialised of the developing countries, the Mexican case is proto-typical. By the time of the state elections in 1985, the PRI was in trouble. A difficult economic situation did not help and it had to resort to vote-rigging (stuffed ballot boxes which were full before voting started, failure to open polling stations or deliver ballot boxes in opposition areas, false counting, and the like) to engineer short-term electoral success. In the 1980s, such tactics involve a much greater loss of legitimacy than they did 50 years ago. In the long-run, non-communist dominant parties may not survive the transition to an industrial and post-industrial society.

Candidate-choice Elections: Kenya

Candidate-choice elections offer electors choice but not between parties offering competing views on national issues. In the context of the Third World, Kenya is a contemporary example of such elections. It is typical of a group of African states with non-communist, one-party systems. Others include the Ivory Coast, Tanzania and Zambia. In so far as the choice of elected personnel is a genuinely free choice, yet one in which party cues are absent, Mackenzie would call these elections *muddled*.

Though Kenya has formally been a one-party state since 1982 (and informally since 1969), the position of the Kenyan African National Union (KANU) is much weaker than that of Mexico's PRI. KANU is a political arena rather than an actor in its own right. (The same has been said about United States parties, notably by Ranney, 1978.) KANU barely exists outside election campaigns and lacks any meaningful central organisation. Aspiring politicians experience no difficulty in joining KANU. In 1983, for example, only four out of 995 potential parliamentary candidates were rejected by the party. Theoretically a *one-party* state, Kenya is in reality a *no-party* state. Thus candidate-choice elections in Kenya offer a much more genuine choice than in communist states such as Poland where the ruling party is a controlling force. Whether the voters can do much with a free but unstructured choice is another matter.

In the absence of party competition, political conflict is between individuals. In Kenyan elections, KANU-members compete against each other for voters' support in single-member constituencies. In the 1983 parliamentary election, for example, only five out of 153 MPs were unopposed. The competition is real, the outcome determined in the ballot box. Between 40–50 per cent of Kenyan MPs are turfed out at each election, normally including a few ministers among their number. This is a far higher proportion than in Western democracies. Woebetide a Kenyan MP whose performance is judged unsatisfactory by his constituents.

The pork barrel is the key to electoral victory. Candidates must convince local patrons (and hence the clients they control) of their skill at extracting resources from central government for the benefit of their constituency. Just as United States Congressmen try to attract Air Force Bases to their districts, so too do Kenyan MPs set out to obtain rural development projects for their constituencies. Indeed, the United States and Kenya both have muddled, candidate-centred elections as a result of weak national parties. But for three reasons it is even more vital for the Kenyan MP to bring home the bacon. First, even in the 1980s the American Congressman may still be protected from failure by his party label. In Kenya's one-party state, there is no party umbrella to protect the unpopular candidate from the electoral rain. Secondly, many American voters are oriented to national events whereas Kenyan villagers judge their MPs purely on a local basis. If the next village has electricity, but this one does not, the solution is simple – get a new MP. Thirdly, the policy of rural development through self-help, laid down originally by President Kenyatta, required MPs to become involved in community projects rather than to deliberate national policy, which became the preserve of the presidential court. Kenyatta knew full well that muddled elections, which exclude party competition, place few limits on national policy making.

Successful MPs can expect appointment as Assistant Minister which improves access to resources and thus helps re-election prospects. Assistant Ministers can in turn become Cabinet Ministers with better access to the biggest patron of them all – the President. Thus the entire political system forms an elaborate hierarchy of patrons and clients, as shown in Figure 2.1. Elections confirm and strengthen this network.

Figure 2.1 *The patron–client network in Kenya*

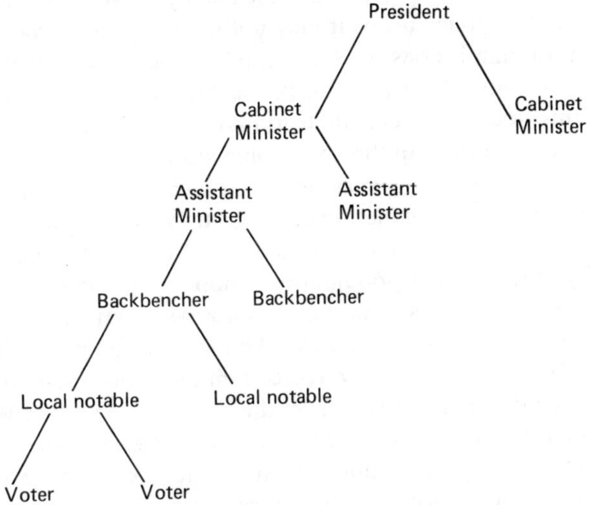

President
Cabinet Minister
Cabinet Minister
Assistant Minister
Assistant Minister
Backbencher
Backbencher
Local notable
Local notable
Voter
Voter

SOURCE: adapted from Barkan and Okumu (1978).

The nature of elections in Kenya has been summarised by Hyden and Leys (1972):

> They are a game in which the candidate may be awarded a licence to improve his personal fortunes by becoming an MP in return for pledges and tokens of his intention to help improve the fortunes of his constituents by the improvement of government amenities in his area.

When judged against the standard of a choice between national programmes, Kenya's elections are inherently muddled; but they are none the less a game with its own clearly defined rules

Conclusion

Non-competitive elections are a mixed bunch. They vary far more than competitive contests in organisation, function and consequencies. One of the few common themes of this chapter has been that elections without choices are rarely central to the political systems of which they form part. In communist states, decisive events usually unfold within the *party* rather than through *elections*. In the developing world the capacity of governments is so limited that in policy terms it may not matter greatly who wins an election, though it does matter greatly – indeed, it matters excessively – in terms of rewards for particular client networks.

But this does not mean that non-competitive elections can be dismissed altogether. In the developing world, elections encourage links between central government and local elites. To an extent, they are an agency of national integration. More generally, the right to vote is undoubtedly the only political right available to a majority of the world's population. In non-competitive systems the cash value of a vote is small but it is always positive. Throughout the Third World, individuals use their vote to gain a little extra security from their patrons while communities use their collective vote to extract small benefits from the centre. Even in the Western democracies, individuals and communities sometimes use elections for just that purpose, though Western elections can be used to advance policies as well as protect interests.

Analysing the functions of elections without choice broadens our perspective on competitive elections. In the Soviet Union elections tell citizens that they do not govern but Western elections convey a somewhat similar message – that voters are permitted to choose but not to rule. In Poland ballots are counted in a way that favours the communist party – but, as we shall see in the next chapter, electoral systems in the West generally favour governing parties. In Mexico, state employment has been expanded to provide jobs for people who deliver votes to the PRI – but Western parties also use the public sector to help their own election prospects. In Kenya electricity generators are distributed to constituencies in accordance with the political clout of MPs – but the same game is played in the United States with missile manufacturing plants.

The difference between competitive and non-competitive elections is an obvious matter of definition – but the similarities are less obvious matters of fact. We do not imagine that our readers will have any difficulty distinguishing the *differences* between the competitive elections of Western democracies, the made elections of Eastern Europe or Mexico, the acclamatory elections of the USSR, and the spoils-oriented elections of many developing countries. But in a book which is mainly about free elections we seek to highlight the less obvious *similarities* between these different kinds of elections. Asking what elections have in common, whether competitive or not, is a more informative exercise than asking how they differ. And the answer shows that elections about choice are about much else besides.

Further Reading

On the classification of elections, see Mackenzie (1958). The collection edited by Hermet, Rose and Rouquie (1978) is the best introduction to non-competitive elections. The chapters by Rouquie on clientelism and by Pravda on communist states are particularly useful. An updated version of Pravda's chapter appears in the reader edited by White and Nelson (1986). White, Gardner and Schöpflin (1982) is a good introduction to the politics of the USSR, Eastern Europe and China which also gives a brief description of their electoral systems. Lawson's (1980) edited work also contains much helpful material on elections though her focus on party-society linkages goes beyond elections. The chapters on Mexico and Colombia are especially interesting. Patron-client relationships are examined in a political and comparative context in the book edited by Eisenstadt and Lemarchand (1981). Similar themes are explored in a fascinating book by Scott (1972) on political corruption.

On elections in specific communist states, see Friedgut (1979) and White (1985) on the Soviet Union, Townsend (1969) on China before the recent reforms and, if you can find it, Pelczynski (1959) on the famous election of 1957 in Poland. On the Third World Chazan (1979) or Cohen (1983) cover African elections while Macdonald (1971) is still a helpful source on Latin America. Clapham (1985) makes shrewd comments on elections in an intelligent if rather abstract analysis of Third World politics. On Mexico, see Padgett (1976) or Levy and Szekely (1983). On Kenya, see Bienen (1974) and Barkan with Okumu (1979).

References

ARIAN, A. and BARNES, S. (1974) 'The Dominant Party System: A Neglected Model of Democratic Stability', *Journal of Politics*, vol. 36, pp. 592–614.

BARKAN, J. and OKUMU, J. (1978) 'Semi-Competitive Elections, Clientelism and Political Recruitment in a No-Party state: The Kenyan Experience', in G. Hermet, R. Rose and A. Rouquie (eds), *Elections Without Choice* (London: Macmillan).

BARKAN, J. with OKUMU, J. (1979) *Politics and Public Policy in Kenya and Tanzania* (New York: Praeger).

BIENEN, H. (1974) *Kenya: The Politics of Participation and Control* (Princeton: Princeton University Press).

BUTLER, D. (ed.) (1959) *Elections Abroad* (London: Macmillan).

CHAZAN, N. (1979) 'African Voters at the Polls', *Journal of Commonwealth and Comparative Politics*, vol. 17, pp. 136–58.

CLAPHAM, C. (1985) *Third World Politics: an Introduction* (Beckenham: Croom Helm).

COHEN, D. (1983) 'Elections and Election Studies in Africa', in Y. Barongo (ed.), *Political Science in Africa* (London: Zed Press).

CORBETT, J. (1980) 'Linkage as Manipulation: the Partido Revolucionaria Institucional in Mexico', in K. Lawson (ed.), *Political Parties and Linkage: A Comparative Perspective* (New Haven: Yale University Press).

CROAN, M. (1970) 'Is Mexico the Future of East Europe?', in S. Huntington and C. Moore (eds), *Authoritarian Politics in Modern Society* (New York: Basic Books).

EISENSTADT, S. and LEMARCHAND, R. (eds) (1981) *Political Clientelism, Patronage and Development* (London: Sage).
FRIEDGUT, T. (1979) *Political Participation in the USSR* (Princeton: Princeton University Press).
HERMET, G., ROSE, R. and ROUQUIE, A. (eds) (1978) *Elections Without Choice* (London: Macmillan).
HYDEN, G. and LEYS, C. (1972) 'Elections and Politics in Single Party Systems: the Case of Kenya and Tanzania', *British Journal of Political Science*, vol. 2, pp. 389–420.
LAWSON, K. (ed.) (1980) *Political Parties and Linkage: A Comparative Perspective* (New Haven: Yale University Press).
LEVY, D. and SZEKELY, G. (1983) *Mexico: Paradoxes of Stability and Change* (Boulder: Westview).
MACDONALD, R. (1971) *Party Systems and Elections in Latin America* (Chicago: Markham).
MACKENZIE, W. (1958) *Free Elections* (London: Allen & Unwin).
PADGETT, L. (1976) *The Mexican Political System* (Atlanta: Houghton Mifflin).
PELCZYNSKI, Z. (1959) 'Poland 1957', in D. Butler (ed.), *Elections Abroad* (London: Macmillan).
PRAVDA, A. (1978) 'Elections in Communist Party States' in G. Hermet, R. Rose and A. Rouquie (eds), *Elections without Choice* (London: Macmillan).
PRAVDA, A. (1986) 'Elections in Communist Party States', in S. White and D. Nelson (eds) *Communist Political Systems: a Reader* (London: Macmillan).
PURCELL, S. (1981) 'Mexico: Clientelism, Corporatism and Political Stability', in S. Eisenstadt and R. Lemarchand (eds), *Political Clientelism, Patronage and Development* (London: Sage).
RANNEY, A. (1978) 'Political Parties: Reform and Decline', in A. King (ed.), *The New American Political System* (Washington, DC: American Enterprise Institute).
ROUQUIE, A. (1978) 'Clientelist Control and Authoritarian Contexts', in G. Hermet, R. Rose and A. Rouquie (eds), *Elections without Choice* (London: Macmillan).
SCHMIDT, S. (1980) 'Patrons, Brokers and Clients: Party Linkages in the Colombian System', in K. Lawson (ed.), *Political Parties and Linkage* (New Haven: Yale University Press).
SCOTT, J. (1972) *Comparative Political Corruption* (Englewood Cliffs, NJ: Prentice-Hall).
SHARKANSKY, I. (1975) *The United States: A Study of a Developing Country* (New York: McKay).
TAYLOR, C. and JODICE, D. (1983) *World Handbook of Political and Social Indicators: Volume I* (New Haven: Yale University Press).
TOWNSEND, J. (1969) *Political Participation in Communist China* (Berkeley: University of California).
WHITE, S. (1985) 'Non-competitive Elections and National Politics: the USSR Supreme Soviet Elections of March 1984', *Electoral Studies*, vol. 4, pp. 215–30.

WHITE, S. (1986) 'Economic Performance and Communist Legitimacy', *World Politics*, vol. 38, 462–82.

WHITE, S., GARDNER, J. and SCHÖPFLIN, G. (1982) *Communist Political Systems: an Introduction* (London: Macmillan).

WHITE, S. and NELSON, D. (eds) (1986) *Communist Politics: A Reader* (London: Macmillan).

ZASLAVSKY, K. and BRYM, J. (1978) 'The Functions of Elections in the USSR', *Soviet Studies*, vol. 30, pp. 362–71.

3

Political Choice: Competitive Electoral Systems

In this chapter we look at electoral arrangements in countries where elections *do* offer a choice, and a choice that is given structure and meaning by the existence of genuinely competitive parties. Our focus here is on the liberal democracies of Western Europe, North America and parts of the British Commonwealth.

What is an Electoral System?

An electoral system is a *set of rules* for conducting an election. These rules specify which public officials are subject to election, who is eligible to vote, how those eligible can claim their right to vote, how the candidates must be selected, and how the votes are to be counted so as to produce an overall result.

But an electoral system is more than this. The rules are *applied* in a specific *context*. How the rules are applied can matter as much as the rules themselves. Fair rules can be applied unfairly as we saw in the last chapter; and even unfair or illogical rules can be applied so sensitively that the system works well. The impact of an electoral system also depends on the social and political context. The same set of rules, applied in the same way, can none the less produce political stability in one society but instability in another. The same electoral system has produced regular changes of government in Britain but permanent Protestant hegemony in Northern Ireland. It is not inconsistent to argue for one kind of electoral system in one country and a different system somewhere else: there are 'horses for courses' in electoral systems as in much else.

So electoral systems in the real world have three important elements: *rules, application, and context*. We cannot properly assess any system without taking account of all three.

What is Required of an Electoral System?

Elections are multi-functional: they must perform a variety of tasks simultaneously. No one set of electoral rules is best for all functions in all contexts. In our view a good electoral system is one that performs a range of tasks reasonably well in a specific context even at the expense of doing none of these tasks superbly well. And a bad electoral system is one which performs none of these tasks satisfactorily.

But what tasks? We suggest that an electoral system should ideally satisfy three main requirements. First, an electoral system should help to make government possible for those at the top but acceptable to those underneath. It should give the government the authority it needs for effective action while offering the people the choice on which legitimacy depends. It should encourage stability and continuity, discourage erratic or capricious change, yet still permit change when that is the clear and persistent popular will. Secondly, the electoral system should help to reduce political frustration and encourage tolerance. To reduce frustration, it should enable the voters to 'throw the rascals out'. This is a safety valve for reducing tension irrespective of changes in policy. To encourage tolerance, an electoral system should draw people into the political system, not shut them out. Thirdly, the election system should not itself add to the problems that already exist. The content and application of electoral rules should convince all the people that the government was 'fairly' elected. Minorities must be reassured that they will not be ignored or neglected.

Unfortunately the requirements of firm government and fair representation, of majority rule and minority reassurance, pull in opposite directions. A system can only meet one requirement at the expense of another. The choice between these yardsticks depends on circumstances. For example, the protection of minority rights may be crucial when such rights are under threat, as in

Northern Ireland, but elsewhere the priority may be firm government and clear policy choices. We repeat: *there is no such thing as the best electoral system*.

We begin this chapter by describing some of the important aspects of electoral systems – the scope and powers of elective office, registering voters, translating votes into seats, and choosing candidates. Then we examine the interaction between the electoral system and politics, looking first at partisan manipulation of electoral rules and secondly at the impact of electoral systems on party systems.

The Scope and Powers of Elective Office

Before we get lost in the mechanical details of electoral systems, we have to remind ourselves that one of the most important characteristics of any system is its scope. Which offices are subject to election is as important as who has the right to vote. And the powers of elected officials are as significant as the freedoms of the voters. A free choice in the voting booth and a fair count of the votes can be worthless if many offices of state are filled by inheritance or examination, or if those officials who are elected must defer to a powerful monarch, a threatening army council, or an overbearing neighbour.

The United States electoral system is unique in its combination of a massive number of elective offices with real freedom of action for those elected. True, the Soviet Union fills an enormous number of posts by election but Soviet elected officials are responsible to their superiors in the party, not to their electorates. In Britain, on the other hand, relatively few positions are filled by election and many officials who would be subject to election elsewhere hold their positions by inheritance, examination, or patronage appointment – as hereditary members of the House of Lords, as non-elected civil servants (selected primarily by examination), as appointed members of the House of Lords ('life peers'), or as members of government-appointed quangos. Local councillors are elected from below but they can be dismissed or heavily fined if they fail to carry out central government policy. It can be argued that elective control of government in Britain *begins and ends* with the 650 members of the House of Commons – though their power, collectively if not individually, is as great as their numbers are small.

Registration: An Effective Franchise

In principle, all citizens aged at least 18 have the right to vote in most contemporary democracies. In many countries women did not get the vote until after the Second World War. Indeed they had to wait until the 1970s in Switzerland, Portugal and Spain. But now restrictions in the West are typically confined to criminals, the mentally incompetent, non-citizen residents and those convicted of electoral corruption. The extent of the franchise is no longer an issue. But having a right in principle is one thing; being able to exercise it effectively is another. The United States led the way to universal suffrage by extending the right to vote but now lags far behind most other nations because of the practical difficulties it places in the way of Americans claiming and exercising that right.

Two rules have a major influence on participation: *compulsory voting* and *automatic registration*. Where voting is legally compulsory, as in Australia, Belgium and Italy, turn-out is high even though the penalties for not voting are low or even, as in Italy, non-existent. Most countries do not have compulsory voting but they do have automatic or compulsory registration, which ensures that citizens can in fact vote when election day arrives. Among the major countries, Australia, France and the United States put the burden of registration on the individual, but class-based party systems in France and Australia mobilise the poor and uneducated who might not be personally motivated to register.

In the United States, however, there is neither compulsory voting nor automatic registration, nor even a class-based party system to mobilise the naturally apathetic or disaffected poor. So among Western democracies America is unique in the extent to which its system keeps the poor, the uneducated, the geographically mobile and minority ethnic groups shut out of the electoral process. Until the mid-1960s, poll taxes (typically $2–$3 for registration in one election), literacy tests and questions on understanding the Constitution were used to deny the vote to 'undesirables', especially Southern blacks. These restrictions have now been swept away but because the burden of registration still rests on the individual, and states still have considerable say in their electoral law, registration and turn-out remain abysmally low. The average American is entitled to do far more electing – by a factor of about three or four – than the citizen of any other democracy. But the right is less likely to be exercised than elsewhere (Crewe, 1981, p. 232).

We recognise that the registration system by itself is not the only cause of low turn-out in the United States. Indeed the system embodies *values* of individualism and self-help which are perhaps more fundamental causes of low turn-out. None the less personal registration is one of the mechanisms by which the dominance of individualistic values operates. The decline in turn-out since the 1960s largely reflects changing attitudes to government and parties, but the major transition from nearly complete turn-out in nineteenth century America to low turn-out in the twentieth century was brought about by laws specifically designed to *exclude* rather than (as with British registration laws) *include*.

Britain is at the other extreme. In contrast to the USA, few public officials are elected but compulsory registration procedures are effective, and a class-based party system mobilises the poor. Local government officials show great diligence in compiling an annual electoral register. But even this process is far from perfect. By the end of a register's life, only 84 per cent of eligible electors are both registered and still living where they are registered. Moreover, non-registration is concentrated among the politically alienated. In 1981 almost a third of new Commonwealth immigrants were not registered. In inner London, a huge 47 per cent of unemployed people up to age 30 were not registered (Todd and Dodd, 1982, p. 8). The ultimate test of a registration procedure is its ability to enfranchise these politically cynical and non-integrated citizens.

Translating Votes into Seats

European traditions of democracy were based originally on majoritarian principles: the candidate (or candidates in a multi-member constituency) with the largest number of votes won the election, and those who had supported other candidates were morally bound to accept the result. In Britain there was traditionally only one round of voting and no requirement that the winning candidate must get over half the vote – that is, a *plurality* was sufficient, an *absolute majority* unnecessary. Within the Roman Catholic church there was also a long tradition of majoritarian elections but one that focused more on absolute majorities achieved by *repeated ballots*. This practice served as the model for various continental European countries. Under a repeated ballot system a candidate was only elected on the first ballot if he won over half the votes, otherwise a second ballot was held. This might restrict candidates to the top two candidates from the first round (i.e. a *run-off*) or it might allow candidates to do their own deals with each other about who should withdraw from the second ballot. Sometimes more than two ballots were allowed. But in order to bring the process to a conclusion the rules for the final ballot either had to restrict the number of candidates to two or had to allow election by plurality. France used a three-ballot system in 1789. Since then it has tried several other methods, always returning to the repeated ballot. It now uses a *second ballot* for presidential elections and, until 1986, for parliamentary elections also. Austria, Italy, Switzerland (until 1900), the Netherlands and the German Reich used multiple ballots until the end of the First World War.

The British system of single ballots and pluralities, often called *first-past-the-post* (FPTP), is used in Canada, India, New Zealand, South Africa and the United States – that is, in most of Britain's important former colonies. For elections to its House of Representatives, Australia uses the *alternative vote* which is a device for achieving a multiple ballot result without the trouble of going back to the polling station. Australians list their candidates in order of preference. If no candidate wins over half the first preference votes, the candidate with fewest first preference votes is eliminated and his votes are reallocated according to his voters' second preferences, and so on, until one candidate has over half the vote. The difference between the alternative vote and the *repeated ballot* is that the alternative vote does not allow a candidate to influence the second count by withdrawing his candidature.

All Continental European countries have switched to some form of *proportional representation* (PR) for their parliamentary elections. (The French change their system between proportional representation and the majoritarian double-ballot so frequently that comments about France are often out-of-date. President

Mitterrand is on record as saying that *changes* of electoral system constitute normality in France. The French used the double-ballot in the Third Republic, and again in the Fifth Republic until 1985 when they switched to PR for the 1986 elections. They are likely to switch back to the double-ballot before the end of the decade.) The basic principle of proportionality is to award seats in parliament in proportion to the numbers of votes cast for different lists or groups of candidates. As a result these groups do not *win* or *lose*, they gain more or less *representation*.

What groups? In theory we might specify all kinds of proportionalities – proportional representation by age and sex, for example, is built into some of the procedures by which delegates to United States presidential nominating conventions are selected and is of great concern to those who organise Soviet elections. Proportional representation by area and region is guaranteed by apportionment rules that give a certain number of seats to particular areas or regions in proportion to their population. Such rules apply to both FPTP and PR systems.

Historically PR has been used to provide proportional representation for two kinds of groups: first, *ethnic and religious groups*; and secondly, *political parties*. Before the First World War PR was introduced in Denmark, Switzerland, Belgium, Moravia and Finland to give adequate representation to religious or ethnic minorities and to help integrate these minorities into the wider political system. In Scotland PR was used between 1918 and 1929 for elections to Education Authorities which had to manage both Protestant and Catholic systems of public education. For the same reason the British used PR in Northern Ireland during the 1920s and reintroduced it there in the 1970s.

After the First World War the main reason for introducing PR was to provide *party* proportionality. The extension of the franchise and the growth of socialist parties threatened to eliminate some of the old, middle-class parties and give the socialists a disproportionately large share of parliamentary seats if the number of middle-class parties was not reduced by elimination or fusion. Under FPTP a party with a small vote could only win representation in parliament if its vote was heavily concentrated in a few areas. PR allowed small parties with an evenly spread vote to retain some seats in parliament without the need for electoral alliances.

PR systems necessarily use multi-member constituencies: there is no way of proportionately dividing one MP. The more members per constituency, the more accurately members can be allocated in proportion to votes. (However, disproportionality resulting from a small number of representatives per constituency can be overcome by reserving a pool of seats which are allocated at regional or national level so as to achieve a proportional result overall. Denmark, Sweden and Germany use variants of this idea of *pool seats*.) PR systems usually apply *thresholds* to eliminate very small parties – typically those with less than 4–5 per cent of the vote. Then a *quota* is set. A quota is the minimum number of votes required for a party to be certain of winning one elected representative. This quota can be calculated in many ways, among them the *Droop* quota, the *Hagenbach–Bischoff* quota and the *Imperiali* quota. For example, the *Droop* quota sets the quota at: [votes/(seats + 1)] + 1 (see Lakeman, 1970, p. 139 for details of other quotas). Some of these methods favour very small parties more than others.

Inevitably some seats are not allocated by applying these quotas: some parties do not have enough votes for a quota, others have enough votes for one quota but not enough for two quotas, and so on. PR systems then use a variety of formulae for awarding the remaining seats to parties which do not have a full quota of votes. The three most common formulae are the *largest remainder*, the *d'Hondt highest average*, and the *St Lague highest average*. Some of these systems are quite complex. Once the simple counting rules of majority systems are abandoned the possibilities for intricate and ingenious counting systems are limitless.

Three systems merit a special mention: the *additional member system* (West Germany), the *single transferable vote* or STV for short (Ireland), and the *limited vote* (Japan).

West Germany

In West Germany half the parliamentary seats are filled by FPTP in single-member territorial constituencies like those in Britain. The other half are allocated to parties so as to make the overall result, for the full parliament, party proportional. A party that gets a disproportionately large share of seats in the constituencies gets a disproportionately low share of seats in the PR share-out. Moreover, each voter has two votes which may go to different parties: the first vote is used for the FPTP election within the constituency while the second is used for the national PR calculation. This *additional member* system retains the MP-constituency link while still producing a proportional outcome. A variant of it was proposed for Britain in a Hansard Society report in 1976.

Ireland

Ireland, along with Malta, Tasmania and the upper house of the Australian parliament, uses the *single transferable vote* (STV). STV is therefore a version of PR favoured exclusively by countries with British links. Voters are required to list the candidates in their constituency in order of preference. During the count, votes are transferred to second and third preference candidates either because the voter's first preference has more votes than are strictly required for election, or because the candidate comes bottom in first preferences and is therefore eliminated. As this suggests, STV requires a complex counting process that can go on for days. However, the Irish Republic does not actually apply STV rules in a strictly logical way. It uses a simplified version of an STV count which makes the result depend slightly upon chance. To be specific, the result of an Irish STV count partly depends upon which ballot papers happen to be at the top of a pile and which are at the bottom. When the British reintroduced STV for various elections in Northern Ireland in the 1970s they removed the element of chance completely (McKee, 1983). In general, STV is a complex system which can produce a proportional result with smaller constituencies than list systems. It takes into account considerable information about the voters' preferences and encourages parties to consider the views of other parties' supporters.

Japan

For elections to its House of Representatives, Japan now uses a system called the *limited vote*, a variant of which was used in a few British city constituencies between 1867 and 1885. (These 'undivided' cities had multi-member constituencies.) In Japan each elector has only one vote, although nearly all constituencies have between three and five representatives. The limited vote system is

Figure 3.1 *Types of electoral system*

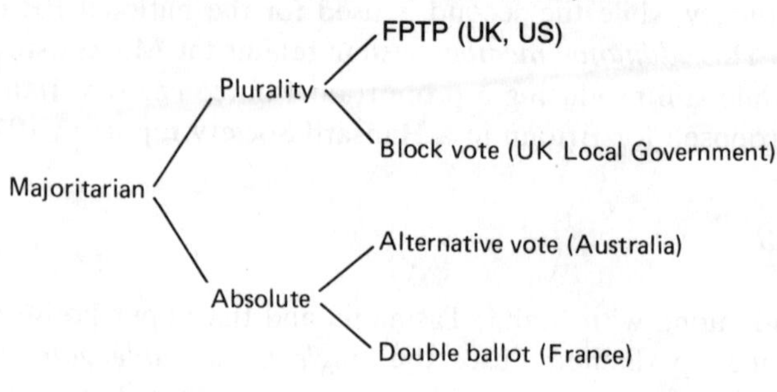

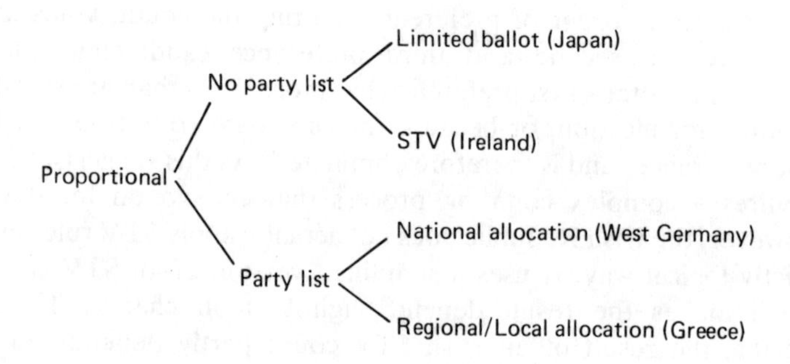

designed to produce a reasonably proportional outcome. Suppose that in a three-member seat one party has 66 per cent of the voters behind it and the other has 33 per cent. Provided the minority party only puts up one candidate it can be sure he or she will be elected, because there is no way of splitting up the 66 per cent among three majority party candidates that will leave each of them with more than 33 per cent. If the minority party is foolish and puts up too many candidates then it could, of course, fail to win any of the three seats. One practical effect of the limited vote in Japan is to intensify competition between candidates of the same party. The limited vote encourages the strongly factional character of Japanese parties.

We can usefully contrast two other kinds of voting system with the *limited vote*. These are the *block vote* and *approval voting*. In Japan, each voter has fewer votes than there are seats in the multi-member constituency. Under the block vote system, often used in British local government elections, each voter has exactly as many votes as there are seats in the multi-member (usually three-member) constituency. Under the approval voting system the voter has even more votes – as many votes as there are candidates, though he does not have to use them all: he is simply asked to vote for every candidate that he finds acceptable. Approval voting can be used even in a single-member constituency (see Brams and Fishburn, 1978 and Brams, 1980 for the advantages of approval voting; see Niemi, 1984 for some disadvantages.)

The limited vote system is an erratic and unreliable form of PR; the block vote usually approximates FPTP since each party usually puts forward as many candidates as seats and voters tend to vote for all the candidates of one party and no others; approval voting is a version of a strictly majoritarian system designed to help the widely acceptable (if often uninspiring!) candidate. For example, in a British single-member constituency contested by Labour, the Conservatives, and the Alliance, advocates of approval voting suggest that the centrist Alliance candidate might come bottom of the poll under FPTP (because he or she was few voters' favourite candidate) yet win under approval voting (because, as a centrist, the Alliance candidate was at least acceptable to both Labour and Conservative voters while Labour voters would not approve the Conservative candidate and Conservative voters would reject the Labour candidate).

Most PR systems do achieve the broad objective of approximately proportional representation for parties in parliament. Most majoritarian systems also distribute seats roughly in proportion to votes for most parties, most of the time, though nothing in the system guarantees this. PR systems usually come a little closer to proportionality than do majoritarian systems and they produce fewer upsets and unusual deviations from proportionality. Exactly *how proportional* a PR system is depends principally on how many members there are per constituency (the more members, the more proportional the result) and on how steep the thresholds are for winning any seats. If electoral systems are ranked in order of the proportionality of their results, majoritarian systems rank with the bottom half of PR systems – they are not so proportionate as the best PR systems, but not much worse than the less proportionate of PR systems (Rose, 1983, p. 41).

The Territorial Dimension

Electoral systems can be divided into those that stress locality and those that stress party – two fundamental and incompatible bases of representation. When the nation is divided up into a large number of small, single-member constituencies the electoral process is necessarily fragmented in space and, as we shall see in the next section, it may also be fragmented in time as well. All kinds of spatial influences – some intended, some barely recognised – come to have an important influence on the results.

For example, campaigning can be done on an explicitly local basis. Thus each United States Congressman defends his own record, not that of his party, still less that of Congress as a whole. Similarly, parties can focus their efforts and resources on particular areas. When the Scottish National Party (SNP) first won seven seats in the British parliament in February 1974 it was perhaps unsurprising that it contested only the seventy-one Scottish constituencies. Less obviously, an analysis of its campaign expenditures shows that it only fought a strong campaign in about twenty seats. In many Scottish seats it had a candidate but no campaign (Miller, 1981, p. 207).

Even the largest parties adjust their efforts to the spatial nature of the contest, using 'regional opt-outs' for their televised election broadcasts, for example. Labour's party election broadcasts on Scottish television in the 1970s were designed to counter the SNP threat; they would not have sounded so good to viewers in Birmingham or London. Similarly, French parties in the Third Republic, or the American Democratic Party in the New Deal years, were notorious for presenting different images in different parts of the country. Such behaviour is not restricted to territorial electoral systems such as FPTP, but it is encouraged by them.

Under FPTP (and somewhat less clearly under double-ballot or alternative vote systems also) there is an enormous advantage in having an efficiently distributed vote. In a two-party system under FPTP a party can, at the limit, achieve a 'seats-to-votes ratio' of 2.0 – that is, its percentage of seats in parliament can be twice as high as its percentage of votes in the nation. To achieve this maximum ratio it must receive no votes at all in the seats where it does not win, and no excess of votes beyond a bare majority in those seats where it does. (In multi-party elections the situation is a little more complex, but see Miller, 1981, ch. 7 for an example.)

The total *size* of the party's vote is irrelevant for this maximum seats-to-votes ratio; all that matters is its *spatial distribution*. It is true that in post-war Britain FPTP has tended to inflate the seats-to-votes ratios of the largest parties, Labour and Conservative, and deflate the seats-to-votes ratio of the smaller Liberal Party. And Rae's (1967, p. 89) study shows that FPTP quite generally tends to help larger parties more than small. But the bias towards large parties is fairly weak and inconsistent. For example, in the 1983 British election, the Alliance won almost the same *size* of vote as Labour, but because Alliance support was evenly spread its seats-to-votes ratio remained catastrophically low: it won 26 per cent of the vote but only three per cent of seats in parliament. Conversely, numerous very small parties have gained relatively high seats-to-votes ratios under the same FPTP electoral system because their votes have been concentrated in a few localities – for example, Unionists and their Republican enemies in different parts of Northern Ireland, the Scots and Welsh Nationalists whose votes were concentrated in quite small parts of their national homelands, even the small pre-First World War Labour party whose votes were concentrated in mining areas. The Scottish Liberals enjoyed a very good seats-to-votes ratio (in Scotland) during the 1960s when their vote had collapsed to little more than the personal following of three sitting Liberal MPs – a poor vote, but a most efficiently distributed one. These examples show that there are many different reasons why a party's vote may be efficiently distributed, and size is not the determining factor.

For small parties the most efficient distribution is a very uneven one. But beyond a certain size, an uneven distribution becomes a handicap. The rule is simple and inflexible: a party should waste votes *neither* by scoring sizable minority votes *nor* by winning seats with excessive majorities. In 1951, Attlee's Labour government was thrown out of office despite winning more votes than the Conservatives: it won too many ultra-safe seats with excessive majorities; so the Conservatives took more seats despite a smaller national vote.

The best example of an over-concentrated vote damaging a large party in a FPTP election is the South African election of 1948. That was the fateful election which handed power to the pro-apartheid Nationalist/Afrikaner Alliance. With only 42 per cent of the vote the Nationalists won seventy-nine seats and defeated the United Party/Labour government which won 52 per cent of the vote but only seventy-one seats. Ten years later the Nationalists tightened their grip by winning twice as many seats as their opponents despite approximately equal votes (allowing for unopposed returns). While malapportionment contributed something to the Nationalist success, the main cause was a very inefficient distribution of its opponents' vote which elected too few anti-Nationalist MPs, each with too large a majority.

Under FPTP, the spatial distribution of social and ethnic groups is important for the groups themselves as well as for the parties. Concentrations of Scots, Welsh, Irish, blacks, and miners in particular British constituencies, like the concentrations of Jews in New York and the Irish in Boston, give these groups more direct representation in parliament and more influence in politics than they would have if their vote were dispersed or, equivalently, if elections were held under a nationwide PR system.

Obviously, the spatial distribution of party support is affected by where the natural supporters of each party live; but it is also affected by where the constituency boundaries fall, because for elections it is the distribution *between constituencies*, and that distribution alone, that matters. Other things being equal, the larger the constituencies the more heterogeneous their populations. Streets may be entirely full of workers, but as more and more streets are grouped together to form a constituency the chances of like being grouped with like decline. So the larger the constituency the less likely it is to be socially and politically polarised, and the less safe it will be for any one party. In other ways too, the size of constituencies may have a major effect upon the style and content of elections: the visibility of candidates, for example, depends critically upon whether the shape of a constituency matches the distribution area of a newspaper or the reception area of a television station.

One factor that makes spatial distributions particularly critical under FPTP is the power of the *context effect*. Surprisingly, the spatial variation in party support is usually very much greater than could be explained merely by the spatial distribution of social groups. For example, in 1983 the variation in Labour and Conservative votes did follow variations in the class composition of constituency electorates as we should expect; but the partisan variation was about four times as great as the social variation suggested (see Miller, 1984 for an analysis of the 1983 election;

and Miller, 1978 for a fuller discussion.) Generally, the partisanship of local electorates is much more coherent, much more highly structured, much more polarised and much easier to predict than we should expect purely on the basis of their social composition. It follows that group-based party support tends to be much more spatially variable, and therefore (usually) much more efficiently distributed for FPTP elections than might be expected from the spatial distributions of the groups themselves. (See chapter 7 for a further discussion of this context effect.)

A related phenomenon is that of spatial continuity, which is also surprisingly strong. Where a party whose support is not normally group based, and not normally very variable from place to place, none the less manages to create a cluster of support, the effects may linger for a long time. Thus the Liberal Party, which tends to be more successful in by-elections than in general elections, has managed to retain some seats won in by-elections for years thereafter.

The Time Dimension

One consequence of spatially-based electoral systems is that they allow elections to be spread out in time as well as in space. At the turn of the century British elections were spread over a period of weeks. At the General Election of 1900, for example, the first constituency voted on 1 October and the last on 24 October. This extended period meant that the early results formed a significant part of the campaign oratory in the later-polling constituencies (see Blewett, 1972 for a description of campaigning under these circumstances). On a more compressed time-scale some results from present-day United States elections in the eastern states are known hours before polls close in the western states. Voters in the later elections may take account of the earlier results when deciding whether (and how) to vote.

Space-time interaction is significant in other ways also. Under a PR system the top 100 candidates on a party list may be elected. If one dies during the parliament, then the one hundred and first on the list can take his place. But under FPTP and similar territorial systems, the death of a sitting member leads to a by-election unless: (1) the constituency is left unrepresented, (2) the seat is filled by appointment, or (3) the candidate in the original election campaigned 'in harness' with a deputy or substitute.

All these devices are used in territorial electoral systems. In Britain, Labour's reluctance to call a by-election when the dissident Labour MP, Dick Taverne, resigned in 1972 left his Lincoln constituency *unrepresented* for so long that the rules on by-elections had to be changed. In Canada, a few years later the Liberals were so afraid of by-election defeats that they left fifteen constituencies unrepresented until public anger forced them to hold a 'mini-general election' in 1978, in which they did badly. When a United States Senator dies, the State Governor may *appoint* a replacement. French candidates for parliament under the Fifth Republic's double-ballot system ran in harness with a *substitute* who could take over their seat if they died or resigned. The best example of a substitute running in harness is, of course, the United States vice-president whose principal task is to assume the presidency if the president is incapacitated (as Johnson did after Kennedy's assassination).

Thus even where there is no party list, by-elections are not absolutely necessary, but they are a natural way of filling a vacant seat. They introduce a dynamic element into a territorial electoral system. Though a by-election occurs in a specific place, the local electorate is often seen as speaking for the nation as a whole. Its verdict consists, not in the raw result, but in the change between the last general election and the by-election. Thus even atypical constituencies can deliver a 'national' verdict. They do more: by-elections not only pronounce a verdict on the government of the day, they stimulate a further reaction by the electorate throughout the country. Britain's Liberals have always shot up in the national opinion polls *after* a by-election success; the Canadian Liberals plunged in the polls *after* their defeat in the mini-general election of 1978.

By-elections, even when they occur, attract relatively little national attention in the USA, but the same space-time interaction is visible in that most American of institutions, the presidential primary. From February to June, Democrats and Republicans in different states go to the polls to choose candidates for the parties' nominating conventions. Voters in states with later primaries take account of the results of earlier primaries. A good result in one state has much the same effect on national support as a good result in a British by-election: one good result helps produce another.

Choosing Candidates

The extent of democracy depends as much on participation in selecting candidates as in choosing between them. In Western democracies, the most common pattern is selection by constituency parties under supervision of the national party; the next most frequent pattern is national selection after consideration of suggestions from lower party levels (Ranney, 1981). But the relationship between the selectorate and the electorate varies between electoral systems.

The selectorate is generally a small group in democracies employing first-past-the-post electoral systems. Nowhere can this be more true than in Britain. Conservative, Labour and Liberal candidates are chosen by small groups of local activists and officials in each constituency. Although the Social Democrats have widened the number of participants in the selection process, every British party, without exception, confines the selection process to its dues-paying membership; none reaches out to its supporters in the electorate. (For recent studies of the selectorate see Bochel and Denver, 1983; Criddle, 1984; and for an international review, Ranney, 1981.)

Until 1983 relatively few candidates were really 'selected' at all. Once elected to parliament, most MPs assumed that they would remain their party's nominee until they were defeated in an election, or until the constituency was abolished by the Boundary Commissioners. Between 1950 and 1964 Ranney (1965, p. 43) estimates that only two dozen MPs were refused re-adoption. The whole process was dominated by parliament and party.

Recent reforms mean that Labour MPs now face *mandatory reselection* during each parliament. This means the opposite of what it appears to mean: it means that no Labour MP will automatically be the party's candidate in the next election. MPs must face a selection committee along with other contenders for the party endorsement. Other parties may eventually follow suit; indeed there are historical precedents in the deselection of Liberal MPs whose views offended groups within the party in the 1860s and 1870s (Berrington, 1985). Even so it is most unlikely that any British party will ever open up the selection process in the manner of a United States primary.

Although the United States employs the same basic electoral system as Britain, the unique institution of the *primary* vastly extends participation in candidate selection, albeit with some undesirable consequences. It is used for nominations to Congress and State offices and for the selection of delegates to presidential nominating conventions. It allows potential candidates to appeal to party sympathisers over the heads of party office bearers and so *impose* themselves on parties rather than get *chosen* by them. Primary elections were introduced into many states early in the century. They then fell out of favour until the 1970s, when both parties reacted against Humphrey's nomination in 1968 as Democratic candidate despite the fact that he had not won a single primary. By 1980, 75 per cent of both Republican and Democratic convention delegates were chosen by primary elections. Both parties moved away from primaries in 1984 though both still chose a majority of convention delegates that way.

Primary elections take control of candidate selection out of the hands of party caucuses but distribute that important power in an haphazard way. Each individual state has its own laws about primaries; there is no uniform system. The usual scheme is for interested electors to declare themselves Democrats or Republicans when they register to vote. That does not bind them to vote one way or the other in the presidential election itself but registered Republicans will not be allowed to vote in the Democratic primary and registered Democrats will not be allowed a vote in the Republican primary. Delegates selected in primaries are usually bound to support one or other nominee at the party convention, at least in the early stages of convention deliberations, though in 1984 Democratic delegates were bound by nothing stronger than their word.

Turn-out at primaries is even lower than at elections, and those who participate in Democratic primaries are better educated, more affluent and younger than those who vote for the Democrats in presidential elections (Polsby, 1983, p. 158). On the other hand, participation is sufficiently widespread to ensure that many who do vote have only a scant knowledge of either the character or the policies of potential nominees. Since a primary election takes place within a party, not between parties, party itself cannot give any structure to the choices made. As a result primary elections are subject to the ill-informed whims of the moment. Support for one potential nominee or another can change enormously and without any rational basis. One of the important factors is 'big mo' –

momentum. Primary elections are spread over several months and an unexpectedly good showing in one of the early primaries can cause a huge surge of support in later primaries. Volatility and mindless momentum are likely to be based on a cheerful smile or a catchy slogan because so many primary voters' choices are not anchored in either partisanship or knowledge.

Proportional representation systems differ in how much influence they give voters over which candidates are elected from within a single party. At once extreme stands the *closed party list* system used in Israel. The voter has no choice between candidates but simply votes for the party he or she prefers. Candidates are elected in the order in which they appear on a party's list until the party has received the number of seats to which it is entitled. This gives the central party bureaucracy enormous power over political recruitment, though the low threshold of representation in Israel means that excluded candidates can always hope to gain a seat or two by forming a new party. Rather more common is the *flexible list* system of which Belgium is a clear example. This allows the elector choice between voting for a party or for a specific candidate from the party's list. The extent to which voters use their power to override the party's choice varies considerably from country to country; it also varies between parties and regions within countries (Marsh, 1984, p. 369). One significant example of voters taking advantage of the flexible list was the heavy personal vote in the 1974 Belgian election for Leo Tindemans, the Christian Social leader. This helped him to win acceptance as head of a coalition government (Lakeman, 1982, p. 40). *Open list* systems give even more choice to the voter. In Finland the candidates on the party list are ordered alphabetically and the voter chooses a particular candidate as his only way of voting for the list. In practice, this gives an advantage to well-known candidates such as incumbents, media personalities and sports stars. Finally, the *free lists* of Luxembourg and Switzerland offer the elector the most choice of all the list systems. The elector can cast votes for candidates from different lists and even give two votes to one candidate. The number of votes won *by a list* determines how many candidates of that party are elected; the number of votes gained *by the individual candidates* determines which candidates are elected. In general, list systems give more power to *both* the central party *and* the ordinary voter than the British approach which concentrates influence on local activists; and they can give the ordinary voter some choice between candidates without having the divisive effect of an American primary.

The single transferable vote system (STV) also gives the voters considerable influence over which candidates are elected from a particular party. In STV the voter ranks all the candidates (of all parties) in order – from most preferred to least preferred. Typically a party-oriented voter will rank all candidates of one party higher than any candidates of another party, but the voter is still able to discriminate between candidates of the preferred party. Although early advocates of STV wanted to weaken party organisations this has not always happened in the few countries where STV has been used. In practice competition between candidates of the same party is limited by reducing their multi-member constituencies to a series of individual bailiwicks into which party colleagues do not enter.

Manipulating the System

Electoral rules are framed and applied by established political authorities. Perhaps the government wishes to protect or inflate its share of seats in parliament. Perhaps it wishes to be fair to 'worthy' minorities or suppress 'unworthy' minorities. Frequently the authorities are motivated by a combination of self-interest and a conception of the common interest. But it is abundantly clear that electoral systems are chosen and changed, not for their abstract qualities, but for their anticipated effects on politics in the here and now. Electoral engineering may not always succeed but it usually has a very concrete purpose.

Powerful groups manipulate electoral systems in three ways: first, by *changing the rules*; secondly by *bending the detailed application* of the basic rules; and thirdly, by *refusing to change the rules* despite changing conditions.

Changing the rules

Sometimes electoral systems are changed to strengthen a single party but more often the purpose is to maintain established parties at the expense of threatening outsiders such as Communists in

Europe and blacks in the United States. In Greece and France, among other countries, electoral engineering is a highly developed science; politicians in these (and other) countries show a technical grasp of the electoral system which quite eludes them on other, less sensitive issues.

The Greek electoral system has been repeatedly adjusted to reduce the representation of left-wing groups. The 1950 election using PR produced a hung parliament split among ten parties. So the system was changed to inflate the representation of the larger parties and another election was held in 1951. Unfortunately, this election still produced no clear majority for one party, though two centre parties did form a coalition government. At that point the United States Ambassador announced that further economic aid was contingent on Greece adopting FPTP. The Greeks obliged and in 1952 held a FPTP election which at last produced the desired result. A right-wing party, led by Civil War victor Field Marshal Papagos, won 49 per cent of the vote and 82 per cent of the seats in parliament. When Papagos died in 1955 his successor Constantine Karamanlis produced yet another new electoral system. This used FPTP in the rural areas where his party was strong, but PR in the urban areas where he was weak. So at the 1956 election Karamanlis *lost* the popular vote 47 per cent to 48 per cent but *won* outright control of the parliament with 55 per cent of seats to his opponents 44 per cent. The system used in contemporary Greece still under-represents the communists by discriminating against small parties. In 1981, the two wings of the Communist Party received 18 per cent of the vote but only 4 per cent of the seats.

France has also specialised in manipulation of the electoral system. Since 1875 single-member constituencies have been replaced by PR on three occasions; but three times they have been restored. In 1985 President Mitterrand's by then unpopular Socialist government used its parliamentary majority to reinstate PR once again and thereby minimise its losses in the 1986 parliamentary election. General de Gaulle's revisions of the constitution provide another example of purposeful manipulation of the electoral system. With scant regard for legal niceties, he changed the system for electing presidents and established a powerful, directly-elected presidency, using the double ballot. This meant that the large minority of communist voters could never elect a Communist president by default. Non-communist parties might oppose each other on the first ballot but on the second there would only be one non-communist candidate (unless, of course, the communist candidate was eliminated by the first ballot). So France would get strong government by widely acceptable non-communist politicians.

Bending the rules in territorial systems

The methodology of manipulation depends on whether an electoral system is based on the representation of territory or parties. In territorial systems, such as FPTP, the two main techniques are malapportionment and gerrymandering.

Apportionment. Apportionment is the question of constituency size, as measured by number of electors. There is an obvious advantage to a party in having small constituencies in its strong areas and large ones where it is weak. Historically, unequal constituency sizes have been used to favour rural and therefore conservative areas in Australia, Britain, France, Japan, South Africa and the United States. American states have deliberately biased their electoral systems against the supposedly corrupt and immigrant-dominated cities, either by ignoring constitutional requirements to take account of population changes, or – as in California, Michigan and Illinois – by changing their constitutions. The 1962 Supreme Court case of *Baker* v. *Carr* changed all that by requiring equal apportionment (i.e. constituency populations of equal size) for elections to the Tennessee legislature. Further cases widened the scope of this ruling to other states and also indicated that equal meant *exactly* equal to within a per cent or so, despite the fact that census statistics which form the basis for apportionment are not that accurate. Ironically the United States Senate has two members for each state, whether the population is half a million (Arkansas) or twenty five million (California). This gross malapportionment, a natural consequence of federalism, is part of the Constitution and therefore beyond both party manipulation and judicial review.

Britain adopts a more relaxed approach to the problem of malapportionment. Traditional notions of community representation are held to justify variation in constituency size. The Boundary Commission (which makes recommendations that are normally implemented by government, albeit sometimes after an electorally significant delay) normally achieves considerable equity in its reviews which take place every ten to fifteen years. Because variations in constituency size do not consistently favour one party, deviations from equal apportionment are not a major cause of controversy. (For a comparison of different approaches to the apportionment problem in Britain, the USA and the Commonwealth, see Butler and Cain, 1985.)

In principle, malapportionment is relatively easy to detect and correct. The practical problem is that the cure rests with those who benefit from the disease – elected politicians. The solution is to take responsibility for treatment away from the politicians, though this is easier said than done.

Gerrymandering. Under FPTP there is an obvious advantage in having an unevenly distributed vote. In a two-party system we have seen that a party can, at the limit, achieve a seats-to-votes ratio of 2.0 – its percentage of seats can be twice as high as its percentage of votes, provided that it receives no votes at all in the seats it does not win, and no excess of votes beyond a bare majority in those which it does.

Gerrymandering is the art of maximising the efficiency of a party's vote. The basic principle is to draw constituency boundaries in such a way that a party has no votes at all where it loses and a bare plurality where it wins. The term itself comes from the shape of one constituency designed by Governor Gerry of Massachusetts in 1812 to help his political allies. It was so long, narrow and wiggly that it reminded one journalist of a salamander – hence gerrymander.

Contemporary America provides some fine examples of gerrymandering. The Supreme Court's insistence on equal apportionment removed the constraints associated with the need to observe community boundaries and it also required frequent boundary revisions which remained in the hands of state legislatures. As a result, politicians have gerrymandered to their heart's content. For example, before the 1982 Congressional elections Republicans openly boasted of their intention to gerrymander and of their superior skills in doing so. The Republican National Committee had spent several years coordinating preparations for redistricting and fed computer files of precinct data to their politicians in the states (Ehrenhalt, 1983, p. 48; Jacobson, 1983, pp. 13–14). Unfortunately for the Republicans the Democrats, with less noise and less hi-tech computer back-up, none the less did an equally effective partisan gerrymander in the states where they controlled the legislature. In California, Congressman Phillip Burton quietly produced a map designed to increase the Democratic majority from 22–21 to 27–18 (California gained two additional Congressional seats in 1982 because of population increases). In the end it seems the Republicans made no net gain through gerrymandering in 1982. None the less, the sheer extent of partisan manipulation of district boundaries was a disastrous by-product of the Supreme Court's intervention in the electoral process.

Three kinds of political self-interest are apparent in United State gerrymanders. First, the party that controls a state legislature draws boundaries to help itself. Secondly, boundaries are drawn so as to help incumbents of both parties, increasing the number of safe seats, and decreasing the number of marginals. Thirdly, dominant individuals and factions redraw boundaries to help their racial, ethnic, ideological, or even personal cliques within the party.

The British method of drawing boundaries is more successful. Local agents of the Boundary Commission do not operate with a single set of principles. In some places their reports happen to help Labour, in others they help the Conservatives. Waller (1983) concludes that it is the chaos of these decisions, unmotivated either by partisanship or consistent logical principle, which produces a fair result. Partisan motivation would produce intentional gerrymandering but any consistent principle applied uniformly throughout the country would also be likely to produce an unintentional gerrymander by accidentally favouring one party or another. In this instance British justice has been blind, incoherent and therefore successful. Those who seek an example of British 'muddling through' need look no further.

The only way to detect gerrymanders is to look at outcomes, and the only way to prevent intentional gerrymanders is to keep politicians out of the redistricting process.

Bending the rules in proportional representation systems

Adopting PR as a principle does not end arguments about electoral fairness, it intensifies them. The Scandinavian countries especially have had long experience of proportional representation but an almost continuous debate about the best PR formula to use. When they have changed their rules it has always been in order to achieve specific party objectives – to help one party or hurt another rather than to pursue some abstract idea of fairness.

Corresponding to gerrymandering and malapportionment, we find such techniques in PR systems as: (1) manipulation of thresholds and constituency sizes; (2) cartels; and (3) bonuses.

Thresholds and constituency size. Most architects of PR want representation to be proportional for serious, pro-regime parties. They want to keep trivial splinter groups and tiny anti-regime parties out of parliament for fear that parliamentary representation might help them destabilise the political system. Effective thresholds to exclude very small parties may be *explicit* or *implicit*. In Germany no party with less than 5 per cent of the national vote is included in the PR share-out of seats; in Denmark the explicit threshold is 2 per cent; in Sweden 4 per cent.

Implicit thresholds are influenced by the number of members returned per constituency: the smaller the number, the less proportional the result – and it is small parties that suffer. At one extreme Israel and the Netherlands group all their parliamentary seats into a single national constituency. Hence a party can get an MP elected to the Dutch parliament even if it scores less than one per cent of the national vote. By contrast Ireland uses 41 constituencies to elect a total of only 166 MPs: some Irish constituencies have three MPs, others five. No PR system for allocating seats will give any seats to a party with few votes in a constituency when there are only three seats to allocate: under most systems, a party with less than 25 per cent of the vote is unlikely to win any seats in a three seat constituency.

Manipulating the size of constituencies, and therefore the number of seats, is a form of gerrymandering. Throughout its long years of power in Eire, Fianna Fail drew and redrew constituency boundaries so as to maximise its representation in parliament. When its Fine Gael and Labour opponents were in office in 1974 they also tried to manipulate the boundaries in their favour. The Minister in charge was James Tully who contributed the term Tullymander to the Irish political vocabulary. A Tullymander is a blatant gerrymander which fails. Tully divided the areas of Fine Gael/Labour strength into three-seat constituencies so that his National Coalition could win two-thirds of these seats with 50 per cent of the vote, and all of them with 75 per cent. In areas of relative weakness he arranged to have more four-seat constituencies: in these four-seat constituencies he could still hope to win fully half the seats as long as his Coalition scored at least 40 per cent of the vote. Unfortunately for him, the swing of popular support to Fianna Fail was so large that what had been strong Coalition areas (the three-seat constituencies) became marginal Fianna Fail areas and the small constituencies in these areas now produced a bonus of seats for Tully's opponents.

Sometimes PR systems are designed to discriminate against one specific party, most often the communists. In Sweden in 1952, the ruling coalition of Social Democrats and Agrarians wanted a new system that would benefit both of them without the need for a formal electoral pact. That meant a system which would give the Social Democrats, as the largest party, a modest degree of over-representation while not penalising the small Agrarian Party. In addition, they wanted to continue to penalise the smallest party of all, the Communists, and in this they succeeded. By altering the method of setting quotas for the allocation of seats, albeit in a way that had no rationale in mathematics or justice, the desired result was obtained. Compared to the previous election, the Social Democrats gained two seats, the Agrarians gained four and the Communists lost three. The new rules had been scrupulously applied but the Communists were cheated none the less (Sarlvik, 1983).

Cartels. Although PR is basically proportional representation for parties, various PR systems allow parties to group themselves into electoral coalitions called *cartels*. Outside Scandinavia the system is often described by the French word *apparentement*. The cartel system has been used in Scandinavia, France, Italy and Greece. The principle of the cartel is that parties are allowed to declare themselves linked for electoral purposes if that alters the PR allocation of seats in their favour, but they are under no obligation to act as a responsible political coalition in parliament. The device begins and ends in arithmetic. It has no implications for policy or responsibility.

In Fourth Republic France, the system used for the elections of 1951 and 1956 allowed a cartel of parties to take *all* the seats in a multi-member constituency if, collectively, they won over 50 per cent of the vote. Similarly, the Italian electoral law in 1953 offered two-thirds of the seats in parliament to any cartel that won over 50 per cent of the national vote. (The governing cartel's vote dropped to a fraction of a per cent under 50 per cent when this law was introduced; so it had no effect and was later repealed.)

In Sweden and Norway the cartel system helped the fragmented anti-socialist parties combine against the socialists for electoral purposes without having to resolve their political differences. Socialist governments abolished the system in 1947 in Norway and 1952 in Sweden. This Scandinavian version of cartels worked within constituencies. Where two locally weak parties each received insufficient support to obtain any seats within a multi-member constituency, their combined vote might entitle them to one.

Bonuses. FPTP systems usually produce a significant bonus in seats for the party with most votes. These bonuses are usually smaller under PR although PR systems have occasionally been explicitly designed to provide a *governing bonus* for the leading party (or cartel). Those who stress fairness as a criterion for electoral systems are not necessarily opposed to government bonuses provided they are fairly and reliably calculated. That means the bonus should go to the party that is in the lead in terms of votes: it should *reinforce* the PR result, not *override* it. Gudgin and Taylor (1979) quote, with approval, Dutch proposals to allocate parliamentary seats in proportion to the *squares* of the parties' shares of the vote (a voting split of 40:30:20:10 in a four-party system would give seats in proportion to 16:9:4:1, i.e. an absolute majority for the top party). The method would appeal to any mathematician but has not yet been adopted by politicians. However, cruder, less elegant systems of reinforced PR have been used to favour governing parties in Greece since 1958, and were enshrined in the 1953 Italian law on cartels.

Bending the rules by doing nothing

Governments sometimes engineer elections by failing to change the rules instead of actively manipulating them. A particularly widespread practice is the technique of the *passive gerrymander*. This means that governments refuse to redraw constituency boundaries to take account of population shifts. In the past, right-wing governments used the passive gerrymander by ignoring the movement of population from conservative rural areas into the more progressive urban areas. The Kaiser's pre-war German Reich used it with crushing effect against the socialist SPD. Similar passive gerrymandering, giving undue representation to conservative rural areas, prompted the United States Supreme Court to take an interest in apportionment in 1962 and 1964.

Population trends have now changed in mature industrial societies. Instead of the old drift from the countryside to the towns, more recent population movements have been from the inner city to the suburbs and rural fringes. Consequently, the passive gerrymander now helps left-wing parties against their conservative opponents. Britain provides a good example of this reversal. In 1969 the Labour Government persuaded parliament to postpone implementation of the Boundary Commission's proposals until after the 1970 election. The excuse was that a reform of local government was pending. The effect was to give Labour six extra seats (a larger effect had been expected) in the 1970 election by failing to abolish or merge decaying inner-city constituencies that returned Labour MPs. Labour lost the 1970 election none the less and the new Conservative government promptly implemented the new boundaries.

Another form of electoral manipulation through inaction is failure to adjust the electoral system to a changing pattern of party competition. Again, Britain provides a good example. In 1955 the Liberals won 3 per cent of the votes and 1 per cent of the seats. At that time Britain was still a two-party system and under-representation of trivially small parties, such as the Liberals, was arguably an appropriate outcome under any system, PR or FPTP. But in 1983 the Liberal/SDP Alliance won 26 per cent of the votes but only 4 per cent of the seats. Britain's FPTP system can perform capriciously when there are three or more major parties. By refusing to change the electoral system, Conservative and Labour governments have relied on growing distortions in the electoral system to protect their own positions from a third-party challenge.

Do Electoral Systems Influence Party Systems?

Views have changed on the consequences of electoral systems for party politics. Before and immediately after the Second World

War PR received a bad press. It was blamed for the rise of fascism in Germany and Italy. By contrast, Britain's FPTP system was praised for producing firm decisive democratic governments able to resist fascism internally and externally. In a classic work, Duverger (1954) claimed that FPTP favoured a two-party system; indeed he argued that this proposition approached the status of a true sociological law. PR, on the other hand, he believed was associated with multi-party systems though he did not elevate this to law-like status. Today we hear more criticism and less praise for FPTP, especially in Britain. Electoral systems are often judged guilty by association. There is a strong urge to praise anything connected with a stable, prosperous democracy and criticise anything connected, however tenuously, with a faltering economy or an unstable government.

Do electoral systems have a major political impact? In the very short term there is no doubt at all that they do. If Britain's 1983 election had been fought under pure PR, the Conservatives would not have won an overall majority in Parliament and the Alliance would have won almost as many MPs as Labour. Indeed the Alliance might have become the second largest party if the introduction of PR led more people to vote for previously small parties. This issue of whether electoral systems affect votes as well as their conversion into seats complicates discussion of electoral system effects. But the even more difficult question is whether electoral systems have more than this immediate, short-term effect. Early studies of electoral systems attributed a much wider influence to them. Electoral systems were said to influence party systems – that is, the number of significant parties, their campaign strategies, their willingness to cooperate, their cohesion. Above all the electoral system supposedly had a major influence on the stability of the political system.

Certainly there are notable correlations between the type of electoral system, the number of major parties and the stability of the political system. Douglas Rae's study (1971) of twenty Western democracies in the years 1945–65 showed that 90 per cent of elections involved *either* a combination of a majoritarian electoral system and a two-party system *or* a combination of a PR electoral system and a multi-party system. The only exceptions in his survey were Austria and Canada. In Austria, two parties predominated despite PR while in Canada, the regional/territorial dimension to voting allowed more than two parties to prosper despite FPTP. We can point to a few other places where two parties predominated despite PR (Malta and West Germany, for example) or where territorial parties made FPTP compatible with multi-partyism (nineteenth century Ireland or twentieth century Scotland, for example, have made Britain a multi-party as well as a multinational state). But Rae's basic point stands.

More recently, Powell (1982) has studied twenty-eight democracies over the period 1958–76 and looked at the relationship between electoral systems and voting participation, majority control, government stability and political violence. He concludes that majoritarian systems (such as FPTP) do tend to produce stable, durable governments backed by disciplined legislative majorities. Even when they fail to produce a majority government the *ethos* of single party government associated with such electoral systems leads to a minority caretaker government rather than a coalition. Powell also finds that PR systems allow easy entry into parliament for small, new and extremist parties. Such systems encourage a multiplicity of small parties, and a representational strategy of campaigning which produces close links between parties and social groups. PR systems are associated with negotiation-oriented politics and a low level of turmoil. Voting participation is high partly because of the close links between social groups and parties, and partly because most PR systems also include incentives or requirements to vote. But PR systems were also associated with extremist representation in parliament and relatively unstable governments. Lack of a stable majority government, in turn, makes PR systems especially vulnerable to military intervention (Powell, 1982, p. 225; he instances Greece, Brazil and Turkey).

Neither Rae's nor Powell's static analysis can answer questions about causation. Does PR cause or reflect a multi-party system? Is FPTP a *determinant* or just a *reflection* of stable government? To answer such questions, historical analysis is needed. This reveals that the impact of electoral systems is easily exaggerated. Rokkan (1968, 1970) has pointed out that social cleavages produced multiparty systems in many continental countries *before* they switched from majoritarian to PR systems. The switch did lead to an increase in the number of small parties getting at least 1 per cent of the vote, but it did not fragment the major parties which survived relatively unscathed (Shamir, 1985). The Weimar

Republic's PR system did not cause multi-partyism – that was inherited from the old Reich despite the Reich's majoritarian electoral system. Similarly, FPTP hardly accounts for the two-party system in the United States. Pomper (1980, p. 38) notes that the present electoral system was not established until 1842 by which date a two-party system already existed. In Britain, FPTP did not prevent several reconstructions of the party system culminating in the displacement of the Liberal Party by Labour. Nor has it prevented the recent surge of support for the Liberal/SDP Alliance. Electoral systems are far from omnipotent.

In their reaction against the idea that electoral systems determine party systems writers such as Rokkan suggested that electoral systems were merely the result of party systems which were themselves the consequence of social divisions. Where society was split by a single powerful cleavage a two-party system was the result, irrespective of the electoral system. However, where society was split by multiple cleavages – especially where ethnic and religious cleavages as well as class cleavages were important – the result was a multi-party system. PR was the only system that would satisfy all the major contenders in a multi-party system. PR was a response to the party system and its attendant political problems, not a cause.

This approach was almost as simple as the one it replaced. Contemporary writers (such as Bogdanor, 1983) caution against easy generalisations about the relationship between electoral and party systems. In reality electoral systems are neither cause nor consequence but both. Electoral systems often do reflect political cleavages or, more strictly, they reflect their architects' decisions to make them reflect political cleavages. But electoral systems do have an independent effect of their own. After a period of time an electoral system becomes part of the political furniture. The political circumstances which the electoral system was designed to fit may change but the system remains, operating rather differently in changed circumstances and certainly no longer a mere reflection of contemporary political cleavages.

Britain and France illustrate how the operation of electoral systems depends on political circumstances. Both countries have been affected by the *nationalisation of party competition* – the emergence of the same basic pattern of party competition in all parts of a country. In Britain during the 1920s, Liberal candidates stood a decent chance of victory in the considerable number of constituencies where one of the major parties did not stand. Now, of course, three-party contests are the norm, a factor which reduces the Liberals' ability to win seats. Equally, under the double-ballot system in France during the Third Republic electoral alliances before the second ballot were forged on a local basis, with the centre Radical Party joining forces with the left in some areas but with the right in others. By the time of the Fifth Republic, pacts had become national rather than local, a development which reduced the room for manoeuvre of centre parties and the same electoral system had a different effect upon the fortunes of centre parties. Thus the emergence of nationwide patterns of party competition altered the operation of the electoral system, especially in territorially-based systems.

The moral is that it is easier to point to a vast variety of specific consequences arising from the application of particular electoral systems in particular circumstances than to enunciate some simple general rule. Moreover, these consequences often depend upon the fine details of electoral systems rather than their gross features. Characterising systems simply as PR or majoritarian can be misleading. Just as attention to detail is the essence of electoral engineering, so too should it provide the basis for analysing the impact of electoral systems.

Further Reading

Too much of the writing on electoral systems and their effects is polemic rather than analytic. Beware of enthusiasts.

A review of arguments for and against different systems can be found in Lijphart and Grofman (1984). For a superbly readable account of several particular electoral systems operating in their social and historical contexts see the collection of essays edited by Bogdanor and Butler (1983). The chapter by Rose is a clear, overall description that sets out the basic definitions and statistics of current European systems, while the chapter by Bogdanor is an informed and balanced account of the interaction beween electoral systems and party systems. For more on that critical interaction see the classics by Rae (1967, 1971) and Rokkan (1968, 1970), the more comprehensive and up-to-date study by Powell (1982), and the special issue on electoral systems of the *European Journal of Political Research* (December 1985). The history of Duverger's 'law' linking FPTP with two-party systems is well reviewed in Riker (1982). On the vexed issue of reapportionment see Butler and Cain (1985). The *International Almanac of Electoral History* by Mackie and Rose (1986) gives useful historical sketches of various countries' electoral laws, and charts the trends in party support through changing electoral systems.

References

BERRINGTON, H. (1985) 'MPs and their Constituents in Britain: the History of the Relationship', in V. Bogdanor (ed.), *Representatives of the People* (Aldershot: Gower).

BLEWETT, N. (1972) *The Peers, the Parties and the People: the General Elections of 1910* (London: Macmillan).

BOCHEL, J. and DENVER, D. T. (1983) 'Candidate Selection in the Labour Party: What the Selectors Seek', *British Journal of Political Science*, vol. 13, pp. 45–70.

BOGDANOR, V. (1983) 'Conclusion: Electoral Systems and Party Systems', in V. Bogdanor and D. Butler (eds), *Democracy and Elections* (Cambridge: Cambridge University Press).

BRAMS, S. J. (1980) 'Approval Voting in Multi-candidate Elections', *Policy Studies Journal*, vol. 9, pp. 102–8.

BRAMS, S. J. and FISHBURN, P. C. (1978) 'Approval Voting', *American Political Science Review*, vol. 72, pp. 831–47.

BUTLER, D. (1981) 'Electoral Systems', in D. Butler *et al.* (eds), *Democracy at the Polls* (Washington, DC: American Enterprise Institute).

BUTLER, D. *et al.* (eds) (1981) *Democracy at the Polls* (Washington, DC: American Enterprise Institute).

BUTLER, D. (1983) 'Variants of the Westminster Model' in V. Bogdanor and D. Butler (eds), *Democracy and Elections* (Cambridge: Cambridge University Press).

BUTLER, D. and CAIN, B. (1985) 'Reapportionment: a Study in Comparative Government', *Electoral Studies*, vol. 4, pp. 197–214.

CREWE, I. (1981) 'Electoral Participation', in D. Butler *et al.* (eds) *Democracy At The Polls* (Washington, DC: American Enterprise Institute).

CRIDDLE, B. (1984) 'Candidates', in D. Butler and D. Kavanagh (eds), *The British General Election of 1983* (London: Macmillan).

DUVERGER, M. (1954, 1959) *Political Parties* (London: Methuen).

EHRENHALT, A. (1983) 'Reapportionment and Redistricting', in T. E. Mann and N. J. Ornstein (eds), *The American Elections of 1982* (Washington, DC: American Enterprise Institute).

GUDGIN, G. and TAYLOR, P. J. (1979) *Seats, Votes and the Spatial Organisation of Elections* (London: Pion).

JACOBSON, G. C. (1983) *The Politics of Congressional Elections* (Boston: Little Brown).

LAKEMAN, E. (1970) *How Democracies Vote: a Study of Majority and Proportional Systems* (London: Faber).

LAKEMAN, E. (1982) *Power to Elect: the Case for Proportional Representation* (London: Heinemann).

LIJPHART, A. and GROFMAN, B. (eds) (1984) *Choosing an Electoral System* (New York: Praeger).

MCKEE, P. (1983) 'The Republic of Ireland', in V. Bogdanor and D. Butler (eds), *Democracy and Elections* (Cambridge: Cambridge University Press).

MACKIE, T. T. and ROSE, R. (1986) *International Almanac of Electoral History* (London: Macmillan).

MARSH, M. (1985) 'The Voters Decide? Preferential Voting in European List Systems', *European Journal of Political Research*, vol. 13, pp. 365–78.

MILLER, W. L. (1978) 'Social Class and Party Choice in England: A New Analysis', *British Journal of Political Science*, vol. 8, pp. 257–84.

MILLER, W. L. (1981) *The End of British Politics? Scots and English Political Behaviour in the Seventies* (Oxford: Clarendon Press).

MILLER, W. L. (1984) 'There Was No Alternative: the British General Election of 1983', *Parliamentary Affairs*, vol. 37, pp. 364–84.

NIEMI, R. G. (1984) 'The Problem of Strategic Behaviour under Approval Voting', *American Political Science Review*, vol. 78, pp. 952–8.

POLSBY, N. (1983) *The Consequences of Party Reform* (Oxford: Oxford University Press).

POMPER, G. M. (1968, 1980), *Elections in America: Control and Influence in Democratic Politics* (New York: Longman).

POWELL, G. BINGHAM (1982) *Contemporary Democracies* (Cambridge, Mass.: Harvard University Press).

RAE, D. W. (1967, 1971) *The Political Consequences of Electoral Laws* (New Haven: Yale University Press).

RANNEY, A. (1965) *Pathways to Parliament* (London: Macmillan).

RANNEY, A. (1981) 'Candidate Selection', in D. Butler *et al.*, *Democracy at the Polls* (Washington, DC: American Enterprise Institute).

RIKER, W. (1982) 'The Two-party System and Duverger's Law', *American Political Science Review*, vol. 76, pp. 753–66.

ROKKAN, S. (1968) 'Electoral Systems', in D. L. Sills (ed.), *International Encyclopedia of the Social Sciences*, vol. 5 (London: Macmillan).

ROKKAN, S. (1970) *Citizens, Elections, Parties* (Oslo: Universitetsforlaget).

ROSE, R. (1983) 'Elections and Electoral Systems: Choices and Alternatives', in V. Bogdanor and D. Butler (eds), *Democracy and Elections* (Cambridge: Cambridge University Press).

SARLVIK, B. (1983) 'Scandinavia', in V. Bogdanor and D. Butler (eds), *Democracy and Elections* (Cambridge: Cambridge University Press).
SHAMIR, M. (1985) 'Changes in Electoral Systems as Interventions: Another Test of Duverger's Hypothesis', *European Journal of Political Research*, vol. 13, pp. 1–10.
TODD, J. E. and DODD, P. A. (1982) *The Electoral Registration Process in the United Kingdom* (London: Office of Population Censuses and Surveys).
WALLER, R. J. (1983) 'The 1983 Boundary Commission: Policies and Effects', *Electoral Studies*, vol. 2, pp. 195–206.

4

The Electoral Message: Interpreting Election Results

Introduction

In the opening chapter we classified elections into free competitive elections, dominant-party elections, candidate-choice elections, and elections by acclamation. When freedom is curtailed we naturally focus on how much, if any, is left; and we classify elections according to the way they are organised and conducted. Elections without choice tell us about the regime, not the electorate. Indeed such elections are designed to prevent us finding out about the opinions, attitudes, prejudices and choices of the electorate.

But the free, competitive elections of liberal democracies are *not* designed to muffle the voice of the electorate – quite the contrary. So it should be easy to interpret the result of a free election in terms of the choices and aspirations of the electorate. Alas, the information content of an election result is very low, even when the election is free and competitive. The result itself tells us how many votes went to each candidate and which candidates were elected to office. By itself, however, the result provides little insight into the nature of politics or the state of the parties, and it conveys no clear message from the public to the politicians. As Dahl (1964, p. 126) comments:

> In no large nation state can elections tell us much about the preferences of majorities and minorities beyond the bare fact that among those who went to the polls a majority, plurality or

minority indicated their first choices for some particular candidate or group of candidates. What the choices of this electoral majority are, beyond that for the particular candidates, it is almost impossible to say with much confidence.

A loud voice often serves as a substitute for empirical confidence, however. The simple fact is that all kinds of people do interpret elections, often in a very self-interested way. Without in any way contradicting Dahl, Kelly (1983, p. 3) writes:

> The belief that elections carry obvious messages is widely shared in democratic nations. It is held by many protest voters, surely, and evidently by those politicians, reporters, editors, scholars and promoters of causes and interests who, in the immediate aftermath of an election, say with great assurance what it means.

It is useful to distinguish between insight and message according to the motivations people have for interpreting elections. The public, journalists and scholars need to interpret elections primarily to understand: that is, in order to gain *insight*. For the public, this reflects a natural curiosity about the world; for journalists and scholars, insight is the nature of their business. Political actors, on the other hand, have a more immediate motivation for interpreting elections. Some seek guidance as to their own future behaviour: they respond to the *message* of the election. Others want to use the election message to influence or control the behaviour of others. To use a religious metaphor, politicians are like the faithful gathered in church to seek the guidance of the Holy Spirit – but some are on their knees in the pews while others are on their feet in the pulpit.

The importance of insight into an election result is to protect against misinterpretations of its message. After Ronald Reagan's massive victory over Jimmy Carter in the United States presidential election of 1980, opinion polls showed that by a majority of 63 per cent to 24 per cent the public interpreted the election as a simple rejection of President Carter rather than as a mandate for more conservative policies (see, for example, Schneider, 1981, p. 247). But this did not prevent George Bush, the victorious vice-presidential candidate, claiming that the victory was:

> Not simply a mandate for change, but a mandate for peace and freedom; a mandate for prosperity; a mandate for opportunity

> for all Americans regardless of race, sex or creed; a mandate for leadership that is both strong and compassionate . . . a mandate to make government the servant of the people in the way our founding fathers intended; a mandate for hope; a mandate for hope for the fulfilment of the great dream that President-elect Reagan has worked for all his life.

Such crude misinterpretations are often a more powerful influence on the course of events than careful, well-documented analyses. Many Congressmen agreed that Reagan had been given a mandate for change and were restrained in their opposition to his proposals for fear of incurring the wrath of the new, conservative electorate. Whether there *was* a new, conservative electorate became irrelevant; the interpretation had been established. Interpretations of elections, however unreal, have real political consequences. Drew (1981, p. 345), commenting on the 1980 result, noted that:

> The important thing in politics when it comes to determining the behaviour of politicians, is not necessarily what happened but what people think happened – what becomes the accepted truisms. The truisms guide behaviour. There is little question that most of the Democrats, and even those moderate Republicans, who remain in Congress will poke their heads out of the trenches very cautiously.

This chapter first reviews a classification of competitive elections according to the voting patterns in the electorate. It then discusses the importance of politicians' and commentators' expectations in framing interpretations of the actual result. Subsequent sections examine the most common *mis*interpretations of national elections and the particular problems of interpreting 'non-national' elections.

How to Classify Competitive Elections

Confronting the bare facts of an election result, the most useful starting point is to place the election in one of the categories developed by political scientists. This can be tricky, for these categories have multiplied in response both to the weaknesses of

Table 4.1 *A classification of competitive elections*

	Levels of support	
Patterns of voting support	*Normal majority party wins*	*Normal majority party loses*
Continuity in pattern of electoral cleavages	Maintaining ('Normal')	Deviating
Change in pattern of electoral cleavages	Converting	Realigning ('Critical')

Other types of election:

Reinstating elections are elections which reverse the effect of a deviating election.

Dealigning elections show a weakening of existing alignments but no new cleavages developing. Old alignments are broken but are replaced by volatility rather than new alignments. Numerical majorities may be large in an era of dealignment but they are unstable and swings between elections can be large.

early classifications and to recent changes in the nature of elections themselves. The four main types are shown in Figure 4.1: realigning, converting, maintaining and deviating elections.

The starting point is Key's (1955) concept of *critical* elections. These are *realigning* elections which break the existing political mould. To use Key's own words, they are 'elections in which the depth and intensity of electoral involvement are high, in which more or less profound readjustments occur in relations of power within the community and in which new and durable electoral groupings are formed'. Realigning elections have long-term consequences; they set a new mould as well as breaking the old one. In the USA the 1930s provide the most recent period of realignment, when Roosevelt put together the New Deal Coalition which made the Democrats the 'natural majority party' for at least a generation thereafter.

But sometimes the bases or patterns of support for parties change without altering their levels of support. Theoretically, two equal parties might swop all their voters without changing their relative strength. This distinction between bases and levels of support is valuable in practice: for example, Sweden's Social Democrats have remained remarkably successful in the 1970s and 1980s even though their electoral base has moved from blue-collar workers towards those employed by, or otherwise dependent on, the state. Elections which change the bases of support for parties without radically affecting their level are termed *converting* elections. They 'convert' the existing parties to new patterns of support.

The other types of elections are more straightforward. *Maintaining* or *normal* elections occur when party shares of the vote change little and political alignments remain unaltered. In countries with a natural majority party, that party wins a normal election. *Deviating* elections are where a party suffers a sharp loss of support but one which is spread evenly over all social groups, so that the pattern of political alignments is unaffected even though the levels of party support change. In a deviating election, the majority party's defeat is due to short-run factors such as a poor candidate. Despite speculation about the new conservative majority in the United States after Ronald Reagan's victory in 1980, that election is an example of a deviating election, that is one in which Jimmy Carter failed to rally enough natural Democrats. *Reinstating* elections reverse the impact of deviating elections and mark a return to normal. A reinstating election is nothing more than a normal election after a deviating one – for example, Jimmy Carter's victory in the United States election of 1976 returned a Democrat to the White House after eight years of Republican presidents. Finally, *dealigning* elections witness a weakening of party attachments among voters and a declining relationship between social groups and particular parties. Dealignment rings out the old without ringing in the new.

Practical application of this classification depends very much on the availability of data. Analysts have used three main techniques to measure 'alignments' and variations around them. The *first* is to ask people directly about their psychological identification with political parties (see Chapter 6 for a further discussion of the concept of party identification). In the United States, such questions invariably show a Democratic lead over the Republicans, indicating that a 'normal' election will yield a Democratic victory. But surveys of US party identification also reveal a growing number of non-partisans, showing the emergence of dealignment since the 1960s. A *second* treatment of alignments is to use survey findings on the relationship between social groups and party support. When social groups are tightly linked to parties (as in Northern Ireland) this is evidence of alignment; when the links decay (as in Britain since the 1970s) this is evidence of dealignment.

In combination these two methods of self-assessed partisanship and its link with social groups are ideal; but application presupposes the availability of modern survey data. For earlier periods, it is necessary to use a *third* method, analysing aggregate election results in regions, states or constituencies rather than the votes of individual voters. When a particular result is highly correlated with previous results, such as for example when the most Labour regions at one election continue to be the most Labour at the next, there is evidence of continuity in alignments. Sharp discontinuities, on the other hand, are a sign of a break in the electoral pattern. (Note that correlations are unaffected by changes in the overall levels of party support, provided that a party gains, or loses, support *uniformly* in all regions.)

Even changes in the level of party support may provide some insights, however. For example, Dean Burnham (1978) examined swings in British constituencies at elections held between 1880 and 1974. By this rather crude method he identified 1886, 1906, 1918, 1931 and 1945 as realigning elections, while 1910 and 1935 were reinstating elections which at least partly offset the huge changes that occurred in 1906 and 1931.

There are several problems with the classification scheme shown in Figure 4.1. *First*, it is often difficult to classify an election without the benefit of hindsight. In particular the distinction between deviating and realigning elections is defined in terms of their *long-term* consequences. Both are elections in which the governing party is defeated but in a realignment the defeat is permanent and marks the start of a new electoral era while in a deviating election the majority party's defeat is reversed at the next election. Although it is impossible to reach a firm decision about whether any recent election is deviating or realigning, there are likely to be several clues awaiting the political detective.

Deviating elections are 'low-stimulus' campaigns in which some short-term factor – an unpopular candidate, a scandal, unfavourable economic conditions – causes majority party supporters to stay at home, or perhaps to defect temporarily to another party in terms of their vote, but not to alter their partisan self-image, their sense of party identification. In the United States presidential election of 1980, a shift in the last two days of the campaign in the public's rating of President Carter's handling of the economy largely explains why he became the first Democrat to be voted out of the White House since 1888. In contrast, realigning elections are 'high-stimulus' campaigns which debate major national issues, forge new links between voters, groups and parties and end in a high turn-out, often involving the participation of newly-enfranchised electors. In Britain, realignment between the world wars was marked by the collapse of the Liberal Party and the rise of Labour. But whether another realignment is now underway, with the SDP/Liberal Alliance replacing Labour as the major party of the left, will not be known until well into the 1990s.

There is a *second* difficulty with the whole concept of critical elections. Is any one election ever critical? Can a major change in patterns of alignment take place that quickly? The answer is no. The idea of a single crucial election is just too elegant for the real world. Great changes in political alignments usually take place over a sequence of elections.

The last major realignment in the United States occurred during the 1930s but it was not all concentrated into the celebrated 1932 campaign, when Roosevelt defeated the Republican President Herbert Hoover. Over a decade, the bases of the major parties' support changed, as did the balance of support between them, though the number and names of the major parties remained (confusingly) the same. Roosevelt's New Deal coalition of urban working class, Catholic and ethnic areas in the north allied to the Democrats' traditional strength in the south changed the pattern of socio-political cleavages, put New Deal issues at the head of the political agenda, and made the Democrats the natural majority party (hence the 1930s was a realigning rather than a converting decade). But the realignment of forces into a Democratic New Deal coalition backing Roosevelt versus an anti-New Deal Republican opposition did not come about, all at once, in 1932. It began to take shape earlier, in 1928, when the (unsuccessful) Democratic candidate was (like Roosevelt) a New Yorker and (unlike Roosevelt) a Catholic. The realignment certainly continued with Roosevelt's election in 1932, but it gathered pace thereafter because of fierce Republican resistance to his New Deal measures.

Had these policies been enacted with cheerful bipartisan support, the outcome for US voting patterns in the late 1930s and 1940s might have been very different. There are realigning *periods* rather than realigning *elections*.

If we are going to pick out just one election as the critical election in realignment, we might pick the first or the last in the realigning sequence – the one that disrupts old patterns of voting, or the one that fully establishes the new pattern. With hindsight, we can see that 1932 marked a break with old cleavages but it did not fully implement the new structure. Indeed as Broder (1980) notes, the very gradual shift of Southern whites to the Republicans since the 1950s represents the long-delayed falling into place of the New Deal party system. Realignment was continuing in the South even as it was overtaken by dealignment elsewhere. Jeanne Kirkpatrick (1983, p. 8), by contrast, regards the *final* realigning election as critical. She suggests that 'when such realigning or critical elections occur, they reflect trends that have been building for years, perhaps for a decade, and are finally expressed in a single dramatic election'. She suggests, almost certainly incorrectly, that Ronald Reagan's victory in 1980 was such a turning point. But whether we regard the first or last election in the sequence as critical, it is clear that realignment takes time.

A *final* problem with the classification of elections is its applicability to an era of *dealignment*. With the exception of dealigning elections, all the categories presuppose clear alignments between voters, social groups and parties. Particular elections then create, exemplify, or deviate from this pattern. But what happens when such links fade away or at least weaken in intensity? This is the problem of the disappearing baseline. It helps to explain the paradox that only one of the last five United States presidential elections has been 'normal' in the sense of yielding a victory for the majority party, the Democrats. If dealignment continues without realignment (and this may depend more on political leadership than anything else), new classifications will be needed which place election results in new categories, not defined in terms of partisanship or social groups – perhaps classifications based upon distinctions between the various factors that have hitherto been lumped together under the dismissive heading of 'short-term' factors: candidates, issues, media coverage and the like. We discuss the growing importance of short-term factors in Chapter 8.

In summary, political scientists have classified elections by whether they create, maintain, deviate from, or show a weakening of, links between parties and either individual voters or social groups. The classification depends both upon the levels of party support and the patterns of party support. Difficulties in applying this classification are that the categories are not wholly exclusive, that categorisation often requires hindsight, and that changes in alignments take more than one election to work through. None the less, the classification is still a useful starting-point for interpreting specific elections.

Why Expectations are Crucial

Expectations play a crucial role in electoral interpretation. Often results are not judged by any absolute standard. They are judged by whether they fit or upset *prior expectations*. An expected defeat hardly counts, and the same is true of an expected victory. Winning in politics often means 'doing better than expected'. Losing means 'doing worse than expected'.

Expectations coloured the interpretation of the 1980 presidential election in the United States. The margin of Reagan's victory and the defeat of Senate liberals had not been forecast. So the surprise and the impact were all the greater. Understandably, many commentators lost their sense of judgement. Instead of interpreting the figures as the result of a very late, sudden swing, their surprise and perhaps their sense of guilt at failing to foresee the outcome made them inclined to overstate and overdramatise the Republican and conservative sweep. (Reagan's re-election in 1984 was less unexpected and inspired less cataclysmic interpretations.)

Conversely, Labour's disastrous performance in the 1983 British general election brought forth notably restrained commentaries. Most writers (not all) avoided interpreting that election as the end of the road for the Labour Party despite the drop in its vote to a mere 28 per cent. The reason for this restraint was that the quarrels in the Labour Party during the 1979–83 parliament had been so intense that no one really expected it to do very well in the election.

Politicians elected with a majority that falls below expectations are elected none the less. True, by exceeding expectations in 1980,

Ronald Reagan was presented with an opportunity to create political capital by claiming a mandate from the people. It was a chance he seized with both hands. But he would have been president even if his margin had been less than anticipated. In this case expectations influenced the resources available to a new government rather than who governed. Where expectations are even more significant is in elections that are a *prelude* to bigger contests rather then decisive in themselves. A sequence of elections allows candidates to rapidly gain (or lose) momentum by exceeding (or falling below) expectations. American presidential primaries are the classic example. An unexpectedly good performance brings a welter of media attention, financial support and general momentum. Doing better than expected in the first couple of primaries is especially important. New Hampshire, traditionally the state that holds the first primary of election year, contributes less than 1 per cent of delegates to the national party conventions, but it receives an excess of media attention because it comes first. In 1980, the New Hampshire primary got three times the television coverage of the New York primary despite the fact that New York had ten times as many convention delegates (Dye and Zeigler, 1983, p. 198). Statistically, George McGovern lost the New Hampshire primary in 1972 as did Jimmy Carter four years later. But because both candidates exceeded expectations, they were set on the road to the Democratic nomination.

Expectations are not quite as important in interpreting British by-elections even though these also stimulate momentum for the winning party, particularly when a general election is in the offing. This is because by-elections, like presidential contests but unlike any one primary election, do have one unambiguous outcome. But low expectations can limit the damage to the loser. Confronting the prospect of a by-election defeat, party managers are well advised to lower media expectations at the start of the campaign and then engineer a last-minute swing in their favour, no matter how small. The result can then be presented as above expectations. Many a by-election wreck has been salvaged thus.

But whose expectations matter? And where and how are they formed? Basically, expectations emerge from journalists' discussions in bars. The collective judgement of the media on such matters is rarely biased by intention, but it is often superficial and volatile. Too many journalists judge the present in relation to the immediate past; they lack awareness of long-term trends; they can talk each other into an empirically-unfounded but reassuring consensus. They often underplay or ignore survey findings altogether, thus enabling winning politicians to get away with wild claims about their 'mandate' from the people.

So it is important to recognise not just that expectations frame election results but that the frame is often misleading, and sometimes deliberately so. When you interpret election results, try to stand back from the superficial judgements of journalists, the self-interested claims of politicians, even the familiar distortions of your own prejudices: messages are not insights.

How to Misinterpret Elections

When politicians misinterpret election results, they do so in a self-interested way. Their views are biased but purposeful. But when journalists and commentators get it wrong, as they often do, they do not have the excuse of prejudice. Their errors are simply mistakes. Misinterpretations on the day after the election are often corrected in the following months by more careful analysis, but by this time the misinterpretations are themselves part of history. Here then is a brief guide to the most common mistakes made in interpreting election results. Watch out for them on the day after the next election.

There is no electorate, only electors

Divining the motives of a single entity called 'the electorate' is a specialist skill of leader writers. We are told that the electorate 'gave the government a clear mandate for change', 'plumped for caution rather than revolution' or even 'gave a confused, uncertain verdict'. These phrases are sometimes totally empty; more often they refer to the political consequences of the election result rather than the motives of the voters. As Stokes (1981) points out, the electorate is 'large, dispersed and heterogeneous'. Further, between individual motives and collective consequences there runs a vast chasm called the electoral system. An election may result in political stalemate without any one elector supporting this outcome. Perhaps half the voters favour left-wing change and the other half right-wing change, producing a collective result of no change. The lesson is: beware assessments of the electorate's intentions because only electors have intentions.

Details do not matter

Election pundits are gravely handicapped in interpreting elections: they know too much. They attribute significance to details – the manifesto content, a particular press conference, the quality of a party's organisation – of which most voters are totally unaware. Individual candidates are especially prone to over-estimate their own significance; they prefer to conclude that the strategy in their constituency was wrong rather than that it was simply irrelevant. A particular problem is that commentators over-estimate the importance of the campaign by seeking the crucial moment. There is no such moment; the campaign is a culmination of events since the last election, not an event in isolation. For most voters, elections are not usually (though they can be occasionally) dramatic events; the voter wants some information but not too much. To understand an election result it is best to stay away from the capital city, confine one's campaign activities to watching television, read a popular newspaper (not an intellectual one) and keep a sharp eye on the opinion polls. The lesson is: understanding the intricacies of a campaign does not mean you understand the voters.

Exceptional elections are the exception

Commentators find it difficult to say 'this was a dull election with no important long-term consequences'. Such statements imply the subject is not worth writing about in the first place. But the fact is that although elections can be of fundamental importance, many are not. Realigning and converting elections are less frequent than maintaining, deviating and reinstating ones. The mould is seldom broken – and, as we have seen, almost never broken at a single election. In the excitement of the result, as individual careers are made and lost, it is easy for this sense of detachment to disappear. The lesson is: be sceptical of all claims about watershed elections made within five years, let alone twenty-four hours, of the result.

Explaining voting patterns is different from explaining the result

Analyses which explain why different people vote in different ways may not tell us much about why a particular party won an election. Thus an issue may polarise people between two parties without giving either party an advantage. A new issue may erupt which drives some people towards the 'red' party and others towards the 'blue' party. But if it drives equal numbers in each direction the issue will have no effect on the colour of the new government no matter how large an effect it has on structuring the vote. To take another example, analysts in Britain often claim that the decline in class voting has hurt the Labour Party. In itself, such a proposition is nonsense: a decline in class voting implies that both classes henceforth vote in similar ways – no more and no less. If they both vote against Labour then, of course, Labour loses; but if they both vote for the Labour Party then of course it wins. (This elementary point is stressed by Heath, Jowell and Curtice, 1985; it should not have been necessary to emphasise something so obvious.)

Academics often use elections as an opportunity to take a sociological census, indicating which social divisions are most important. There is nothing wrong with this but it contributes little to an understanding of why this overall result differs from the previous one: it does not tell us why the victor won. The lesson is: distinguish patterns from levels of support. Patterns, in themselves, seldom if ever help to explain why one party beats another.

More people switch than you think

When the 'blue' vote falls by 5 per cent and the 'reds' gain by the same amount, it is natural to assume a direct switch between the two. But reality is never so simple. Some 'reds' will have gone over to the 'blues' – but these will be hidden by the greater number of transfers in the opposite direction. The extent of this churning can *only* be gauged by *panel surveys*. Panel surveys are those in which the same respondents are interviewed at two or more times. So they identify individual respondents who change their attitudes or behaviour. They measure gross change rather than net change. Panel surveys invariably reveal more people changing their votes than is apparent from a simple comparison of the overall results. Constructing 'flow of the vote' tables from panel data to show the true extent of inter-party traffic is an important skill of the elections analyst (Sarlvik and Crewe, 1983, ch. 2). But panel surveys are expensive and so rare; in consequence, commentators generally overestimate the number of loyalists in the electorate. Two lessons: (1) remember that still waters run deep and (2) do panel surveys.

New voters and non-voters matter

A swing from 'blues' to 'reds' does not require *any* existing voters to change the party they vote for. 'Blue' supporters may decide to abstain; the 'reds' may gather in first-time voters and previous abstainers. Movements in and out of the voting population contribute significantly to short-run electoral change and have in the past been the main influence on long-term alignments. Differential abstention is specially important when only a relatively small fraction of the potential electorate actually vote – in US presidential elections where only half the adult population vote, or in (off-year) Congressional elections, British local government elections and British elections to the European Parliament, in all of which not much more than one-third of the electorate votes.

A major weakness of election-night *exit polls* by the television networks is that they interview voters, but *only voters*, as they leave the polls. Who votes and who stays at home may be more important than the choices made by those who arrive at the polling station. So exit polls only tell part of the story. *Los Angeles Times* polls of the full electorate in the 1980 presidential election showed that 28 per cent of Carter's 1976 voters registered to vote in 1980 but did not actually vote. By comparison only 7 per cent of those who had voted for the Republican Gerald Ford in 1976 registered but did not vote in 1980. Thus Schneider (1981, p. 225) concludes that 'abstention siphoned off even more former Democratic voters in 1980 than did defection to other candidates'. Television exit polls provide no data on such important flows of voters. The lesson is: study all the electors, not just voters.

Change matters more than levels

Commentators frequently assert that a party lost votes because opinion polls showed it had unpopular leaders, policies or both.

But just as a party's votes are compared with the last election, so also should the opinion polls be considered in relation to the previous campaign. Perhaps its leaders and policies were even *less* popular last time, in which case we would have to look elsewhere to explain the party's further loss of support. For example, in the British election of 1983 Labour had a sixteen-point lead over the Conservatives as the best party to deal with unemployment – but this did not help Labour improve on its 1979 standing because its lead was exactly the same then. When seeking to explain *changes* in votes, one must examine *changes* in (not levels of) other factors. The lesson is: compare like with like.

Watch the government's performance, especially on the economy

When voters think the governing party has performed badly, and the economy is sluggish, oppositions tend to win elections. When voters believe the governing party has performed satisfactorily, and the economy is sound, governments win. Elections are referendums on government performance in general and its handling of the economy in particular. Many an election deemed to be about some major policy controversy turns out to have been decided by such mundane issues as the cost of living (see the section on retrospective voting in Chapter 6). The British election of February 1974 was decided as much by the rate of inflation as by the miner's strike. The United States election of 1980 was as strongly influenced by perceptions of President Carter's handling of the economy as by his fumbling over the American hostages in Iran. As a rule, commentators exaggerate the importance of issues on which the parties have different objectives and underestimate issues such as prices, jobs and economic growth where parties differ primarily over means or performance. The familiar lesson is: oppositions do not win elections, governments lose them.

Keep an eye on the long-term

A final point concerns the distinction between studying elections and analysing long-term electoral change. Looking at the waves of a single election can easily obscure the long-term tides. A current election is compared with the previous one – as was that one, in its day. But comparison of adjacent elections will not pick up all the changes that take place between the first and last election in a long sequence. Developments in the class structure, the replacement of the generations, rising educational levels – none of these may determine the outcome of a single election even though over time they transform the nature of electoral choice. The lesson is: make long-term, as well as short-term comparisons.

Interpreting Non-National Elections

National elections send a message to the same level of government as they elect. A president or parliament is chosen and those elected receive a message, no matter how obscure, about how they should govern. But this is not always the case with 'non-national' elections. These include *sub-national* local elections and *supra-national* elections in Europe to the European Parliament. Voters use both kinds of non-national elections to send messages to the national government. Similarly, in a referendum, voters often ignore the topic on the ballot paper and use the occasion to send a message to the national government which primarily reflects their overall assessment of its performance.

Non-national elections (and non-election votes like referendums) lead to two opposed errors of interpretation. On the one hand those involved in non-national elections are prone to exaggerate their own importance; they fail to recognise the full extent to which the voters are using the opportunity to send a message to the national government. On the other hand, many nationally-oriented commentators, especially those journalists who work for the national press or nationally networked television programmes, make the opposite error of assuming that non-national elections tell us exactly what the result of the national election would have been if one had been held at the same time. This is dangerous because turn-out is generally much lower in non-national elections. Non-national elections may not even cover the whole country: for example, a by-election in a single constituency, or local elections which may cover different areas of the country in different years. Moreover, local and other non-national issues may have *some* influence, even if not the dominant influence, on the results. In particular places and at particular times non-national issues can be important even though they are not generally so. Hence the problem with simple extrapolations to a hypothetical national result. The message sent by non-national elections resembles the noise we get from a radio when two stations broadcast on much the same frequency, or the confusion that comes when two telephone wires get crossed: the mingling of two signals makes it difficult to interpret either one.

Elections to the European Parliament are an example of how votes can be cast on a national basis even in non-national elections. Reviewing the first campaign held in 1980 in the nine member countries, Blumler and Fox (1982, p. 140) conclude:

> This was essentially an *ambiguous* election. Each campaign was nationally unique: in that sense it was not an *integrated* election. Party arguments and public debate rarely identified issues central to the future of Europe: in that sense it was not much of a *Community* election. When casting ballots many voters evidently responded to domestic party loyalties: in that sense it was not a fully *transnational* election.'

People with strong views on Europe (for or against) were most likely to vote, but in all countries more voters said their party choice was based on domestic rather than European reasons. Using a European vote to send a message to national governments makes perfect sense to the *voter*: national governments matter more. But it makes nonsense of the European *election* when viewed from the perspective of the European Parliament.

Similarly, with local government elections in Britain – and for a similar reason. In essence local councils in Britain administer national programmes: their own room for significant local initiative is small. One consequence is that relatively few people bother to vote; another is that British local government elections are seldom interpreted as an electoral judgement on local governments themselves. Instead they are interpreted simply as a message to central government, and moreover, a message to central government about its national policies rather than its policies towards local government itself (see Miller, 1986, for a detailed survey analysis of the motivations of voters in local elections). Historically, the only adjustment that had to be made to local government results to match the national opinion polls was if a Labour government was in office, when low turn-out among Labour supporters caused the party's share of votes in local contests to drop about 5 per cent below its national opinion poll rating (Berrington, 1972). The best example of British voters casting local election votes on a national basis came in 1979, when local elections were held in England (outside London) and Wales on the same day as the general election. Analysis showed a close relationship between the two sets of results, especially in urban areas, though the Liberals consistently polled better at local level (Waller, 1980). More recently, however, there have been slight signs of 'ticket splitting' in Britain, with voters more inclined to vote for Labour – the party of public services – at local than at national level.

The United States provides a partial exception to the rule that non-national elections are referendums on the performance of central government. Indeed, it has sometimes been claimed that the USA suffers from the opposite problem, that its Congressional elections (not presidential however) are the by-products of local politics. Reflecting the multiplicity of elected offices in the USA, American voters have many opportunities to split their ticket – and an increasing number of them do so. As a result of weakening party loyalties, the proportion of American voters casting a straight ticket (that is, voting for the same party for all the offices elected on the same day) declined from 65 per cent in the 1960 presidential election to 33 per cent in 1972. By 1980, even a third of strong party identifiers voted for different parties at state and local level (Flanigan and Zingale, 1985, p. 30). Ticket-splitting is most common when a Republican wins the White House, since many Democrats continue to vote for their party's candidates at the state and local level.

On the other hand, there has been a vigorous debate about whether mid-term congressional elections are anything more than a message to the president about *his* performance rather than the performance of the Congressmen up for election. Mann (1978, p. 2) notes that 'in recent years many scholars have turned to the view long held by politicians and journalists that mid-term elections are referendums on the performance of the President and especially on his handling of the economy'. Tufte (1975, 1978) has shown that there is a strong relationship between congressional voting in mid-term elections and measures of national economic performance and presidential popularity. But although the overall swing of votes in congressional elections is a response to national factors the variation around this average is very high. Some individual Congressmen do very much better than the average for their party while some do very much worse. Thus Mann argues that:

> increasingly, congressmen are responsible for their own margins of victory or defeat and the electoral constraints they face are defined largely in their individual districts. National economic conditions and presidential popularity go far towards explaining aggregate national change, but to the individual member concerned about his own vote, they are secondary.

There is some evidence that good candidates will not stand when they believe that national conditions are unfavourable to their party. This is because they believe the now-dated literature that individual candidates do not matter. But the decision of these high-calibre candidates not to stand damages their party so that conditions which seem unfavourable really do become unfavourable. Here then is another illustration of how interpretations of elections affect the reality itself (Jacobson, 1983).

Overall, non-national elections are in large measure a response to the performance of national government but how precise the response and how direct the mechanism of response is varies across countries and time. Europeans are more likely to use local elections to send a message to the central government than Americans, where split-ticket voting has increased considerably.

Using elections to one office to send a message to another is unsatisfactory because it weakens the link between the politicians' actions and their electoral performance. It destroys the politicians' responsibility to their electorates. But there is no point in castigating the voters for failing to hold their elected representatives responsible. They use elections to send a message to what is, in their (and our) view, the real seat of government power. Criticism should be reserved for those who set up elected offices which lack real discretionary power.

Conclusion

The classification of elections discussed in this chapter is still the main analytical contribution of political scientists to the interpretation of elections. The categories of maintaining, deviating, converting and realigning elections locate particular results in the context of underlying cleavages. But the scheme assumes that links between groups, parties and voters are the natural order of things; it does not cope so well when confronted with increasingly dealigned Western electorates. Party identification is declining as both a direct influence on votes and as an indirect influence exercised through the voter's attitudes to issues and leaders. In interpreting contemporary elections political scientists need to pay more attention to explicitly political influences on the result – and especially to the ambiguous concept of 'issues'.

But however political scientists develop their classifications in the future, their task is given added importance from the deep impact of accepted interpretations of an election result on the political process itself. Interpretations which influence reality should themselves be based on reality – though often they are not.

Further Reading

For early academic studies classifying elections and focusing on realignment see Key (1955) and Campbell *et al*. (1966). For more recent work, focusing more on periods of realignment than on critical elections, see Beck (1982) or Carmines and Stimson (1984). Dealignment in Britain and America is discussed in Sarlvik and Crewe (1983) and Nie, Verba and Petrocik (1976) respectively, though in our opinion Nie overstates his case somewhat. The collection edited by Crewe and Denver (1985) considers alignment and dealignment in a range of Western countries and reaches a more qualified conclusion.

On the message of elections, which is frequently distorted but none the less powerful, see the (undistorted) studies by Kelly (1983) and Schneider (1981).

Every change of government in Britain or president in the United States brings forth a deluge of interpretive writing. Start by looking up the newspaper files for the week or two after an election. Most libraries should have the (London) *Times*, the *Guardian*, the *Economist*, *Time*, *Newsweek*, the *New York Times* or the *Washington Post*. *Keesing's Contemporary Archives* will have the basic facts. But journalists do not have to write for a world-status paper to express their opinion. Read the election interpretations in whatever newspapers your library keeps – local, national or international. Do not forget the low-brow tabloids. Remember that interpretations do not have to be correct to be politically important. For more considered interpretations of single elections look at Schneider (1981), Drew (1981), Miller (1984), any of Theodore White's *Making of the President* series or any of David Butler's more cautious *British General Election* series. Good examples, though not the most recent, are White (1961, 1973), Butler and Rose (1960), and Butler and Pinto-Duschinsky (1971).

References

BECK, P. (1982) 'Realignment Begins?', *American Politics Quarterly*, vol. 10, pp. 421–37.

BERRINGTON, H. (1972) 'Local Swings and National Roundabouts', *Swinton Journal*, vol. 13, no. 3, pp. 27–33.

BLUMLER, J. and FOX, A. (1982) *The European Voter: Popular Responses to the First Community Election* (London: Policy Studies Institute).

BRODER, D. S. (1980) 'The Democrats', in R. Harwood (ed.), *The Pursuit of the Presidency* (New York: Berkley Books).

BURNHAM, W. D. (1978) 'Great Britain: the Death of the Collectivist Consensus?', in L. Maisel and J. Cooper (eds), *Political Parties: Development and Decay* (London: Sage).

BUTLER, D. and ROSE, R. (1960) *The British General Election of 1959* (London: Macmillan).

BUTLER, D. and PINTO-DUSCHINSKY, M. (1971) *The British General Election of 1970* (London: Macmillan).

CAMPBELL, A., CONVERSE, P. E., MILLER, W. E. and STOKES, D. E. (1966) *Elections and the Political Order* (New York: Wiley).

CARMINES, E. and STIMSON, J. (1984) 'The Dynamics of Issue Evolution: The United States' in R. Dalton *et al*. (eds), *Electoral Change in Advanced Industrial Societies* (Princeton: Princeton University Press).

CREWE, I. and DENVER, D. (1985) *Electoral Change in Western Democracies: Patterns and Sources of Electoral Volatility* (Beckenham: Croom Helm).

DAHL, R. A. (1964) 'Minorities Rules', in L. J. Fein (ed.), *American Democracy: Essays on Image and Realities* (New York: Holt, Rinehart & Winston).

DREW, E. (1981) *Portrait of an Election* (New York: Simon & Schuster).

DYE, T. R. and ZEIGLER, L. H. (1983) *American Politics in the Media Age* (Monterey: Brooks Cole).

FLANIGAN, W. and ZINGALE, N. (1985) 'United States', in I. Crewe and D. Denver (eds), *Electoral Change in Western Democracies: Patterns and Sources of Electoral Volatility* (Beckenham: Croom Helm).

HEATH, A., JOWELL, R. and CURTICE, J. (1985) *How Britain Votes* (Oxford: Pergamon).

JACOBSON, G. C. (1983) *The Politics of Congressional Elections* (Boston: Little, Brown).

KELLY, S. (1983) *Interpreting Elections* (Princeton: Princeton University Press).

KEY, V. (1955) 'A Theory of Critical Elections', *Journal of Politics*, vol. 17, pp. 3–18.

KIRKPATRICK, J. J. (1983) *The Reagan Phenomenon and Other Speeches on Foreign Policy* (Washington, DC: American Enterprise Institute).

MANN, T. E. (1978) *Unsafe at Any Margin: Interpreting Congressional Elections* (Washington, DC: American Enterprise Institute).

MILLER, W. L. (1984) 'There Was No Alternative: the British General Election of 1983', *Parliamentary Affairs*, vol. 37, pp. 364–84.

MILLER, W. L. (1986) 'Local Electoral Behaviour', Committee of Inquiry into the Conduct of Local Authority Business, *Research, Vol. III: The Local Government Elector*. Cmnd 9800 (London: HMSO).

NIE, N. H., VERBA, S. and PETROCIK, J. R. (1976, 1979) *The Changing American Voter* (Cambridge, Mass.: Harvard University Press).

SARLVIK, B. and CREWE, I. (1983) *Decade of Dealignment: the Conservative Victory of 1979 and Electoral Trends in the 1970s* (Cambridge: Cambridge University Press).

SCHNEIDER, W. (1981) '*The November Vote for President: What Did it Mean?* in A. Ranney (ed.), *The American Elections of 1980* (Washington, DC: American Enterprise Institute).

STOKES, D. (1981) 'What Decides Elections?' in D. Butler *et al*. *Democracy at the Polls* (Washington, DC: American Enterprise Institute).

TUFTE, E. R. (1975) 'Determinants of the Outcomes of Midterm Congressional Elections', *American Political Science Review*, vol. 69, pp. 816–26.

TUFTE, E. R. (1978) *Political Control of the Economy* (Princeton: Princeton University Press).

WALLER, R. (1980) 'The 1979 Local and General Elections in England and Wales: Is There a Local/National Differential?', *Political Studies*, vol. 28, pp. 443–50.

WHITE, T. H. (1961) *The Making of the President 1960* (New York: Atheneum).

WHITE, T. H. (1973) *The Making of the President 1972* (New York: Atheneum).

Part II

Voters: Loyalty Versus Choice

Now we look at the voters themselves. Once again our overall theme is the tension between freedom and constraint. But now we focus on the internal constraints imposed on the voters by themselves.

In the real world voters do not approach a competitive election with an open mind about candidates, parties and issues. So they cannot be fully responsive to an election campaign. In that sense they do not make a free choice. Instead they are bound by ties of conviction and loyalty, and their attitudes and political choices are further conditioned by the social and geographical environment in which they live. For brevity, we have used the word loyalty *to emphasise both the restrictiveness and the internal nature of these restrictions. They contrast with the external restrictions and controls, imposed by governments and institutions, which we discussed in the first part of the book.*

We begin with a chapter on how voters think, how their commitments to ideologies or belief systems structure their approach to issues. We conclude that this logical kind of constraint extends to only a small minority of the voters. Next we compare models of voting that emphasise the voters' freedom of choice with others that emphasise the constraints of social position and psychological commitment to parties. We continue our discussion on these topics in Chapters 7 and 8. We conclude that these non-institutional factors still exercise enormous constraint upon the voters' choice, though their impact is declining, and voters are becoming a little more responsive to the issues and appeals of election campaigns. But the era of the rational voter, unconstrained by ties of loyalty and fellow-feeling, is still a long way off.

5

How Voters Think About Politics: Ideologies, Issues and Images

Do People Think About Politics?

Ordinary voters do *not* think very long or very hard about political questions. Their lives are dominated by private and personal concerns – their health, their family, their friends. These are the things that give them most pleasure and most pain, the things that demand their most immediate attention. For most people most of the time, politics is peripheral.

Although surveys seldom ask people directly about their thinking, they do ask about political conversation and political knowledge. Answers to these questions give clues to how voters think. In the mid-1970s Barnes and Kaase (1979) asked respondents in five countries whether they discussed politics *often*, *sometimes*, *rarely* or *never*. Americans seemed to discuss politics more than Europeans, but political discussion was intermittent everywhere. Most people discussed politics on occasion but only around 15 per cent in Britain, the Netherlands, West Germany and Austria discussed it 'often'. In the USA, 27 per cent reported frequent political discussions.

When people are asked about real political leaders, and especially about policies, their responses still show limited awareness. Most Americans can name the president and the governor of their state, most Britons can name the top leader of each party, but knowledge of secondary political figures is very limited. Ignorance about policies is even greater. In their study of the 1948 United

States election Berelson, Lazarsfeld and McPhee (1954) found that although Truman and Dewey had taken up sharply opposed positions on trade union legislation and price controls, only 16 per cent of the electorate knew the positions of both candidates on both issues. In 1974, at the height of the devolution debate in Britain, roughly a third of the Scots electorate said they did not know what Liberal Party policy was on devolution or North Sea Oil – despite the party's commitment to Home Rule ever since Victorian times, and despite its very specific policy for sharing oil revenues between Scotland and England.

Most people think about politics *some* of the time and most people know a *little* about it. But relatively few think *very much* about politics or have *extensive* knowledge about parties, policies or personalities.

Why Do People Think About Politics?

Why do people think about politics at all? What functions are served by holding political views? Adapting the schemes of Brewster Smith, Bruner and White (1958) and Katz (1960), we suggest three functions for political thinking: understanding, social adjustment, and self-expression.

The need to *understand* is the most obvious but certainly not the only motive for political thought. By understanding the political process, people can make sense of the information thrust upon them by the media, they can appreciate their own role as voters – and ironically they can avoid further thought. As Lane (1969, p. 33) writes: 'Political ideas are the means of economising time and effort, for they give the means of habitual and easy responses.' It is notable here that when people are asked why they watch party broadcasts on television, seeking confirmation and reinforcement of their existing ideas looms almost as large as the desire for new information (Blumler and McQuail, 1968; Blumler, McQuail and Nossiter, 1975, 1976; Patterson and McClure, 1976). The need to understand is easily satisfied.

Political thought also serves non-political purposes. Political opinions ease *social adjustment* – the process of entry into and acceptance by social groups. Typically this process is a subtle one, as with the emergence of shared political views among members of a family. One British survey found that only 27 per cent of young voters and a mere 12 per cent of older ones reported that their families typically disagreed when they talked politics (Blumler, McQuail and Nossiter, 1975). Political discussions with like-minded family members and friends can be a way of maintaining rapport, solidarity and identity with people who are close to us. As politics is rarely a central interest, people are more willing to change their politics to fit in with their friends than to select their friends on the basis of their political opinions.

Ordinary voters discuss politics the way they discuss the weather – not so much because they are intensely interested in either topic, but because they need something to talk about in social situations.

Finally, both the extent and the content of political thinking reflect the need to *express* self. Many aspects of self can be expressed in politics – not just personality and its conflicts but philosophy, morality, esteem and core values. The radical child of conservative parents expresses emerging *independence* in political form; the authoritarian expresses repressed *anger* in a desire for strong government; the environmentalist expresses ecological *values* by supporting the Green Party. Generally, the greater the political involvement, the more that involvement expresses aspects of self. For the typical voter, relatively unengaged in politics, the external demands of social adjustment shape political thinking more than the internal demands of self-expression.

Who Thinks About Politics?

Although politics is peripheral to the typical citizen, any large electorate shows considerable variability in the extent and manner of its political thinking.

Education is a crucial influence on both the *quantity* and the *quality* of political thought. Higher education in particular has a striking effect on political interest, knowledge and sophistication. In a five-nation survey conducted in Austria, Britain, Holland, the USA and West Germany, Klingemann (1979) found that education had more effect than other social variables on the ability to think about politics in an ideological way. Education also increased issue voting: among the more highly educated, issues and ideology counted for more, and the candidate's personal qualities for less, when it came to deciding how to vote. (For similar findings on the USA, see Dye and Zeigler, 1981, p. 209; and Pomper, 1980, pp. 204–5. For Canadian findings see Clarke *et al*., 1979).

Carmines and Stimson (1980) distinguish between *easy issues* – emotional issues such as racial questions which require little information, and *hard issues* such as economic questions which require more information instead of just a gut reaction. Those with low levels of education are particularly likely to be *easy-issue* voters rather than *hard-issue* or even *non-issue* voters. Analytical skills, more information and greater interest in politics enable the highly educated to adopt clear positions on hard issues and vote in accord with them. But gut feelings alone are enough to make the poorly educated vote on issue lines provided the issues in question are simple, intellectually undemanding and emotive.

This distinction between easy and hard issues points to the value of the idea of *issue publics* – those people who share a concern about a particular topic. In their 1970 survey, Butler and Stokes found that the British electorate quoted a large number of different issues as 'most important'. The most frequently mentioned issues were taxation and inflation, but both of these got no more than 12 per cent of all mentions. Among those people who named an issue as 'most important', a majority were usually able to see a difference between the parties on that issue – hence the notion of diverse 'issue publics', each motivated by special issue concerns. Yet public perceptions of the most important issues are not usually so fragmented. Surveys have revealed remarkable unanimity among the British electorate in recent years: unemployment has usually been, by common consent, the most important issue. Even when such consensus is lacking, it is simplistic to divide voters into watertight compartments on the basis of the single issue they label 'most important'. Voters may not be concerned about a vast multitude of detailed issues but many voters are concerned about two or three major issues, so that 'issue publics', defined as those who are concerned about particular issues, are overlapping, not mutually exclusive, subsets of the electorate.

We might expect more evidence of political thought among *floaters* who change their vote than among *stand-pats* who stick with the same party year after year. After all, nothing more than habit is necessary to explain repeated voting for the same party. Early studies in the 1950s, however, characterised the floating voter as a person with low interest and little knowledge about politics. Floaters looked more like habitual abstainers than rational voters. It seemed then that committed partisanship not only kept voters loyal to the same party year after year but also provided the motivation for taking an interest in politics and acquiring knowledge about it. Since then the evidence has been accumulating that some floaters, at least, are indeed motivated by issue concerns. In Britain, voters who switch to the Liberals during campaigns have scored well on political information; in Scotland, voters who deserted the SNP between 1974 and 1979 had less commitment in 1974 to Scottish self-government than SNP loyalists; and in the United States, defectors to George Wallace in 1968 were clearly motivated by issue concerns. In short, large electoral changes in recent decades have produced clear evidence that floaters can be as motivated by issues as loyal partisans. The clear distinction between informed, interested partisans and ignorant, feckless floaters has been eroded by events and research since the 1950s. But we should not go too far the other way and hastily conclude that floating voters are paragons of issue-based rationality.

When Do People Think About Politics?

Although the level of interest and information is generally low, it does vary. Long-term trends are sometimes visible. A particularly striking example is post-war Germany where a steady rise in political interest (from a very low starting point) has gone along with greater acceptance of political institutions. Over a shorter time-span there is clear evidence of an electoral cycle which raises both interest and knowledge as an election approaches, though the depth of that knowledge and the quality of that interest should not be overestimated.

Elections raise the political temperature. In Australia, Aitkin (1977, p. 257) found that political interest, political discussions, following politics in the media and even perceptions of party differences all increased in the campaign period. In Britain, though not so much in Australia, even the strength of partisanship among the voters also intensifies dramatically during election years (Butler and Stokes, 1974, p. 470).

The election cycle also influences *how* people think about politics. In the mid-term there is an atmosphere of 'the people versus the government' but as the election approaches political thinking becomes more comparative: instead of merely reacting to the government, the voters think more in terms of choosing between parties. This is one explanation of the tendency for governments to pick up support in the build-up to an election: voters have to confront the alternatives. The *when* of political thinking affects the *how*, which in turn influences levels of party support. Between 1969 and the election year of 1970, Butler and Stokes' surveys show that British voters' attribution of blame for current economic difficulties switched from the current Labour government to the preceding Conservative government – which had been out of office for six years (Butler and Stokes, 1974, p. 391).

Dramatic events force themselves on the public. But the nature of the event determines the kind of reaction it evokes. For example, at election time people tend to think about politics more in terms of party than in terms of issues and ideology (Miller and Shanks, 1982). In response to a foreign crisis they tend to think very much in nationalistic terms. At the very least, events affect the salience of issues. In April 1982 the Argentinians invaded the Falkland Islands. British opinion polls (by Gallup) on the 'most important' issue facing the country showed that unemployment was *the* issue up to March 1982 when 74 per cent cited unemployment and almost no one mentioned foreign affairs. Then in the next three months 27 per cent, 42 per cent and 30 per cent cited foreign affairs as the 'most important' issue. Following the Argentinian defeat in June, the July poll showed 70 per cent citing unemployment and only 2 per cent citing foreign affairs as the most important issue. By September 79 per cent were citing unemployment as the issue, and almost no-one mentioned foreign affairs. The Falklands, like many foreign issues, was an emergency condition, receiving immediate but short-term attention from the public. But unemployment, like many economic issues, is considered important by the electorate even if there is no special crisis.

What Political Objects Do People Think About?

What are the *objects* of voters' thoughts? In one way or another, the whole of Part II of this book is concerned with that question;

here we begin by summarising our overall view. Voters certainly do not confine their thoughts to weighing up the rights and wrongs of alternative policies. Indeed, only a small part of voters' thoughts are likely to focus on policy. Voters think politically about: (1) political substance (2) institutions (3) politicians (4) groups and (5) themselves.

Political substance

Political substance includes policies and issues but it also includes goals, values and performance. The essential preconditions for mass political thought are that the subject must demand neither detailed knowledge nor penetrating powers of analysis. Most people have neither the time nor the motivation to acquire specialist knowledge and analytical skills. There is a tremendous need to simplify. So thoughts about political substance tend to focus on values, goals and performance rather than on issues as such. Few voters will either know or care about the details of manpower policies, but they will evaluate the goal of full employment and they will assess government performance (and the likely performance of the opposition) in attaining that goal. Substance, then, is about broadly stated objectives and progress towards them.

Institutions

The main *institutions* which people think about are parties and governments. Parties and governments loom large in political thinking, not least because they are a wonderful simplifying device. Of course they can only perform their simplifying function if each party or government can be regarded as a single entity. Voters tend to see parties and governments as more united and monolithic than they really are. A certain amount of internal debate can be, indeed must be, ignored in order to keep the voter's picture of the political world simple. If the internal debate becomes too intense then voters protect the simplicity of their perspective on politics by classifying a party as 'divided' – disunity becomes a description, a characteristic of the single entity. Ordinary voters baulk at the effort involved in thinking in terms of intra-party factions and tendencies. So, for example, British voters reacted to left-right quarrels within the Labour Party in the run up to the 1983 election not by lining up on one side or the other, but by punishing candidates from both wings of the party. Right-wing Labour candidates suffered electorally just as badly as the left. At the election, the sins of one faction were visited upon the other.

Whether people think about the political system as a whole has been the subject of some disagreement. Arthur Miller (1974) claimed that in the late 1960s and early 1970s there had been a precipitous decline in the extent to which Americans trusted their government. The key question put to respondents was: 'How much of the time do you think you can trust the government in Washington to do what is right – just about always, most of the time, or only some of the time?' The problem is how to interpret this question. In their answers, were people thinking about the *regime*, the incumbent *president*, *Congress*, or even about questions of *federal versus state* influence? Miller implied that respondents were thinking about the regime and the constitutional system when he wrote about 'hostility toward the institutions of government and the regime as a whole'. But Citrin (1974) maintained that the focus of people's thoughts when answering this question was on *incumbent officials*, not the *regime*. The distinction is important because a change of officials is routine but a change of regime means revolution. Citrin showed that among those who identified strongly with either the Republicans or the Democrats, levels of trust varied sharply according to which party's candidate was elected president. None the less, and partially confirming Miller's original analysis, there was a large decline in political trust among all kinds of partisans. If nothing else the controversy over Miller's analysis has shown that it is exceedingly difficult to measure attitudes towards the regime. There must be some doubt about how much most people think about the regime in normal times. The legitimacy of a regime resides more in habits of obedience than in conscious support.

Of course, there are certain places, such as Northern Ireland, where people habitually devote much thought to the *regime*, the *constitution*, even the *political community*, and where parties as such are of secondary importance.

Politicians

Policies are technical but *politicians* are not. Although the ostensible choice may be between policies and parties, much of the voters' thinking is about leaders. This is not just a characteristic of presidential systems. In Britain during the 1960s, Butler and Stokes (1974, p. 353) measured the number of spontaneous comments about parties (when respondents were asked about parties) and leaders (when respondents were asked about leaders). They found almost as much comment about leaders as parties. Clarke *et al.*'s study (1979) of the Canadian electorate shows that those without strong partisan commitments and with relatively low interest in politics are especially prone to see politics in terms of political leaders. By contrast, those with higher levels of interest tend to give rather more weight to issues.

Although politicians have a prominent place in the voter's picture of politics, the *number* of politicians who appear in this picture is very small. Voters think about the leader of each major party and occasionally about the leader of a faction within a party, such as Tony Benn in Britain – that is, about leaders and their major challengers. But secondary leaders such as cabinet ministers are not generally well-known. A survey taken just six months after the Conservative victory in 1979 found that a majority of voters could not name *any* cabinet member apart from the prime minister. In general the single top leader of each major party is the focus of most popular thinking about politicians.

Groups

Voters often link political parties to social *groups*. In a famous study, Campbell *et al*. (1960) asked a sample of American voters to say what they liked and disliked about each major party. The largest single category of response (45 per cent) covered the relationships of parties to groups – rich and poor, black and white, immigrants and native-born. Occasionally these groups are remote from the voter's own experience, as with deferential working-class Conservatives in Britain who believe their party is fit for office because of its links with the aristocracy. More often the salient groups are those to which the voter belongs, as with working-class Labour voters who believe Labour represents their class interests. Group thinking can of course shade into ideological thinking: the Marxist also analyses politics in terms of conflicting class interests. But more often than not voters see political parties as simply working *for* a particular group, without any implication that the party must therefore work *against* opposed groups. For example, even in the 1960s only four in ten working-class Labour voters in Britain saw politics as the representation of *opposing* class interests. Rather more saw parties in terms of class but without any overlay of conflict (Butler and Stokes, 1974, p. 91). Compared to party ideologists, voters place more stress on the group representation basis of politics, but they do not normally emphasise the idea of group conflict.

Voters themselves

Finally, people think about *themselves* in relation to politics. Political self-confidence encourages participation and a willingness to consider politics seriously. But self-images often link back to group awareness. As Lane (1969, p. 318) says, 'To be politically conscious is both to ask and to answer, if only in a minor way, such questions as *What groups do I care about?* and *What does this caring imply?*' Self-images provide the connection between group and party loyalties, though as class identification weakens in many democracies, more room is available for other aspects of personal identity to influence political thought. (On the influence of personality factors see Adorno *et al.*, 1950; and Stone, 1974.)

What Kinds of Thoughts Do People Have?

Political thinking ranges in scope from the narrow and specific to the broad and diffuse. In style and mood it ranges from rational calculation to unrestrained emotion. We might classify some relatively simple kinds of thoughts into *salience*, *choice*, *perception*, *evaluation*, *association* and *affect*. Then there are complexes of thoughts, that group together many simple thoughts and organise or structure them in some way. Here we might make a useful distinction between *images* and *ideologies*.

Salience

Salience means importance. The first question to ask about an issue, an event or even a personality, is whether the voter thinks it important. Does it matter? Does the voter consider it important for the country, for his or her own personal life, or for making up his or her mind how to vote? Clearly there are various kinds of salience. But if the voters do not consider an issue important in *any* way then it is very unlikely to affect their view of politics or their voting behaviour (see RePass, 1971).

Choice

The next kind of thought is choice. On some issues, like defence for example, voters may choose a policy position. They may wish to retain nuclear weapons or get rid of them. Similarly with goals and values. Some voters may wish to move towards a society based on free enterprise and self-reliance, others may prefer the ideal of a more caring-sharing society. They may prefer one leader to another, one party to another. Ultimately they have to make a choice when they vote on election day. Choice is not relevant to every issue, however. Butler and Stokes (1974) put forward the concept of *valence* issues on which voters evaluated performance rather than chose objectives – reducing unemployment for example. Somebody somewhere can be found to disagree with any objective, but the distinction between position issues (i.e. choice of policies) and valence issues (i.e. performance on problems) can sometimes be useful. Party competition can still go on even when all the parties and most of the voters are in full agreement about values and objectives.

Perceptions

Perception must be distinguished from knowledge. We use the term perception to describe what the individual voter *believes* to be true rather than what *is* true, if indeed there is such a thing as absolute truth. If there were general agreement about where politicians, parties, organisations and groups stood on goals and issues then there would be no need to discuss voters' perceptions. But perceptions are as much the property of the perceiver as of the perceived. The same politician may look like a liberal (in the ideological sense) to one voter and like a conservative to another. Perceptions vary from individual to individual and from time to time. Sometimes perceptions vary in a systematic and easily explicable way. President Carter was perceived as a conservative when he fought the liberal Edward Kennedy for the Democratic nomination in the spring of 1980; but the same Carter was perceived as a liberal when he ran against Reagan at the Presidential election later in that year. In the more partisan systems of Europe, perceptions are strongly and consistently influenced by party loyalties rather than particular candidates.

But while the attitudes and loyalties of voters may already bias their perceptions, politicians are not entirely unable to change them. Indeed, politicians can sometimes take advantage of the slippage between reality and perceptions. One useful strategy is to make different appeals to different groups or regions – helped by *regional* press and television coverage. Another is the *band-spread* strategy, in which a politician raises an issue and articulates public discontent but avoids committing himself to any particular course of action. With any luck all kinds of discontented voters will think that he agrees with their own solutions. For example, both doves and hawks on Vietnam voted for Nixon, the dovish voters claiming Nixon was a dove and the hawks claiming Nixon was a hawk:

> Those who saw a big difference between Humphrey and Nixon in either direction were generally perceiving each candidate as standing wherever they wanted him to stand. They projected their own opinions onto their favoured candidate. Among Republicans, who mostly favoured Nixon, extreme hawks thought that Nixon was an extreme hawk; extreme doves thought that he was an extreme dove.
>
> (Page and Brody, 1972)

Evaluations

Choices and perceptions are the raw material for evaluations, that is conscious or unconscious calculations of which party or candidate comes *nearest* to the voter's own goal or issue choice. Pollsters ask questions like: 'Which party has the best policy on defence?' This is an evaluative question. It is not the same as simple party choice, even if the answers are biased towards the party the voter prefers overall. Typically, one party is rated best on some issues but not on others. This pattern makes it logically impossible for evaluations to be no more than simple reflections of overall party preference.

Rational choice theorists attempt to reconstruct or simulate the process by which choices and perceptions are turned into evaluations. One way is to ask survey respondents to place both themselves and the parties on policy scales. For example, we may show each respondent a line labelled with policy alternatives:

Get rid of all nuclear weapons in Britain	Increase British nuclear weapons

We may then ask him or her to mark positions on the line to represent party policies and their own position. We will then be able to calculate the *proximity* (nearness) of each party to the voter on this particular policy issue. A rational choice theorist would assume that a voter would evaluate the party nearest to himself on the policy line as the one with the 'best policy on defence'. In fact many voters do not respond in this way. Their reasoning must be more complex or less rational than the rational choice theorist would expect.

Evaluations of governments and oppositions, incumbents and challengers, involve different time perspectives. To overstate the contrast a little, the voter must compare the *past record of the incumbent* with the *future promises of the challenger*. Judgements on governments are *retrospective*, while judgements on oppositions are *prospective*. Moreover, it is a lot easier to apply the logic of issue positions and policy proximities to the challenger's prospectus than to the government's record. This is because retrospective evaluation of the government's record may be largely in terms of its *performance on valence issues* rather than its *policy on position issues*. Never mind whether the government has the right policy on defence or education or health, the question may be: 'Are you better off than you were four years ago?' – to quote the 1980 campaign slogan of Ronald Reagan which invited voters to pass a retrospective, valence-issue judgement on Jimmy Carter's Presidency.

Associations

We now move on to other kinds of thoughts, less rational, less calculative, more emotional but no less powerful. One such form of thinking is simple association. A man is known by the company he keeps. And the objects of political thinking 'keep company' in the voter's mind. The written word is not the best medium for discussing this topic. Words are too sharp, too clear, too precise. Pictures would be better. John Tyndall of the neo-fascist National Front put it thus:

> What is it that touches off a chord in the instincts of the people to whom we seek to appeal? It can often be the most simple and primitive thing. Rather than a speech or printed article it may just be a flag; it may be a marching column; it may be the sound of a drum; it may be a banner or it may be the impression of a crowd. None of these things contain in themselves one single argument, one single piece of logic . . . [yet] they are recognised as being among the things that appeal to the hidden forces of the human soul.
>
> (Walker, 1977, p. 145)

The British election of 1983 provides another example of the importance of associations. It was held on the anniversary of the Falklands war, and during the campaign Margaret Thatcher had herself photographed in front of an aircraft hanger which was painted with the world's largest Union Jack. There was no need for her to raise the Falklands war as an issue, or argue the superiority of her defence policies, or stress the virtue of firm government, or question the patriotism of her opponents – one picture made all the right associations.

Associations do not depend entirely upon the modern technology of photo-calls and television, however. British and Australian voters associate the Labour Party with trades unions. No amount of clever advertising is likely to change that association, which years of history have made. Significantly, the psychological association of Labour and the unions in the voters' minds goes beyond the realities of history. Labour is associated with unions in general, irrespective of whether or not a particular union is organisationally affiliated to the party.

The significance of associations is that positive and negative feelings towards one political object are easily transferred to other political objects with which it is associated; in fact, 'guilt by association' is the rule.

Affect

Affect means positive or negative emotion: liking or disliking. It may or may not correspond to more calculative evaluations. Indeed affect may spring from deep emotional needs and then be cloaked in a veneer of rationality. Rational explanations of likes and dislikes need to be treated with scepticism; they are often rationalisations rather than reasons. Affect is typically measured in surveys by asking respondents to give 'feeling thermometer' ratings to various political objects, on the basis of 'how warmly' they feel towards them. In Butler and Stokes' (1974) 1970 election survey, the British police topped the list with an average score of 82 degrees (on a thermometer with a maximum of 100), parliament got 73, the outgoing Prime Minister Harold Wilson got 56, coloured immigrants 38 and unofficial strikers 22. Such findings fit Disraeli's observation that 'what we call public opinion is generally public sentiment'.

Images and ideology

Images and ideologies are complexes of political thought which bring together and organise or structure the simple component thoughts. At first they seem almost unrelated. Ideology, at least in the sense in which we use the term in this chapter, means a coherent arrangement of attitudes towards groups of issues that is characterised by constraint: the positions taken on individual issues by the ideological voter must 'hang together' in some logical way. Attitudes on the detailed and transitory issues of the day must fit in with general principles of some kind, though the validity of these general principles is irrelevant to the question of whether ideologies exist. We shall examine whether voters do have ideologies later in this chapter.

Images also organise and structure political thinking. But images are complexes of perceptions, rather than complexes of issue positions. Images relate more to political objects and actors rather than issues. They are more about the way the world *is*, rather than about the way it *should be* – though that is more of a logical distinction than a behavioural one since political perceptions and political prescriptions are intimately related. Nimmo and Savage define an image as 'a human construct imposed upon an array of perceived attributes projected by an object, event or person' (Nimmo and Savage, 1976, p. 8). That definition emphasises that (1) images come from reality but (2) they are projected and perhaps biased by the projector (3) they are perceived, and perceptions may be biased by the perceiver (4) they impose order and simplicity on the chaos of a multitude of perceptions.

Party images are the voters' mental pictures of the parties. They cover more than issue and ideological perceptions. In particular, images include perceptions of style as well as perceptions of policy. The content of party images is by definition quite unconstrained and frequently asymmetric – one party may be pictured in terms of its ideology while another is pictured in terms of its leadership. Similarly, the image of one politician may depend upon public perceptions of his competence (or lack of it) while another politician has an image which is dominated by his reputation for honesty and integrity (or lack of it).

Milne and Mackenzie (1954, 1958) used the concept of images in their studies of the Bristol electorate. They stressed the importance of long-term, enduring party images based on the parties' historical association with certain symbols or generalised policy orientations. Labour was seen as 'standing for the working class', the Conservative Party as 'standing for free enterprise' and the Liberal Party as 'standing for compromise'. Three decades later Heath, Jowell and Curtice (1985) again emphasised the importance of images, general policy orientations, underlining the enduring nature of these images by claiming that the content of British party images had hardly changed in thirty years. Advocates of the rational choice model of voting argue that these general images are (1) accurate and (2) a sensible basis on which to decide how to vote.

Trenaman and McQuail (1961), and later Butler and Stokes (1974), broadened the concept of images to include more transient aspects, related to style rather than ideology, malleable rather than enduring, derived from clever presentation as much as from historical reality. Thus Butler and Stokes asked their respondents whether the parties were 'modern, expert, powerful, wise, middle-class, united, good, left-wing, strong-minded, honest, exciting, or new'. This takes us a long way from policy evaluations of the parties yet many voters are motivated more by their reactions to such kaleidoscopic images than by calculations of policy positions. Images make the incommensurable commensurable: competence can be weighed against integrity, good policies against exciting policies, policies against personalities. Thus in the early 1960s Harold Wilson attempted to change the working-class cloth-cap image of the Labour Party by associating it with the 'white heat of technological advance' – something that did not deny the working-class image but turned attention away to another more exciting, more modern image. Twenty years later, Neil Kinnock was again attempting to revive the party's fortunes by image adjustment as much as by policy change.

Do People Use Ideological Concepts?

The problem of ideology is important in electoral studies. If voters do think in ideological terms, this will influence both our understanding and our evaluation of the quality of electoral choice. Our assumptions about how to communicate with voters, and how to word survey questions, will also be affected. Broadly speaking, political scientists have adopted two approaches to the problem. First, they have investigated whether voters understand and use *abstract concepts* such as left and right, liberal and conservative. Secondly, they have studied whether voters' political views form an overall package or *system of beliefs*. Both approaches are based on a definition of ideology as a system of relatively abstract ideas about politics and society. Both approaches show a similar history: an initial generation of studies claiming that Western electorates lacked ideology; a second phase pointing to major increases in ideological thinking; and the current third phase which suggests that these changes, though real, were exaggerated. This section examines electors' understanding of political concepts; the question of belief systems is considered in the following section.

The use of ideological concepts by the electorate has itself been examined from various perspectives. First, researchers have measured how many voters make meaningful, *active use* of ideological concepts such as left and right, liberal and conservative. Secondly, they have tried to measure how many voters can *recognise* such terms, even if they do not use ideological concepts spontaneously. Thirdly, they have tried to determine the *basis* of ideological thinking – does it merely reflect partisanship or is it based on broader philosophies and principles? If voters describe themselves as 'left-wing' purely because they vote for the socialist party, then ideology becomes a consequence rather than a cause of electoral decisions and its significance is much diminished.

The *active use* of ideological concepts has been assessed by asking survey respondents to discuss, in their own words, what they like and dislike about the main parties. Interviewers record the respondents' spontaneous comments. Then the chief researchers read through all of these interview reports, noting the types of concepts voters use in evaluating the parties and classifying the voters according to their *level of ideological conceptualisation*.

This procedure was first adopted in a study of the 1956 Presidential election in the United States (Campbell *et al*., 1960, ch. 8). Only 3.5 per cent of the voters emerged as ideologues – people who described the parties in terms of abstract conceptions such as liberal and conservative, the balance between federal and state power, or between government support and individual initiative. An additional 12 per cent were near-ideologues – people who referred to such concepts in a peripheral way. The authors concluded that 'the concepts important to ideological analysis are important only for that small segment of the population equipped to approach political decisions at a rarefied level'.

During the early 1970s, Klingemann (1979) applied this procedure to electorates in Britain, the USA, Austria, West Germany and the Netherlands. Despite his efforts to detect a variety of ideological concepts, the only concepts used with any frequency were those related to the left-right or liberal-conservative dimension. Overall, ideological concepts were used in only about one-tenth of party evaluations. Klingemann classified voters as *ideologues* if they used *both* left and right concepts in evaluating the parties. The number of ideologues was very small, ranging from 4 per cent in Britain and Austria up to 9 per cent in the Netherlands. He classified as *non-ideologues* those who used *neither* left nor right concepts. Non-ideologues made up about 80 per cent of the electorate in Britain, the USA and Austria and about two-thirds of the electorate in Germany and the Netherlands. (The remaining voters used *one* of the concepts of left or right.) Government performance, domestic policies and relationships with social groups were a more common basis of party evaluations than ideology.

Recognition of ideological terms is more common than their active use but is still confined to a minority. In his five-country survey, Klingemann asked his respondents to place themselves on a left-right scale and to explain what they meant by the terms left and right. Overall, 19 per cent did not recognise the concepts at all; a further 15 per cent gave no meaning or a completely wrong meaning to the terms; 19 per cent explained both left and right by reference to parties or social groups; and a further 17 per cent explained one of the terms by reference to parties or groups. So the proportion of voters who explained *both* concepts in unambiguously ideological terms, with references to political change, to a particular organisation of state and society, or to ideological movements, came to only 23 per cent. Britain stood out as exceptionally non-ideological, with only 11 per cent. (For comparison, see also Eijk and Niemoller, 1983, pp. 227–8.)

When a voter says he or she is 'left-wing', does this reflect a commitment to a particular party or to a set of political principles? What is the *basis* of ideological thinking? Overall, party loyalty seems to be a more important influence on ideological self-placement than views on issues though this does vary across countries and social groups. In a survey conducted in eleven Western democracies in 1973, Inglehart and Klingemann (1976) found that in all the European nations except Ireland, partisanship accounted for at least four times as much variation in left-right self-placement as did issues. In the USA, however, the two components were of almost equal strength.

Some Americans clearly use ideology as a partial alternative to party as a means of making sense of political choices. For a long time the value of the liberal-conservative distinction in the United States has been to allow Americans to link conservative southern 'Democrats' with the Republican Party rather than with the rest of the Democratic Party. Ideology is a way of internally *dividing* American parties, especially the Democrats. In continental Europe, by contrast, ideology is much more useful for *grouping* parties in multi-party systems so as to make politics more comprehensible. This is especially so in European countries with unstable parties such as France: there parties changed their labels so frequently that it was difficult for voters to form attachments to parties as such and at one time the left-right dimension almost took over the role of making sense of electoral choice (Converse and Dupeux, 1962). In short, the fewer parties there are, and the more united they are, the less important such terms as 'left' and 'right' become.

The relative influence of party and issues on ideological self-placement also depends on education and political interest, according to Inglehart and Klingemann. For the highly involved and educated, left-right self-placement reflects issue attitudes while for the less politically involved and less educated it does not. However, partisanship influences left-right self-placement among all groups.

The use of ideological language is not a constant: it can vary over time in response to political stimuli. In *The Changing American Voter* (1979) Nie, Verba and Petrocik suggest that the percentage of ideologues rose from 12 per cent in 1956 to 33 per cent in 1972 before falling back somewhat in 1976. They argue that more polarised contests between Goldwater and Johnson in 1964 and between Nixon and McGovern in 1972 stimulated an increase in ideological thinking in the American electorate. Although they measure ideological thinking differently from Campbell *et al.* (1960), their trend analysis certainly shows that Americans were using a more ideological language in the 1970s than in the 1950s. The voters had at least picked up some *terminology* from the ideological candidacies of 1964 and 1972. But there are some doubts about whether the voters' thinking has really become much more ideological in *structure*. When the original technique of reading through respondents' reasons for liking and disliking the parties was applied to the 1970s, the increase in the proportion of ideologues was less dramatic though still substantial. For example, Klingemann (1979) found that the *use* of ideological or near-ideological thinking doubled rather than tripled between 1956 and 1974. Klingemann also notes an increase in the *recognition* as well as the *use* of ideological concepts in both Britain and the United States.

But the growing number of 'ideologues' revealed by these studies do not share the richness of political thought which is taken for granted among elites. Kinder (1983, p. 394) notes that the

> use of an ideological vocabulary in no way guarantees that the underlying ideas are deeply understood or even that the terms are correctly used. It appears that Nie, Verba and Petrocik have

demonstrated increases only in what might be called the non-ideological use of ideological terminology.

That is an overstatement. All studies agree that the level of ideological thinking *did* increase after the mid-1950s; the dispute is about whether it increased anywhere near as much as the growing popularity of ideological terminology. Levitin and Miller (1979) show that liberal/conservative self-placement in the elections of 1972 and 1976 was closely linked to voting behaviour, but there was little agreement among voters about what was a liberal or conservative issue position. In fact many voters perceived the ideological position of their favoured candidate to be close to their own simply because he was their preferred candidate. The tail of party loyalty was still wagging the dog of ideology. To Levitin and Miller it seemed that many voters now using ideological labels still lacked coherent and well-articulated views of the political world.

Do People Have Belief Systems?

Political thinking can be assessed in statistical as well as linguistic terms. In a classic article, Converse (1964) looked for evidence of belief systems in the United States electorate – that is, for a structure of attitudes characterised by constraint. Attitudes are constrained when the voter's position on one issue is related to the position he or she adopts on other issues. The result is a *structure* of beliefs, a *belief system*. For example, people in favour of nationalisation might be expected to be sympathetic to trade unions; those opposed to immigration might support capital punishment. A belief system is more general than an ideology since its elements may be connected psychologically rather than logically, and the elements need not be derived from some set of first principles. Converse found that the issue attitudes of American congressional candidates in 1958 were somewhat constrained. However, the correlations between ordinary voters' attitudes to different domestic issues were substantially lower, and there was no correlation at all between their attitudes to foreign and domestic policy.

One possible explanation for these low correlations was that there were several different belief systems applying to different groups of voters, each group committed to rather different packages of issues. High correlations would only show up if voters were divided into two opposed ideological camps. However, a third group that sided with the first on some issues and the second on others could be highly ideological yet its presence would reduce the correlations between issue attitudes among the sample as a whole. For example, classic liberals do not fit into a single left-right scale since they tend to support the left on social policy but the right on economic policy. However, if voters did have well-developed belief systems of any sort, we might at least expect them to be *consistent over time*. So Converse went on to look at the correlations between attitudes on the *same* issues over time. Using a panel survey conducted between 1956 and 1960, Converse showed that the stability of party identification was high while the stability of *all* issue attitudes was very much lower. The most stable of the issues he analysed was attitudes to racial segregation in schools. Other issue attitudes with less clear-cut group associations were very unstable. Least stable of all were attitudes on foreign aid and on federal government involvement in housing. Converse claimed that this instability was 'eloquent proof that signs of low constraint among belief elements in the mass public are not products of well-knit but highly idiosyncratic belief systems . . . Great instability in itself is *prima facie* evidence that the belief has extremely low centrality for the believer'.

Moreover, Converse found that the correlation between attitudes in 1956 and 1960 was no lower than the correlations over the shorter periods 1956–58 and 1958–60. He argued that this somewhat surprising pattern was consistent with a model in which a very few voters have well-developed and perfectly stable attitudes while most voters have *non-attitudes* – that is they give random responses to interviewers' questions about issues.

Butler and Stokes' study of British voters in the 1960s broadly confirmed this view of the electorate. These authors also found substantial instability in attitudes over time. For example, only 43 per cent were consistent in supporting or opposing nationalisation over four interviews spread between 1963–70. Even when Butler and Stokes restricted their analysis to the minority with stable opinions, they still found only limited constraint between issues. For example, there was only a small correlation between attitudes to nationalisation and the Common Market. There were, however, stronger relationships between attitudes to political parties and attitudes to party leaders. This suggests that parties rather than issues structure political thinking.

Other statistical studies which allow the possibility of several ideological dimensions have shown some structure to the electorate's political opinions. Luttbeg (1968) found five dimensions underlying attitudes in the United States; for Britain, Alt (1979) came up with three factors, Sarlvik and Crewe (1983) with five, Robertson (1984) and Harrop (1982) with two, while Scarborough (1984) produced six core profiles and six action profiles which combined into five belief sets! In nearly all these studies, two dimensions recur. The first is a 'left-right' factor covering government involvement in the economy and society, particularly for redistributive purposes. Nationalisation falls squarely into this factor. The second dimension is a 'tough-tender' factor covering such issues as law and order, capital punishment, immigration and race relations (for an early study of this type, see Eysenck, 1951). Uncovering these dimensions does not invalidate the original findings of Converse. These additional studies merely show that there is *some* structure to political thinking (involving more than one dimension) rather than no structure at all. Converse's point was that the structure is not strong enough to justify the conclusion that most voters have structured belief systems.

Despite the qualifications, Converse's view of the mass electorate remained predominant until the publication of Nie, Verba and Petrocik's *The Changing American Voter* in 1976. These authors did not dispute the accuracy of Converse's view of the American electorate in the 1950s. However they claimed to find an enormous increase in attitude constraint in 1964 followed by a steady but slow decline from 1964 to 1976. They interpreted this as a 'response to the changes in the political stimuli voters have been receiving – in particular to the heightened intensity of political issues in the 1960s'. After 1964, the level of attitude constraint among ordinary American voters was higher than the level of attitude constraint had been among congressional candidates in 1958. If elites had been ideological in the past, it seemed that the masses were now ideological as well.

Unfortunately, this apparent jump in issue constraint in 1964 coincided with changes in the format of survey questions about issues. Up to and including 1960 respondents were simply asked to agree or disagree with a statement putting one side of an issue; in 1964 and 1968, they were asked to choose between statements putting both sides of the issue; and from 1972 onwards, they were asked to give a number representing how much they agreed with one side or the other. Although these later questions are more sophisticated, the *changes* in format produce artificially inflated estimates of the rise of issue constraint. Several recent studies have used split samples, some respondents being asked questions in the pre-1964 format, the rest being asked questions in the post-1964 format. Some of the results suggest that when questions were put in a 1950s format the level of attitude constraint in the late 1970s was no higher than in the 1950s (Abramson, 1983; Bishop, Oldendick and Tuchfarber 1978; Sullivan, Pierson and Markus, 1978). Petrocik (1980) argues that while part of the increase in apparent issue constraint may have been due to changes in question format, some of the increase was real. Even using 1950s-format questions, attitude constraint was somewhat higher in 1974 than in the 1950s: 'at worst the increase in issue consistency has been exaggerated'. Exaggerated it certainly was. Even if we accept the figures given by Petrocik it would appear that a modest rise in issue constraint in 1964 was gradually dissipated thereafter; so that by 1976 issue constraint was no higher than in the 1950s.

The real value of recent research is that it shows how poor question-wording led to an underestimate of the extent of issue constraint in the 1950s. It is not so much that the United States electorate has suddenly sprouted belief systems; it is more that the structure to political thinking went undetected in the 1950s.

A similar conclusion emerges from recent studies of the stability of attitudes over time (Converse and Markus, 1979). On the kinds of issues studied in the 1950s stability remained low in the 1970s. But the replies to new questions on such moral issues as marijuana and abortion showed high stability over time. Thus the stability of attitudes was probably underestimated in the early studies because the wrong issues were investigated. Attitudes are not entirely 'non-attitudes'. People do hold real views on some issues and they hang on to them over lengthy periods of time. Issue constraint seems to reflect some logical and historical associations – but only the clearest and most unambiguous of such associations. More subtle, well-developed and structured ideologies, derived from basic principles and exercising a powerful constraint on attitudes to individual issues, remain absent from the political thinking of the great mass of voters in Western democracies.

Conclusion

In normal times at least, ordinary people have a very *part-time* involvement with politics. Their political thinking is intermittent and lacks both detail and structure. Their most complex political thoughts are unstructured collages of heterogeneous and often self-contradictory images rather than logically structured and constrained ideologies or belief systems. Over the last two decades many voters have adopted a more ideological language but to a large extent that simply reflects the terminology and slogans of politicians. None the less poor techniques in early survey research during the 1950s and 1960s probably led us to underestimate public understanding of issues and public concern for issues at that time. In addition, there is some evidence that the public has become a *little* better able to handle issue-politics since the 1950s – though more because of the emergence of simple emotional issues and issue-based (instead of interest-based) political campaigns than because of any increase in the sophistication of the electorate.

Further Reading

Good statements of the 1950s and 1960s orthodoxy appear in *The American Voter* (Campbell *et al*., 1960) and *Political Change in Britain* (Butler and Stokes, 1969, 1974). Converse's (1964) article in *Ideology and Discontent* is an important starting point – frequently attacked and frequently defended, it is worth reading in the original. Nie, Verba and Petrocik's (1976, 1979) *Changing American Voter* overturned the old orthodoxy briefly but has since come in for devastating criticism. Abramson (1983) gives a clear account of the voluminous and confusing literature on issues, ideology, and issue voting. Klingemann's chapters in Barnes and Kaase's (1979) five-nation study are particularly good on levels of ideological conceptualisation. While United States researchers have emphasised issues, and European researchers have been fascinated by ideology, British researchers have consistently emphasised the importance of images but have seldom attempted a comprehensive analysis of the image concept. There is a chapter on images in Butler and Stokes (1974) but it is not the best chapter in that book. Images are at the core of Heath, Jowell and Curtice's (1985) discussion of British voting, but they offer little by way of evidence to support their view.

References

ABRAMSON, P. R. (1983) *Political Attitudes in America* (San Francisco: Freeman).

ADORNO, T. W., FRENKEL-BRUNSWIK, E., LEVINSON, D. J. and SANFORD, R. N. (1950) *The Authoritarian Personality* (New York, Norton).

AITKIN, D. (1977) *Stability and Change in Australian Politics* (Canberra: Australian National University Press).

ALT, J. E. (1979) *The Politics of Economic Decline* (Cambridge: Cambridge University Press).

BARNES, S. H. and KAASE, M. (1979) *Political Action: Mass Participation in Five Western Democracies* (Beverly Hills: Sage).

BERELSON, B. R., LAZARSFELD, P. F. and MCPHEE, W. N. (1954) *Voting: a Study of Opinion Formation in a Presidential Campaign* (Chicago: University of Chicago).

BISHOP, G. F., OLDENDICK, R. W. and TUCHFARBER, A. J. (1978) 'Effects of Question Wording and Format on Political Attitude Consistency', *Public Opinion Quarterly*, vol. 42, pp. 81–92.

BLUMLER, J. G. and McQUAIL, D. (1968) *Television in Politics: its Uses and Influence* (London: Faber).

BLUMLER, J. G., McQUAIL, D. and NOSSITER, T. J. (1975) *Political Communication and the Young Voter 1970–71* (London: Report to Social Science Research Council).

BLUMLER, J. G., McQUAIL, D. and NOSSITER, T. J. (1976) *Political Communication and the Young Voter in the General Election of February 1974* (London: Report to Social Science Research Council).

BREWSTER SMITH, M., BRUNER, J. and WHITE, R. (1958) *Opinions and Personality* (New York: Wiley).

BUTLER, D. and STOKES, D. (1974) *Political Change in Britain: the Evolution of Electoral Choice* (London: Macmillan).

CAMPBELL, A., CONVERSE, P. E., MILLER, W. E. and STOKES, D. E. (1960) *The American Voter* (New York: Wiley).

CARMINES, E. G. and STIMSON, J. A. (1980) 'The Two Faces of Issue Voting', *American Political Science Review*, vol. 74, pp. 78–91.

CITRIN, J. (1974) 'Comment: The Political Relevance of Trust in Government', *American Political Science Review*, vol. 68, pp. 973–88.

CLARKE, H. D., JENSON, J., LEDUC, L. and PAMMETT, J. (1979) *Political Choice in Canada* (Toronto: McGraw-Hill Ryerson).

CONVERSE, P. E. (1964) 'The Nature of Belief Systems in Mass Publics', in D. Apter (ed.), *Ideology and Discontent* (New York: Free Press).

CONVERSE, P. and DUPEUX, G. (1962, 1966) 'Politicization of the Electorate in France and the United States', *Public Opinion Quarterly*, vol. 26, pp. 1–23; reprinted in A. Campbell *et al.*, *Elections and the Political Order* (New York: Wiley).

CONVERSE, P. E. and MARKUS, G. B. (1979) 'Plus ça Change . . . : the New CPS Election Study Panel', *American Political Science Review*, vol. 73, pp. 32–49.

DYE, T. R. and ZEIGLER, L. H. (1981) *The Irony of Democracy: an Uncommon Introduction to American Politics*, (5th edn) (Belmont, Ca.: Wadsworth).

EIJK, C. and NIEMOLLER, C. (1983) *Political Change in the Netherlands* (Amsterdam: Erasmus University Press).

EYSENCK, H. (1951) *The Psychology of Politics* (London: Routledge & Kegan Paul).

HARROP, M. (1982) 'Labour-voting conservatives: Policy Differences between the Labour Party and Labour Voters', in R. Worcester and M. Harrop (eds), *Political Communications: The General Election Campaign of 1979* (London: Allen & Unwin).

HEATH, A., JOWELL, R. and CURTICE, J. (1985) *How Britain Votes* (Oxford: Pergamon).

INGLEHART, R. and KLINGEMANN, H. (1976) 'Party Identification, Ideological Preference and the Left-Right Dimension among Western Mass Publics', in I. Budge, I. Crewe and D. Farlie (eds), *Party Identification and Beyond* (London: Wiley).

KATZ, D. (1960) 'The Functional Approach to the Study of Attitudes', *Public Opinion Quarterly*, vol. 24, pp. 163–204.

KINDER, D. R. (1983) 'Diversity and Complexity in American Public Opinion', in A. W. Finifter (ed.), *Political Science: the State of the Discipline* (Washington: American Political Science Association).

KLINGEMANN, H. D. (1979) 'Measuring Ideological Conceptualizations' in S. H. Barnes and M. Kaase (eds), *Political Action* (Beverly Hills: Sage).

LANE, R. (1969) *Political Thinking and Consciousness* (Chicago: Markham).

LEVITIN, T. E. and MILLER, W. E. (1979) 'Ideological Interpretations of Presidential Elections', *American Political Science Review*, vol. 73, pp. 751–71.

LUTTBEG, N. R. (1968) 'The Structure of Beliefs among Leaders and the Public', *Public Opinion Quarterly*, vol. 32, pp. 398–403.

MILLER, A. H. (1974) 'Political Issues and Trust in Government: 1964–1970', *American Political Science Review*, vol. 68, pp. 951–72.

MILLER, W. E. and SHANKS, J. M. (1982) 'Policy Directions and

Presidential Leadership: Alternative Interpretations of the 1980 Presidential Election', *British Journal of Political Science*, vol. 12, pp. 299–356.

MILLER, W. L. (1981) *The End of British Politics? Scots and English Political Behaviour in the Seventies* (Oxford: Clarendon Press).

MILNE, R. S. and MACKENZIE, H. C. (1954) *Straight Fight 1951* (London: Hansard Society).

MILNE, R. S. and MACKENZIE, H. C. (1958) *Marginal Seat 1955* (London: Hansard Society).

NIE, N. H., VERBA, S. and PETROCIK, J. R. (1976, 1979) *The Changing American Voter* (Cambridge, Mass.: Harvard University Press).

NIMMO, D. and SAVAGE, R. L. (1976) *Candidates and Their Images: Concepts, Methods and Findings* (Santa Monica: Goodyear).

PAGE, B. I. and BRODY, R. A. (1972) 'Policy Voting and the Electoral Process: the Vietnam War Issue', *American Political Science Review*, vol. 66, pp. 389–400.

PATTERSON, T. E. and McCLURE, R. D. (1976) *The Unseeing Eye: the Myth of Television Power in National Politics* (New York: G. P. Putnam's Sons).

PETROCIK, J. R. (1980) 'Contextual Sources of Voting Behaviour: The Changeable American Voter', in J. C. Pierce and J. L. Sullivan (eds), *The Electorate Reconsidered* (Beverly Hills: Sage).

PIERCE, J. C. and SULLIVAN, J. L. (1980) *The Electorate Reconsidered* (Beverly Hills: Sage).

POMPER, G. (1980) *Elections in America: Control and Influence in Democratic Politics* (New York: Longman).

REPASS, D. E. (1971) 'Issue Salience and Party Choice', *American Political Science Review*, vol. 65, pp. 389–400.

ROBERTSON, D. (1984) *Class and the British Electorate* (Oxford: Blackwell).

SARLVIK, B. and CREWE, I. (1983) *Decade of Dealignment* (Cambridge: Cambridge University Press).

SCARBOROUGH, E. (1984) *Political Ideology and Voting: An Exploratory Study* (Oxford: University Press).

STONE, W. F. (1974) *The Psychology of Politics* (New York: Free Press).

STOKES, D. E. (1966) 'Some Dynamic Elements of Contests for the Presidency', *American Political Science Review*, vol. 60, pp. 19–28.

SULLIVAN, J. L., PIERSON, J. E. and MARKUS, G. B. (1978) 'Ideological Constraint in the Mass Public: a Methodological Critique and Some New Findings', *American Journal of Political Science*, vol. 22, pp. 233–49.

TRENAMAN, J. and McQUAIL, D. (1961) *Television and the Political Image* (London: Methuen).

WALKER, M. (1977) *The National Front* (Glasgow: Fontana).
WORCESTER, R. and HARROP, M. (1982) *Political Communications: The General Election Campaign of 1979* (London: Allen & Unwin).

6

Psychological, Economic and Sociological Models of Voting

Is voting an act of affirmation or of choice? This is the fundamental question on which models of voting disagree. In the *party identification model*, the act of voting is seen as expressive, not instrumental. It is a way of demonstrating a deep seated loyalty to a party. One no more chooses a party than one chooses a religious or national identity. In the *rational choice model*, by contrast, voters choose the party which comes closest to their own interests, values and priorities. They make rational choices by working out which party is the best means to achieve their ends.

The party identification model springs from social psychology. It is sometimes known as the 'Michigan model', because it was developed at the University of Michigan in the 1950s. At other times it is described as the 'socialisation model', because it emphasises the impact of family on partisanship. The rational choice model comes from economics and is often referred to as the 'economic model'.

There is also a third, more purely *sociological approach* to voting in the political science literature. One variant of this is termed the 'structural' or 'radical model'. The sociological approach emphasises the impact of social structure on political parties. It tends to by-pass the individual elector altogether and, to the extent that it does focus on people, it emphasises the social base of values and interests rather than the mechanisms by which they translate into voting behaviour. Compared to the other models, this approach provides questions rather than answers; hence we call it an approach rather than a model.

In this chapter we describe and evaluate these various frameworks. Our own preference is for the party identification account, backed by sociological and historical analysis of the origins of partisanship, but it is important to note that the models diverge more in their assumptions than in their application. Reality keeps breaking into the tidy worlds of theory. In practice the party identification school has to allow choice into its model to explain why *some* electors change their vote. In practice the rational choice school has to allow voters to have a standing commitment to a party to explain why *so few* electors change their vote. So different models of voting end up identifying similar factors as influencing the vote, but they use distinct vocabularies to describe these factors.

The Party Identification Model

Propositions

The concept of party identification denotes the long-term feelings of attachment which many electors develop to a particular political party. To identify with a party in this psychological sense it is not necessary to be a formal member. Just as many English people think of themselves as Church of England, even though their links with the church are exceedingly tenuous, so many electors see themselves as Labour or Conservative even though they do not belong to the party in a formal sense or even vote for it consistently. Thus identification with a party forms part of the citizen's self-image, initially inherited through the family but then strengthening with its duration, as adult voters rely more and more on their partisanship to help them make sense of the continuing barrage of political information which assails them. The American voter accepts the Republican Party's arguments *because* he is a Republican, and not (as the rational choice model would have it) the other way round.

The party identification model received its first full outing in *The American Voter*, a classic study of the Presidential elections of 1952 and 1956 (Campbell *et al.*, 1960). According to this model, electoral choice is directly shaped by the voter's attitudes to three aspects of politics: candidates, policies, and links between parties and social groups.

Each of these three attitude forces has some independent effect on electoral choice, especially in the short-term. However they are in large measure channels through which party identification affects voting behaviour (see Figure 6.1). Having adopted a Democratic self-image, for example, voters will be inclined to believe that party best represents the interests of their social group, even if they do not have any information on which to base such an assessment.

Figure 6.1 also shows a *direct* effect of party identification on electoral choice. This link is important because a significant minority of the electorate vote for 'their' party without any rationalisation at all in terms of attitudes to issues or candidates.

The figure shows influences *on* as well as *from* party identification. These flow from family and group memberships. This side of the model is not as well-developed by the Michigan authors; they are more concerned with the *consequences* of party identification than with its *origins*. Thus in their treatment of group influence, Campbell *et al*. are more concerned with the psychological meaning of group membership than the group's position in the social structure. Even in the United States, where social groups are less significant or at least more diverse than in Europe, this

Figure 6.1 *The Michigan model of voting*

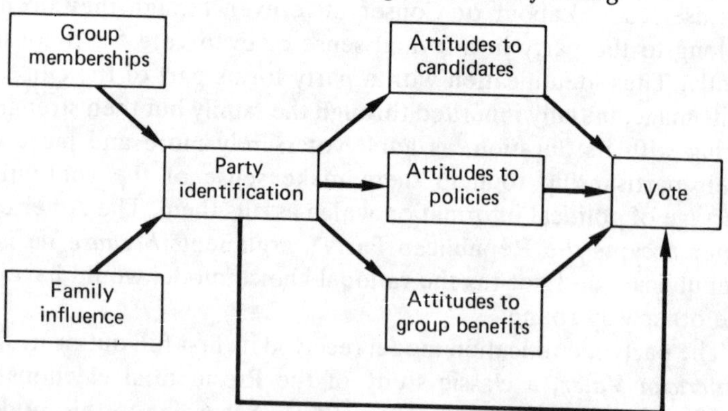

NOTE: This is the model developed in *The American Voter*. For a more recent but fundamentally similar version, see Markus (1982, p. 538). Note that the attitude forces are believed to independently affect votes; they are not just channels through which party identification affects votes.

approach is incomplete. The Michigan model underplays the sociological dimension.

Paradoxically, the best evidence for the value of party identification is that it is *not* a perfect predictor of voting behaviour. In United States presidential elections in particular, a minority of identifiers invariably defect from their 'own' party in order to vote for the 'opposition' candidate. For example, even in the 1952 and 1956 elections on which *The American Voter* was based, many Democratic identifiers voted for the popular Republican candidate, General Eisenhower. Crucially, however, these defectors normally retain a *general allegiance* to their original party and *return to vote for it* at a later date. The ephemeral nature of candidates compared with the enduring nature of parties explains why party identification rather than presidential vote choice provides the best link to the future.

In short, party identification provides a smoothed guide to underlying electoral trends, a way of distinguishing long-term and short-term influences on the vote and thus an ability to classify elections by whether they reflect, deviate from or reshape the partisan structure of the electorate (see Chapter 4 on classifying elections).

Before examining the major controversies surrounding this model, we summarise its five main propositions:

1. Most electors feel a general allegiance to a party and this allegiance is inherited through the family.
2. The function of party identification is to enable the elector to cope with political information and to know which party to vote for. Thus, party identification influences votes not only directly but also indirectly, through its *influence on perceptions* of policies, candidates and the links between parties and social groups.
3. Party identification strengthens with the length of time it is held. (Duration of partisanship is distinguishable from, though related to, the voter's age.) Except in periods of realignment, changes in party identification are personal: they reflect altered group memberships, often associated with geographical or social mobility.
4. Electors who are influenced by the short-term forces of a particular campaign to vote against the party with which they

identify, normally retain their partisanship and return to it in subsequent elections (the *homing* tendency).

5. The distribution of partisanship in the electorate provides a base from which to calculate the *normal* vote – the expected result if short-term forces do not favour one party. Realignments will transform the normal vote, but they occur only very infrequently.

As voting studies have expanded across space and time, political scientists have been exploring the limits of the party identification model. We review these developments under the following headings:

1. Is party identification one-dimensional?
2. How does party identification develop?
3. Does party identification work outside the United States?
4. Dealignment: the fall of party identification?

We conclude with an overall assessment of the model.

Is party identification one-dimensional?

One technical question about the Michigan model has given rise to some controversy in the United States. This is whether party identification is one-dimensional.

The Michigan authors had assumed that electors' attitudes to parties could be plotted on a single dimension with strong loyalists situated at the two extremes:

Strong Democrat	Weak Democrat	Leans to Democrat	Independent	Leans to Republican	Weak Republican	Strong Republican
17%	20%	11%	11%	12%	15%	12%

NOTE: 1984 figures; 2% apolitical.

This assumption was reflected in the now-standard questions: 'Generally speaking, do you usually think of yourself as a Republican, a Democrat, an Independent or what?'; followed by a probe to party identifiers asking the strength of their attachment and a probe to the initially non-partisan asking whether they lean towards one of the parties. (As the figures show, most independents do lean to one or other party.) However, subsequent research has shown this one-dimensional view to be inadequate. In the United States, strong partisans of either party are in some ways similar – for example, in their positive attitudes to the party system. It also proved necessary to distinguish two types of independents – 'negative' independents who lack partisan feeling and are uninterested in politics and 'positive' independents who value their non-partisan stance and are well-educated and involved (Weisberg, 1983).

In the multi-party systems of continental Europe attitudes to each party need to be assessed separately. Knowing that a person identifies with party A does not mean that we can predict with certainty what he or she thinks about parties B, C and D. Even in Britain's adversarial system, 'polarised partisans' who combine positive loyalty to their own party with hostility to the opposition, are by no means universal (Crewe, 1976). Attempts have been made to position parties on a single left-right dimension, giving a space which is defined by ideology rather than by the parties directly; but even here other dimensions such as religious-*vs*-secular or liberal-*vs*-authoritarian need to be included to form a satisfactory picture.

So it is clear that party identification in both the United States and Europe should be viewed as multi-dimensional. The party with which voters identify may provide the cornerstone of their political thinking but it does not determine the *whole* of their outlook. This conclusion involves some modification of the strict party identification model in which simple party loyalty, focused on a single party, explains all. But it is not a fundamental criticism: a *multi-dimensional* view of party identification represents a development of the Michigan model, not a refutation.

How does party identification develop?

The party identification model stresses the role of the family in the transmission of party loyalties. Research in several democracies in the 1960s explored this theme and produced useful results about the development of partisanship in that period (Jennings and Niemi, 1974).

All the evidence suggested: (1) that children developed at least a primitive allegiance to a party at a young age (a majority of

Americans expressed party preferences by the age of ten or eleven); (2) that this first preference was primarily determined by parental loyalties; and (3) that family influence continued, albeit progressively diluted, throughout life.

Compared to other aspects of political socialisation, party identification was unusual in the extent to which it was transmitted across the generations. On general questions of political philosophy as well as specific items of public policy the correspondence between the views of parents and children was much weaker. The fact that party loyalties develop *before* policy preferences was a strong argument against the rational choice view that partisanship is a consequence of policy agreement between voter and party.

More detailed findings showed that the correlation between the partisanship of parents and children was greater for middle-class families. Middle-class parents tended to be more interested in politics and talk more about it. Hence their children were more aware of their parents' views and in many cases awareness seemed to be a sufficient condition for imitation.

Across all social classes, the correspondence between the party identification of father and child was greater than that between mother and child. However this difference arose because children were less likely to be aware of their mother's allegiance. Overall, it appeared as though the mother was, if anything, in a stronger position to influence the child's partisanship if only because she normally spent more time with the child. Yet as a result of women's limited political involvement their potential influence remained largely unrealised.

Socialisation research was not without its critics. How meaningful are the party loyalties of ten year olds? How reliable are voters' reports of their parents' opinions? Is it not social position rather than party identification which is inherited? And surely electoral research should concentrate on voters rather than children? In our view none of these points invalidate the central conclusion that party loyalties were substantially shaped by the family in the period of these studies. The important question is whether the period of the 1960s was typical.

There are two views here. One answer, exemplified in an early article by Converse (1969), used the findings of socialisation studies to construct an ingenious general theory of the development of party identification in democracies. His theory was that in a new regime *three generations* would be needed before partisanship would reach a self-sustaining equilibrium level of about 70 per cent of the electorate identifying with a party. His theory was based on the idea that not all of the first generation would be drawn into a new party system but independents would gradually decline since the absence of partisanship among parents is not passed on to children as successfully as its presence. Thus Converse assumed that the findings of socialisation studies in the 1960s did have general significance.

The second view denies this. In Britain, for example, Crewe (1976) argued that the erosion of commitment to the major parties in the 1970s was not consistent with the Michigan model which predicted a maturing of the two-party system as the electorate came increasingly to be dominated by people whose parents were brought up in an era of Conservative and Labour supremacy. Similar findings from other countries led Beck (1976) to conclude that only the generation which *directly* experiences realignment is sufficiently partisan to transmit its loyalties to the next generation. This new generation possesses at least some attachment to parties but its children have enfeebled loyalties and are ripe for realignment around any new cleavages which may emerge. So Beck postulates a *three-generations* model of long-term *realignments*:

1. The *realigned generation* has strong party loyalties which influence the next generation.
2. The *children of realignment* have weaker but still real party loyalties, though with less capacity to socialise the next generation.
3. The *children of normal politics* have enfeebled party loyalties; they are a dealigned generation open to a new realignment.

Where Beck's third generation is a dealigned group, Converse's third generation is the first to show a mature, equilibrium level of partisanship. Converse gives a three-generation account of alignments while Beck offers a three-generation view of realignments. So these two accounts reflect contradictory conclusions about the power of family socialisation to continue shaping party loyalties as the original period of realignment recedes.

Beck's analysis is broader than Converse's. As the more recent writer, he is able to incorporate the emergence of dealignment into his analysis. But he also carries his work further back in time, arguing that his electoral cycle can be seen in all the major realignments in American history. Overall he makes a strong case for the proposition that the importance of family socialisation in shaping partisanship varies with the stage of the realignment cycle.

Alas, most democracies are too young to have experienced many complete cycles. So Beck's theory is inevitably provisional. It remains to be seen whether it wears any better than the Michigan interpretation of the family's impact on party identification.

Does party identification work outside the USA?

Party identification has now been measured in at least fifteen countries but in nearly all of them its role differs in two main ways from the United States. First, outside the United States a much larger proportion of those who *change their vote* also *change their identification*. (For Britain, see Butler and Stokes, 1974, pp. 39–47; qualified in Cain and Ferejohn, 1981; for Canada, Le Duc *et al*., 1984; for West Germany, Norpeth, 1978; and for Scandinavia, Borre, 1984.) Secondly, outside the United States *far fewer voters think of themselves as Independents*. Together, these findings cast doubt on whether non-American electorates do in fact distinguish party allegiance from current voting. Since the party identification model is built on this distinction, the relevance of the model outside the United States is also called into question.

Several features of United States politics and society explain why party identification is especially useful in the USA. There are many elected offices; voters in many states can register for primary contests as Democrats or Republicans; and the presidential system encourages voters to judge candidates to some extent separately from parties. In addition, the pragmatic nature of American parties discourages voters from using the ideological frame of reference which is more common in the multi-party systems of Europe. Finally, the weakness (or at least the complexity) of *group* loyalties in the United States means that *party* identification has become more than just a reflection of class or religious loyalties. All this suggests that the United States is virtually unique in possessing the characteristics which encourage electors to distinguish partisanship from current vote.

Critics of the party identification model claim that in Europe loyalties to social groups perform the role played by party identification in the United States. They argue class and religious identities explain why voters selectively interpret political events. In addition these critics suggest that long-term trends and short-term influences can be distinguished by postulating a normal vote based, not on party identification, but on the historic voting patterns of major social groups (Robertson, 1976a). Alternatively, issue preferences might be used to estimate a party's expected vote (Budge and Farlie, 1983).

We are not convinced. In Europe as much as in the USA party identification remains a valuable guide to long-term electoral trends. Furthermore, the survey question about *strength* of partisanship helps to explain patterns of turn-out and electoral volatility as well as providing a uniquely sensitive indicator of partisan decay. Questions about ideological self-placement or policy preferences are not viable alternatives because the individual's answers to such questions show too much random variation over time. And indeed they may derive from party loyalties.

Party identification also gives information about the solidity of a party's vote, thus facilitating predictions about its future. And even in Europe there *are* cases where voting and partisanship diverge, as with tactical voting, protest voting or voting for a second-choice party because the elector's preferred party has not put up a candidate. The difficulty of measuring partisanship outside the United States does not mean the concept should be abandoned. European electors are unfamiliar with the *term* party identification, but not with the *concept* or the *spirit*.

Dealignment: the fall of party identification?

Dealignment means the weakening of party loyalties; it is one of the most important electoral trends of the last twenty years. This section examines dealignment in the United States, Britain and continental Europe. The next section considers its implications for the party identification model.

A framework for analysing dealignment is shown in Figure 6.2. This assumes that generational turnover, as discussed by Beck, gradually erodes existing alignments. But this trend is accelerated by changes in the social structure. First, the decline of class and religious loyalties reduces the traditional social base of many

Figure 6.2 *The process of dealignment*

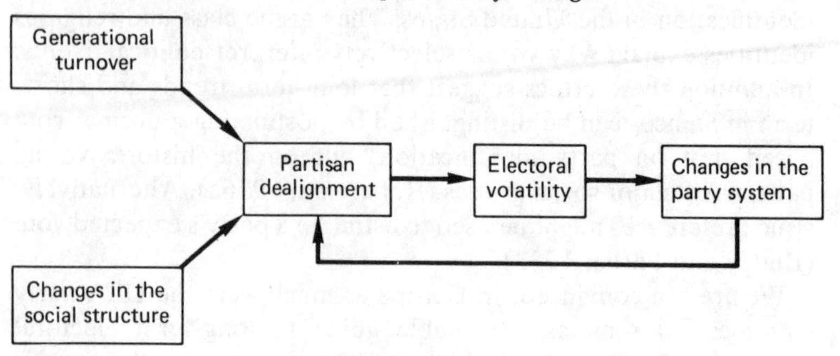

parties. Secondly, the expansion of education encourages the growth of middle-class radicalism and also gives more voters the skills needed to analyse politics in a less partisan fashion. Thirdly, the emergence of television reduces the functional significance of parties as channels of political communication and replaces a partisan medium (the press) with a self-consciously neutral or 'independent' news medium.

Partisan dealignment can lead to electoral volatility which may in turn produce changes in the party system. These may take the form of new parties emerging (such as the Greens), or old ones declining (such as the French Communists). But it is important to note that changes in the party system are as much elite-driven as electorate-driven. This is especially true of the emergence of new parties. For example the birth (if not the growth) of Britain's SDP owed more to conflict within the Labour Party than to social change (Miller, 1987). So the party system is a cause as well as a consequence of dealignment, producing a feedback loop which encourages additional change. In the diagram the causal significance of parties is reflected in the arrow running from right to left.

The *United States* has seen the sharpest fall in party loyalties. Since the mid-1960s, around 30 per cent of the electorate have described themselves as independents – up from 20 per cent in 1954 and an estimated 9 per cent in 1920 (Andersen, 1979). For the last two decades there have been more Independents than Republicans in the electorate (see Figure 6.3). Furthermore, Lipset (1985) argues that up to one in five electors now shift their party

Figure 6.3 *Party identification in the USA since 1937*

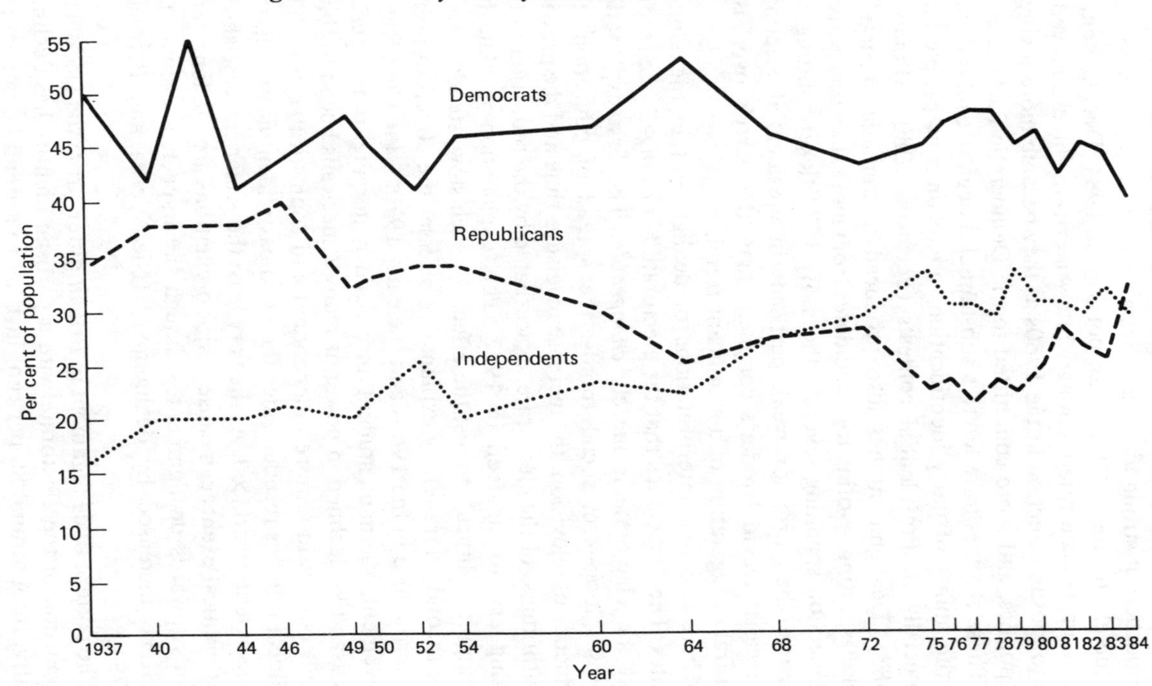

SOURCE: The Gallup Report, Jan./Feb. 1985.

identification in line with their voting behaviour, a finding which suggests that party identification is declining in importance. The proportion of strong identifiers has also declined from 35 per cent of the electorate in 1952 to 26 per cent in 1984. Dealignment is, however, concentrated among white Americans; blacks moved in the opposite direction in the 1960s as they became more involved in politics, and more committed to the Democratic Party.

These changes have led to a substantial though irregular decline in the ability of party identification to explain how people vote, especially in Presidential contests (Petrocik, 1980; Abramson, 1983). Dealignment has also produced a dramatic upsurge in ticket-splitting – voting for candidates from more than one party in an election spanning several offices. By 1972 ticket-splitting had become the norm for weak partisans in presidential elections. Journalist David Broder's comment that 'the party's over' is a natural exaggeration of a significant trend.

There are two interpretations of dealignment in the United States. The first claims that the electorate *has changed*, the second that the electorate is merely *changeable*. The first explanation stresses long-term social trends: the spread of education, the influence of television, the increase in leisure-time and the growing youthfulness of the electorate, exacerbated by the reduction of the voting age to eighteen in 1972. This explanation is plausible though it is difficult to test the effects of such slow, steady trends. The second, more telling explanation stresses the effects of political turbulence in the 1960s and the early 1970s – the Civil Rights movement, Vietnam, student unrest and Watergate. In this period partisan ties declined in power as many Americans began to think about politics in a more independent and sophisticated way. The political tide has receded since then and party identification has to some extent resurfaced. At the very least the American case shows that political events can cause major oscillations around long-term trends towards dealignment – though the impact of events may itself be increased by dealignment (Nie, Verba and Petrocik, 1979).

The pattern of dealignment in *Britain* differs from the USA. The proportion of the electorate with a partisan identity has declined gently, from around 80 per cent in 1964 to around 70 per cent in 1983, but the more dramatic fall has been in the *intensity* of allegiance. Whereas 44 per cent of all British electors in 1964 said their loyalty to one or other of the parties was 'very strong', only 22 per cent did so in 1979, and only slightly more, 26 per cent, in 1983 (Crewe, 1984, p. 190). Dealignment has been reflected in an irregular *decline in turn-out*, a strong performance by *minor parties* at the 1974 elections, growing volatility especially in *by-elections* and *mid-term opinion polls*, and the spectacular performance of the SDP/Liberal Alliance in 1983.

The mechanism of dealignment is also different in Britain. In the USA, as in most countries, young voters have been at the forefront of the decline in party identification. Low levels of partisanship among voters entering the electorate after 1964 account for as much as a third of the overall decline in partisanship between 1964 and 1976. Furthermore, those adults who did move from partisanship to independence were concentrated in the younger age groups (Norpoth and Rusk, 1982).

In Britain, by contrast, the weakening of partisan attachments has been a phenomenon of all ages – and indeed of both sexes and classes. The main exception here is opinion leaders of the future, young voters with a higher education, among whom partisan strength has declined at a particularly sharp rate. The distinctively uniform character of partisan weakening in Britain again probably reflects political events, particularly the perceived leftward lurch of the Labour Party in the early 1980s. This illustrates again how theories of dealignment must incorporate a country's distinctive political experiences and party developments before they can be applied successfully.

In continental *Europe* the picture is blurred by a dearth of good long-term time-series measurements on party identification. This means that partisan dealignment is often confused with its consequence – electoral volatility. As a result, assessments of dealignment in Europe differ largely according to whether the evidence is examined qualitatively or quantitatively. A qualitative review certainly reveals strong signs of dealignment in Europe in the 1970s. Dominant parties were thrown out of office (such as Sweden's Social Democrats in 1976), long-established major parties decayed (such as the various religious parties in the Netherlands), new parties made striking gains (such as Denmark's Progress party in 1973), and almost all governing parties lost ground in elections held during the recession in the late 1970s. But quantitative analyses of electoral volatility and party fragmentation in the post-war period show no evidence of a large, European-wide trend (for a review, see Crewe, 1985).

European countries are at different points in the realignment/alignment/dealignment sequence. Indeed Spain is still at a *prealigned* stage with many voters remaining psychologically outside the post-Franco party system (McDonough and Pinu, 1984). Other countries with relatively new party systems, such as West Germany and Italy, also show few signs of volatility and as yet there is scant evidence of dealignment there. It is in the longest-established party systems – Britain, The Netherlands and Scandinavia – that volatility has advanced furthest. Whether these changes were concentrated in the 1970s, or will continue into the future, remains to be seen. We conclude that most European countries *are* following the path shown in Figure 6.2 – but from different starting-points, at a different pace and with different consequences for their party systems.

Assessment

Dealignment reduces the value of the simple party identification model which undoubtedly worked best in the time and place of its development – the United States in the 1950s. The simple party identification model is in essence a model of stability rather than change; it worked well in the placid electoral conditions of the 1950s but needs modifying and supplementing to cope with the more turbulent 1980s.

First, it is clear that voting behaviour now affects party identification as well as *vice versa*, though voting against one's own party affects the *strength* of partisanship rather more than its *direction*. Dealignment means that party loyalties are more responsive to the prevailing political wind. This point implies that parties can use up their political capital faster than the original party identification model implied. Secondly, the decay of partisanship means that other political attitudes, especially towards candidates and perhaps towards issues, carry more weight in electoral decision making. In the United States the direct impact of party identification on the vote has declined though its indirect effects – through attitudes to issues and leaders – remain substantial. Markus and Converse (1979) suggest that party identification now only affects votes *directly* when evaluations of the candidates are closely matched (see the Appendix to this chapter).

In Europe the party identification model fares less well than in its homeland. In the past European electorates have been anchored in the political waters more by class and religion than by party – which has encouraged sociological rather than social psychological interpretations of voting. And although the social base of voting is declining, this decline has produced volatile, dealigned electorates rather than American-style voters whose party loyalties are important just because they are more than a channel through which class and religion affects votes.

But duly modified, and supplemented by some of the approaches discussed in the next section, the party identification model remains central to the analysis of voting behaviour. The *concept* of party identification provides a precise measure of dealignment and an initial explanation of volatility. It provides the simplest method for distinguishing short-term and long-term electoral trends. It explains much about how voters interpret political information. Above all it explains why even in an age of dealignment most voters go on supporting the same party at election after election.

The Rational Choice Model

If people vote rationally, what is it that they do? Essentially, rational voting consists in supporting the party which is most likely to achieve the voter's political goals. As Enelow and Hinich (1984, p. 3) put it: 'the theory assumes that the voter recognises his own self-interest, evaluates alternative candidates on the basis of which will best serve this self-interest, and casts his vote for the candidate most favourably evaluated'. Three points arise from this definition, each of which contrasts with the party identification model.

The first is that voting is considered to be an instrument – a *means* of achieving some further end. There is no room in the model for citizens who vote for a party because they value such a government for its own sake, still less for citizens who value a partisan vote for its own sake – that would be non-rational behaviour and is outside the scope of the model. In the party identification model, of course, expressive voting is considered the norm.

Secondly, rational choice models usually focus on the voters' *political* goals. Votes are not cast to please one's spouse, to impress one's friends or for any other non-political reason. In the party identification model, much more attention is paid to such social uses of the vote.

Thirdly, rational choice models assume voters are as instrumental in their approach to political *information* as to the vote itself. They acquire as much information as is needed to make their decision and they interpret their information in a cool, collected way. In the party identification model, by contrast, electors react defensively to information, developing a party allegiance precisely in order to short-circuit problems of interpretation.

In this section we begin by summarising the rational choice model proposed by Anthony Downs (1957). This is one of the earliest, simplest and most influential examples of the genre. We then consider two more recent variants: Fiorina's account of retrospective voting and Himmelweit's image of the voter as consumer.

Downs: the rational voter

When information is costless (which it never is), Downs assumes that voters in a two-party system proceed as follows:

1. They assess the *utility income* they have received from the present government. This covers all the benefits of government activity – policing the streets, cleaning the water, defending the shores and so on.
2. Voters assume they will receive the same utility income from this governing party in the future, allowing for any trends such as growing competence or declining vigour. Thus Downs' voters *judge governments on performance*, not promises.
3. Voters work out the utility income they would have received had the opposition been in power. This is a difficult, because hypothetical, calculation; yet it is necessary in order to compare parties in the same way.
4. Electors compute their *party differential* – the difference between the two utility incomes – and vote for the party that comes out ahead.

In a multi-party system, the voter follows a similar procedure but refrains from supporting parties which have no realistic chance of winning.

In the real world, information is inadequate and costly. The time and effort involved in performing the above analysis outweigh the benefit to be had from the results. Indifferent voters have no reason to acquire information at all, while voters with strong preferences will already be committed to a particular party. So Downs suggests several ways in which rational voters cope with uncertainty and reduce information costs. They may judge parties *on ideology* rather than detailed proposals, though this only makes sense if ideology does in fact guide government actions. Rather than forming their own judgements, voters may *rely on the judgements of other people* or media with similar values to their own. Or people may *rely wholly on free information* which comes their way in the course of conversation or watching television. In short the problems of uncertainty and information costs transform Downs' model voter from an omniscient calculating-machine into someone much closer to the voters we are familiar with from the party identification model. Confronting information costs, Downs' voter develops a standing party commitment, relies on trusted social groups to form judgements and does not search systematically for information. Yet these characteristics are also stressed in the party identification model. So here we have an example of how different starting points can lead to the same destination. The problem with Downs' journey is that his conclusion invalidates his premise. His conclusion is really that rational people would not bother to be rational voters – all well and good except that he is supposed to be offering a theory of rational *voting*.

The inability of rational choice models to explain why people turn out to vote has been a particular embarrassment to rational choice models. Let us suppose with McLean (1982) that your party differential is $2000, that is you would pay that much to see the 'reds' rather than the 'blues' elected. You think there is one chance in 30 000 that your vote will change the winner in your constituency and one chance in 300 that your's will be the decisive constituency. The financial value of going to the polls is then $2000 divided by 30 000, then divided again by 300, that is about one fiftieth of one penny! Better to stay at home and save on shoe leather. Much intellectual effort (Meehl, 1977) has not spared the conclusion that there are no rational voters, only rational abstainers and non-rational voters. But once we escape from the straitjacket of a simplistic rational choice model, it is easy to suggest reasons why people vote – such as social pressure, habit, party allegiance and the desire to participate.

A particular limitation of rational choice models is their disinterest in the origins of voters' values. Why do some electors give priority to tax cuts while others prefer public spending? Why are some voters concerned with house prices while others are more interested in reducing malnutrition in the Third World? Where do such priorities come from? Rational choice models take voters' 'tastes' for granted, often even regarding them as fixed. They concentrate on the narrow task of explaining how tastes are translated into electoral choices. By contrast the party identification model locates voters' values in the social context of childhood socialisation and adult experiences. Crucially, research in the party identification tradition also shows that preferences *partly result from* party loyalties, a finding which runs counter to all rational models of voting. (Further details are given in the Appendix to this chapter.)

Excessively narrow in one respect, rational choice models do have breadth in another: they provide a framework which covers parties as well as voters. By assuming that parties seek to maximise votes, just as voters seek to maximise their 'utility income', it is possible to construct models of party competition. Voters' policy preferences provide a 'space' within which parties jockey for position. Where parties end up in this space depends upon the distribution of public opinion, upon whether parties can move into regions of the policy space which have traditionally been occupied by other parties, and upon other assumptions made by the analyst. Downs himself started off this line of research, which essentially sees voters as consumers, and parties as producers, both operating in a political market. (For more recent treatments see Robertson, 1976b; Budge and Farlie, 1977; Enelow and Hinich, 1984.) These models of party competition are formal and deductive but they are becoming increasingly useful in understanding the real world as volatility grows and voters become more responsive to the cues of the political market. Party identification models, in comparison, do not explain the behaviour of parties. They are more static than rational choice theories.

Several political scientists have been unwilling to wait for reality to fully catch up with rational choice models. They have tried to adjust the models by viewing the voter as acting *instrumentally* if not *rationally*. Prominent among these efforts is Fiorina's theory of retrospective voting in the United States, an analysis which is now being applied in other countries as well.

Fiorina: retrospective voting

Retrospective voting means casting one's ballot in response to government performance. It is not a new idea. In the 1960s, the American political scientist V. O. Key (1966) wrote:

> Voters may reject what they have known; or they may approve what they have known. They are not likely to be attracted in great numbers by promises of the unknown . . . The major streams of shifting voters graphically reflect the electorate in its great, and perhaps principal, role as an appraiser of past events, past performance, and past actions. It judges retrospectively; it commands prospectively only insofar as it expresses either approval or disapproval of that which has happened before.

This idea has been recently developed by Fiorina (1981). In Fiorina's account, retrospective evaluations of government performance weigh heavily on citizen choice. These judgements are only discounted if the opposition's proposals are more than usually convincing. Furthermore, Fiorina's voters consider all past experience with the competing parties, including that of previous generations. This explains the 'all-weather' support which still underpins many Western parties; a few recent mistakes by a governing party do not overwhelm its long-term record. Indeed Fiorina argues that voters do not decide anew at each election; instead they develop a party identification, but one which serves as a 'running tally' of *retrospective evaluations*, rather than as an *emotional attachment*. Given that a party's ideology and pool of leaders usually change slowly, Fiorina suggests this is a perfectly sensible policy for voters to follow. However, when new parties emerge or existing parties change radically, Fiorina's voters do recalculate the odds.

How does this account differ from Downs'? After all Downs' voters also search the government's record for clues to its future behaviour. The difference is that in Fiorina's model electors are directly influenced by retrospective judgements; Downs' voters look back just in order to look forward. Comparisons between what the governing party has achieved and what the opposition would have achieved are less important to Fiorina who believes that voters reward governments for good times and punish them for bad times. Fiorina's voters are altogether more brutal than Downs'; they are concerned with results, not policies. As Fiorina puts it, 'what *policies* politicians follow is their business; what they *accomplish* is the voters' business'.

These contrasts reflect a fundamental difference in approach. Downs works deductively. He takes the concept of rationality, and the associated tools of economic analysis, applies the concepts to voting and sees what happens. He tells us how voters would behave if they were rational but not how they do behave in reality. Fiorina is more inductive. He develops an intuitive account of how voters decide into a formal model, then tests the model against survey evidence. (Confusingly, his data show that American voters are more future-oriented than he had supposed.) Fiorina is more concerned with the truth of his theory than with classifying it as a theory of rational voting. 'Whether or not the theory [of retrospective voting] is *rational*', he writes, 'it is at least *realistic*.' There is a place for both deduction and induction in voting studies, though in our view the inductive approach is currently more likely to yield insights into how voters decide.

Fiorina's analysis can also be compared with the party identification model. Again, the two accounts produce some similar predictions about electoral choice from different starting points. Both agree that most voters do identify with a party and that this identification strengthens the longer it is held. But in the party identification model the function of partisanship is to enable the elector to solve the problem of interpreting complicated political information. In Fiorina's model, party identification results from cool reflections on such information; it plays a *more cognitive* and *less emotional* role in electoral decision making; so it reflects *calculations* rather than *feelings*. It is important to recognise that these are differences of interpretation rather than description. There is agreement that party identification influences votes; the debate concerns the status of party identification.

Yet there are areas where the two accounts produce contrasting predictions. The party identification model views partisanship as a long-term affiliation whereas Fiorina's anticipates some voters will change their partisanship in response to a particularly successful or disastrous government. (These will be those voters who believe the parties have been equally good or bad in the past.) There is now no doubt that United States presidents can affect the level of *identification* with their party and not just the level of *voting* support. Thus any model of voting must incorporate a link from vote to partisanship as well as in the other direction. Here Fiorina scores well. On the other hand, the party identification account copes better with the tendency for voters to interpret information so as to sustain their existing partisanship.

And in practice retrospective evaluations are often influenced by later events. For example, ratings of President Kennedy's performance in office rose dramatically after he was assassinated! Or consider Butler and Stokes' findings that over the winter of 1969–70 British voters increasingly blamed the 1951–64 Conservative governments for current economic problems. The past cannot be influenced by the present but *evaluations* of the past certainly can. Yet Fiorina's voters have positive reason not to be biased in this way, for they want their tally of past party performance to be as accurate and cumulative as possible.

Our conclusion is that the retrospective voting model does capture a substantial chunk of electoral reality, though not all of it. Citizens *are* more interested in outcomes than policies; they *do* react more to governments than to oppositions; and they *do* find it easier to assess performance than plans. As developed by Fiorina, Key's insight into electoral behaviour will remain central to the analysis of electoral change.

Himmelweit: the voter as consumer

In *How Voters Decide* (1985), a book based mainly on repeated interviews over fifteen years with a very small sample of British men, a team of social psychologists led by Hilde Himmelweit portrayed the voter as an informed consumer (Himmelweit, Humphreys and Jaeger, 1985). Their model assumes a voter who is active rather than passive, responsive rather than dependent. In contrast to other rational choice models, pride of place in the consumer model is given to the voter's *policy* preferences. The elector searches for the party which offers the best match to these preferences, just as consumers look for the product which best fits their needs. Citizens also take into account the ability of parties to implement their proposals before deciding how to vote, just as the consumer considers the reliability of products before purchase. However voters, like consumers, can develop *brand loyalties*. In Himmelweit's model, this means that past voting does have a small direct effect on current choices. But most citizens treat elections like a shopping expedition; they are on the look-out for fresh ideas and new parties as well as old favourites. Although the voters' information may be skimpy or even wrong electors are at least making a conscious, individual and instrumental choice: *voters decide*!

In defending this model, Himmelweit has to explain why party identification is less important than previously assumed. She argues that party identification is a confusing concept, partly reflecting policy preferences and partly reflecting voting habits, which obscures the fundamental connection between what electors want and who they vote for. Whatever its importance in the past, Himmelweit believes party identification is not central to contemporary voting behaviour.

There is nothing new in the image of the voter as consumer. Lazarsfeld, Berelson and Gaudet (1944) began their path-breaking analysis of the 1940 campaign in the United States with exactly this perspective. But to their own surprise their survey data forced them to conclude that their original consumer model just did not work. Voters were anchored in group loyalties rather than policy preferences, and most votes were committed long before the campaign. The effect of the campaign was *reinforcement rather than change*. Confronting this failure of the consumer model, Lazarsfeld developed an 'Index of Political Predisposition' which in turn paved the way for the development of Michigan's party identification approach. So the question is whether the character of voting has changed sufficiently since 1940 for the consumer model *now* to represent the best point of departure.

We think not. Anticipating the next section, we believe that brand loyalties are much deeper in politics than in the supermarket. Voters still do not choose parties in the way that consumers select detergents. Indeed many electors do not 'choose' a party at all. The consumer model attempts to analyse *how* voters decide without first considering *whether* they decide. By concentrating solely on policy preferences, the consumer model ignores the social context within which these preferences are formed. The influence of family background, group memberships and past voting behaviour (habit) are still under-played. The consumer model stresses the *issues* in issue preferences and neglects the *preferences*. This error is inherent in the metaphor of voter as consumer. Shoppers' purchases may not be determined by their social position or group loyalties (though we suspect Himmelweit's view of the consumer is itself idealised and inaccurate) but voters' decisions certainly are.

There are three specific reasons for supposing that party identification shapes issue attitudes more than *vice versa*. First, a primitive party loyalty develops among children long before they have views on political issues. Secondly, party identification is much more stable over time than policy preferences. By emphasising voters' opinions on the issues, Himmelweit spotlights attitudes which simply do not exist for many electors. Thirdly, when parties do change their policies many supporters adjust their own policy views rather than desert their party. This confirms that party identification should be placed near the core of the voter's belief-system and policy preferences towards the periphery. The barriers to issue voting are much higher than Himmelweit assumes.

None of this means that the party identification approach is all-encompassing. In an era of dealignment, it needs supplementing with an approach which is more sensitive to electoral change in general and to policy influences on voting in particular. But retrospective evaluations are more helpful here than the notion of policy preferences. Fiorina's approach is analytically sharper, less demanding of the voter and intuitively more plausible than Himmelweit's consumer model.

Do issues influence votes?

Models of voting do not work everywhere or nowhere. The character of electoral choice varies across groups, individuals and time. Interpretations of voting must reflect this. In this section we consider the conditions under which issues influence votes; then we turn to the vexed question of whether issue voting is increasing in Western democracies.

Dampening factors. Some conditions encourage issue voting while other conditions restrict it. Let us look at the dampening factors first. If people are not concerned about the issue, or if they do not think the parties differ on the issue, then the issue is unlikely to affect their vote. If an equal number of people support different parties on the issue, then there will be no change in party strength, no matter how many individual votes are affected. More generally, it is useful to specify a list of 'party protection' effects which allow voters to hang on to their existing party loyalties and resist the pull of issues:

1. The parties may fail to differentiate their positions in the eyes of the electorate at large.
2. Once an issue clearly becomes a party issue voters often change their own positions to coincide with their party's policy. This is the *persuasion effect*.
3. Voters may conveniently warp their perceptions of party policies so as to bring their own party closer to their own preference and/or put the opposing party further away from their own issue preference. This is the *projection effect*.
4. Voters may cope with any remaining contradictions by denying the importance of the issue.
5. Voters may succeed in preferring their own party on the issue despite perceiving themselves as closer to another party on that same issue. They may value a party's commitment to principle, or its ability to implement policies in practice, for example.
6. Voters may stay loyal to their party despite disagreeing with it on one particular issue, even a very important issue. Old habits die hard.

The relative importance of these mechanisms varies considerably by issue. In the 1970 British election Enoch Powell's unofficial campaign against immigration succeeded in sharply differentiating Conservative and Labour Party positions on immigration in the eyes of the general public. In the absence of any constraints on vote switching immigration would have produced a massive 26 per cent swing to the Conservatives. In the event it probably contributed less than a 2 per cent swing. On that occasion general party loyalty (condition 6) had the greatest dampening effect, with warped perceptions of party positions (condition 3) also playing a part. But there was little evidence of parties influencing their supporters' own views on the issue; so persuasion (condition 2) did little to dampen the swings. Yet on other issues persuasion has clearly been an important influence: during the 1970s Labour and Conservative partisans very obviously brought their policy preferences into line with their parties' policies on EEC membership and on devolution – especially during the run-up to the referenda on these issues (Miller, 1980).

Amplifying factors. While some factors operate to dampen the influence of issues on voting choice, others work to increase issue effects. Those who have weak party loyalties or no party identification at all are relatively free to vote on issues. By definition young people do not have long-lasting loyalties to abandon; they are particularly susceptible to issue appeals. People who have weak links to others in society – people who do not belong to organisations or whose life-style is private – will lack the reinforcement of traditional loyalties which comes from interpersonal contacts. In Scotland in 1974, for example, there was a strong correlation between attitudes towards Scottish self-government and voting for the Scottish National Party. But this correlation varied in strength across groups. It was especially strong among the young and the irreligious, but markedly weaker among the old and among Catholics. The old and the young, the catholics and the irreligious, did *not* differ greatly in their *attitudes* to self-government. Where they differed most was on the extent to which they *translated* their issue positions into SNP votes.

Has issue voting increased?

Since the 1960s political scientists have come to attribute more influence to issues in the electoral process. This research began in the United States, where increased levels of education, declining partisanship, a series of presidential elections offering clear choices to the voters and some rise in ideological language and issue constraint among the electorate all suggested that issue voting might be on the increase. But what evidence is there that issue voting has become more frequent?

Nie, Verba and Petrocik (1979) claimed to detect a rise in issue voting. They analysed the comments made by voters when they were asked to evaluate presidential candidates. Answers could be classified into references to personal qualities, parties or issues. In the 1950s around three-quarters of respondents mentioned candidates' personal qualities and just over half mentioned issue positions. These proportions changed dramatically in 1964 when Barry Goldwater was the Republican nominee. In that year references to issues became almost as frequent as references to personal qualities; references to party ties dropped sharply. Even after 1964, the number of references to candidates' issue positions remained high, stabilising at about two-thirds of all respondents. Voters clearly adopted a more issue-laden language after 1964.

But was this any more than a change in language? Nie and colleagues show that in 1964 the influence of party identification on voting choice dropped sharply while the influence of issue attitudes rose. Party identification still remained more influential than issue attitudes but the impact of issues was no longer trivial and the impact of party identification no longer overwhelming. This new pattern persisted in 1968 and 1972 but in the 1976 contest between Ford and Carter party identification became, once again, far more influential than issue attitudes. In 1980, however, the influence of issues equalled but did not exceed that of party (Hill and Luttbeg, 1983, p. 50; see also Hartwig, Jenkins and Temchin, 1980).

Several methodological problems bedevil the interpretation of issue voting trends in the United States. (We set out some of these difficulties in the Appendix to this chapter.) One particular difficulty is the improved question format for issues adopted in 1964. Analyses using the new question format imply that *issue voting* as well as *issue constraint* (defined and discussed in Chapter 5) was understated in the 1950s. Bearing this problem in mind, only two firm conclusions emerge from the complex and often contradictory literature on the rise of issue voting in the United States:

1. Party identification is still normally the main influence on electoral choice.
2. Issues are more significant when, as in 1964 and 1972, there is at least one ideological candidate.

In the United States, then, there is still a questionmark over whether the rise in issue voting is a permanent change or a response to specific elections such as 1964. And in so far as there has been any rise in issue voting some researchers attribute it to the emergence of new 'easy' issues – that is emotional, gut issues – rather than to an increasingly sophisticated electorate. If there was more issue voting in the 1960s it was because issues got easier, not because voters got smarter (Carmines and Stimson, 1980).

But a growth in issue voting has also been reported for Britain and the Netherlands, suggesting a broader and more permanent alteration in the nature of electoral choice in several Western democracies. In Britain, for example, Franklin notes a sudden increase in issue voting between 1966 and 1970, with smaller fluctuations thereafter. Franklin (p. 176) suggests that:

> the decline in the class basis of voting choice amounts to a reduction in the strength of forces that previously inhibited volatility and self-expression. The consequence has been to open the way to choice between parties based on issue preferences rather than class loyalty.

And this in turn suggests that the party identification model is now an insufficient, though certainly not a redundant, guide to electoral behaviour.

The Sociological Approach

Main assumptions

The sociological approach rejects the individualistic emphasis of both the party identification and rational choice models. Instead sociologists stress the *group basis* of voting. Electoral sociology is about the rates at which different groups vote for particular parties. The interpretation of group voting patterns is to be found in the group's *position in society*, and how its relationship has developed with political parties, not in the values of its members. Thus the units of electoral sociology are *groups* and *parties*, not *voters*. Advocates of this approach claim to deal with the 'why?' of voting and allege that models based on the individual deal only with the 'how?'.

In its less imperialist versions, we endorse the sociological approach. Indeed Chapter 7 exemplifies it by showing how contemporary voting patterns reflect successive waves of group conflict in Western democracies. Major works in this tradition, such as Lipset and Rokkan (1967), go a long way towards explaining why parties with a particular ideology exist in specific countries, thus accounting for the menu of choice presented to the voter as well as the elector's selection from it.

The presence of large communist parties in France and Italy, for example, can be explained by elite resistance to working-class demands and by late industrialisation. Evidence for this is to be found by contrasting the history of France and Italy with that of countries such as the United States, not in attitude surveys of French and Italian communists.

Although the sociological approach is not itself a theory, it deserves credit for its achievements. Its particular strength is that its variables – class, religion, age, and the like – may perhaps be a *cause* of voting decisions but are certainly not a *consequence* of such decisions: people's age *may* affect their vote, but how they vote *cannot* alter their age. With rational choice and party identification models on the other hand, the direction of causation is not so clear cut: political goals and even a sense of party identification may be a rationalisation of electoral choice rather than a cause. Certainly it is no criticism of the sociological approach to say that votes are more strongly related to electors' attitudes than to their social background. A small correlation indicating a true relationship of cause-and-effect between a social variable and the vote may be more valuable than a large but causally ambiguous correlation showing, for example, that electors believe the party they vote for is 'best for the country as a whole'.

Yet it is absurd to dismiss the individual voter altogether. We have no truck with Dunleavy and Husbands (1985) who argue that 'attitudes do not constitute important causal factors in structuring the way in which people vote'. That is sociology gone mad. First, at the very least, attitudes are mechanisms linking social position with electoral choice. Secondly, attitudes are often useful, though not always decisive, in choosing between alternative interpretations of a sociological correlation. Thirdly, without attitude surveys, it would have been impossible to discover phenomena such as partisan dealignment which sociological skills are then needed to interpret. Again, surveys can reveal whether a party's votes spring from affirmation or calculation, and whether people support a party because of its policies or despite them. Such findings as these influence the kinds of sociological explanations which are relevant to a particular party's support. If voters' beliefs, attitudes and values are ruled out of court, we arrive at a ridiculous position where voting patterns are to be 'explained' solely by the armchair insights of sociologists. No amount of armchair speculation or contemplation of class voting patterns could distinguish, for example, between what Butler and Stokes call *class-representation* (that is, people voting for parties which they feel represent their class interests, without great animosity towards other classes) and *class-conflict* (that is, a polarised system in which people not only regard one party as representing their interests, but regard other parties as antagonistic). So it is worthwhile looking at individual voters' motivations as well as at group behaviour. Indeed, we may have to look at individuals' motivations in order to understand the full meaning of group behaviour.

Dunleavy: the radical model

British political scientist Patrick Dunleavy and his associates have recently attempted to develop the sociological approach into a substantial model of voting (Dunleavy and Husbands, 1985, pp. 18–25). They call it a 'radical' model, perhaps because it counters the party identification orthodoxy, or perhaps because it implies that Western voters do not have a free choice in the ballot box.

In this radical model, people's votes reflect their *position in the social hierarchy*. However, Dunleavy accepts a degree of subjectivity in his model: how groups in the social hierarchy *interpret their position* depends on the mass media and on party competition itself. Thus working-class home-owners in Britain may vote left or right depending on how the media highlight their group interests and on how the parties become linked to particular classes and housing groups. The interpretation of group interests by the media forms part of a *dominant ideology* which is often biased against parties of the left. Electors vote instrumentally in support of their apparent group interests, as defined by the dominant media, whether or not they are aware as individuals of their true motivation. In short, the radical model sees votes as a reflection of the political system's ideological interpretation of social divisions. It is this emphasis on the impact of media and party debate which makes the radical model distinctive within the category of sociological approaches to voting.

This account is interesting as much for its omissions as for its contents. Not only are individual attitudes dismissed but so are social contacts. Dunleavy has no sympathy with the idea that partisanship is formed in the crucible of interpersonal communication. In his view, family, workmates and friends rarely discuss politics so there is no need to postulate some strange process of contagion by which groups develop distinctive voting patterns. Equally there is no need to invoke inter-generational socialisation as the reason why groups show continuity in their electoral support despite the turnover of their members. Instead the answer lies in the continuing *interests* of the group, interests which derive from its position in the social structure. Thus working-class council tenants in Britain do not vote Labour because of discussions in the family or in the local pub, but simply because the Labour Party has represented the interests of these groups over a long period.

This is in sharp contrast to the party identification model. Some early authors in that tradition (Berelson, Lazarsfeld and McPhee, 1954, p. 301) took secondary groups such as trade unions as *indicators* of primary, face-to-face contacts. To be a Catholic in the United States was electorally significant not because of the group membership as such but because it indicated the kinds of people to whom one talked about politics. The radical model suggests that it is group membership itself, as highlighted by the dominant ideology and party competition, which is crucial; political discussion within the group is uncommon and unimportant. In the radical model, media and party debate is the mechanism linking groups with votes; in the party identification model, face-to-face contact is the mechanism. Put differently, the radical model is a theory of *secondary groups* while the party identification model is a theory of *primary groups*.

In criticising the party identification model and constructing an alternative to it, Dunleavy has given a sharper edge to the analysis of voting in Britain. In particular he has shown that party identification theorists often invoke social contact mechanisms in an *ad hoc* way to explain the voting habits of groups. For example, perhaps union members do vote left because they meet working-class people in an additional group context. Yet this mechanism is often assumed but rarely demonstrated. (But see, for example, Verba and Nie, 1972, pp. 176–9, who report on the frequency of political discussion not only in trade unions but in such apparently non-political groups as parent-teacher associations, Boy Scouts,

Bible study groups, and gardening clubs; these apparently apolitical groups seem to encourage even more political discussion than trade unions!) Such evidence as does exist about electoral homogeneity in small groups is usually based on the elector's own reports, a source which exaggerates the degree of convergence. This problem is especially acute when independent confirmation is unavailable, as with voters' recall of parental partisanship when the voter was young.

Although the radical model is still developing, two weaknesses are currently apparent. First, it remains unsuited to the explanation of any aspect of voting which is not socially based. The assumption that voting must be rooted in the social structure leads Dunleavy to overstate the importance of sectoral cleavages and to under-emphasise the extent to which voting now floats free of social anchors and moves with the tides of government performance. Despite the valuable emphasis on the media and party competition, the radical model is a perversely narrow sociological model in an era of increasingly political voting. Secondly, the rigid neglect of voters' attitudes leads Dunleavy into the realm of metaphysical speculation. In explaining how the political debate actually influences the way people vote, Dunleavy speaks of a group's '*collective perceptions*' of its interests, a notion which is far more metaphysical and obscure than the mechanism of social contact it is designed to replace. In general, there is nothing wrong with Dunleavy's emphasis on rates of voting by groups; his error is in the imperialist supposition that this is the only significant topic in the study of voting.

We shall give a fuller account of the social bases of voting in our next chapter.

Conclusion

Models of voting come from different intellectual backgrounds yet tend to converge when applied to the real world of voting itself. This is especially true of the party identification and rational choice models. Most advocates of the party identification model now accept that party identification *reflects* as well as *shapes* voting choices. It is also now widely believed that attitudes to leaders and government performance do not depend wholly on prior loyalties.

Similarly, advocates of the rational choice model agree that in practice voters are neither as calculating nor as ominiscient as pure rational choice models imply. They accept that it is rational for voters to reduce information costs by developing some form of 'party identification'. So both models portray a voter who pays relatively little attention to politics, who develops a standing commitment to a particular party but is also susceptible to influence by major government successes or failures. The concept of retrospective voting is, we believe, a particularly helpful bridge between the two models.

Another way of reconciling the party identification, rational choice, and sociological approaches is to link them to the realignment cycle, thus:

Stage in realignment cycle	*Most useful approach to voting studies*
Realignment	Sociological
Alignment	Party identification
Dealignment	Rational choice

In the period of realignment, social and group cleavages directly influence voting; then, as realignment fades into alignment, party loyalties swing free of their social base; and as dealignment develops, voters become more responsive to political events and more rational in their decision making. This broader approach will become increasingly common as election studies expand across space and time. We will increasingly ask *when* particular models are useful rather than *whether* one particular model has the edge.

Further Reading

The major book on the party identification model is Campbell *et al*. (1960, especially chs 6 and 7). A follow-up by the same authors (1966) extends the original work by focusing more on the consequences of individual voting decisions for the political system as a whole. Markus (1982) contains a more recent if somewhat technical statement of Michigan's approach to voting studies. Abramson (1983) is as good on issue voting as on ideology and belief systems. But the most useful recent collection on United States voting models, containing many of the articles discussed in this chapter, is Niemi and Weisberg (1984). Budge, Crewe and Farlie (1976) presents several critical discussions by Europeans of the Michigan model.

On the rational choice model, Downs (1957) is still the most influential and probably also the least technical work. For a more recent mathematical survey, see Enelow and Hinich (1984). Fiorina (1981, or more briefly 1977) and Himmelweit, Humphreys and Jaeger (1985) are more empirical works. For a very readable and more sympathetic introduction to rational choice approaches than we have offered here, see McLean (1982). Barry (1970, chs 2 and 5) is another sharp discussion. On the sociological approach, see Dunleavy and Husbands (1985).

Two important comparative books on the changing nature of electoral choice are Dalton, Flanagan and Beck (1984) and Crewe and Denver (1985). Both are central to the dealignment debate.

Appendix. Analysing the relationship between partisanship and issue attitudes

In the text we referred to the ambiguity of the evidence linking *issues*, *partisanship* and *voting*. This Appendix describes some efforts which have been made to disentangle the relationships between these three factors. Our aim is to show: (1) that the results obtained by researchers depend crucially on assumptions made *before* their analysis begins; but (2) it is none the less possible to draw some conclusions which most scholars would accept.

The problem

Let us assume we have asked people about their party identification, their issue preferences and their voting behaviour at the last election. No doubt we will find these three factors are statistically related. People who think of themselves as 'red party' supporters will say they prefer 'red' policies and, as a rule, will vote for the 'reds' too. The problem is: what are the *causal* relationships here? What causes what? Are issue preferences a reason for voting choice or just a rationalisation of it? Does partisanship explain (i.e. cause) voting behaviour or just result from it?

Recursive causal models

One 'solution' to the problem is to use a recursive causal model. This links together our three variables in a set of causal relationships but *assumes* that causation only flows in one direction. For example, from partisanship to vote (the Michigan model) or from vote to partisanship (the retrospective model) but not both.

The great disadvantage of recursive causal models is that, intuitively, our variables do seem to feed back on each other. It is just very plausible to suppose that party identification shapes electoral choice in a particular election *and* that voting behaviour in turn influences general party loyalties. Two-way causation, in which one variable simultaneously affects and is affected by another, is surely very common. Given this objection, why are recursive causal models ever used? The main reason is that they allow straightforward statistical techniques (such as regression) to be used to estimate the influence of one factor on another.

Most studies of issue voting have used recursive causal models. They have assumed one-way causation. However, there are several ways in which researchers have tried to cope with the *concept* of two-way causation while still using the relatively simple and robust statistical techniques of recursive models. The basic idea is to break the simultaneity of two-way causal links by adding in a time dimension. Since causes must precede their effects, this is potentially a powerful approach. We list five ways of doing this.

1. Use previous vote as well as current vote. One method, frequently used in British studies, is to distinguish voting choice at the current election from voting choice at the previous election. The assumption is that 'vote last time' influences current issue attitudes and current vote, while current issue attitudes also affect current vote. (Sarlvik and Crewe, 1983, pp. 253–8; Miller, 1980). Because we now have a *time sequence* of variables we can analyse the influence of vote (last time) on (current) issue attitudes, and the influence of (current) issue attitudes on (current) vote, without assuming any *simultaneous* two-way causation. (The analysis therefore includes two-way causation conceptually but not statistically.) Unfortunately, memories of previous voting choices are affected by current political attitudes; so this method requires us to interview the same people at both elections. That is a very expensive way of doing surveys, but memories of past voting behaviour will not do. In addition, this method assumes without evidence that current issue attitudes affect current partisanship rather than vice versa.

2. Use cross-lagged panel analysis. A variant of this first method is known as *cross-lagged panel analysis*. In cross-lagged panel analysis we assume that partisanship and attitudes at the last election may *both* influence partisanship and attitudes at the current election but *neither* current partisanship nor current attitudes influence each other. Miller (1983) used this method to investigate the relationship between attitudes to devolution and party support in Scotland. He found that for the choice between Labour and Conservative the predominant causal influence ran *from party to issue* attitudes: between 1974 and 1979 Labour and Conservative partisans tended to bring their attitudes on Scottish self-government into line with their party's policy rather than change their party. However, in the choice between the Scottish National Party and other parties, party and issue attitudes had some influence on each other, though the *influence of issue attitudes predominated*: the SNP voters of 1974 who held extreme views on self-government at that time tended to stay loyal to the party in 1979, while those with less nationalistic policy views in 1974 defected to other parties in 1979.

3. *Distinguish party identification from vote.* American authors have used a different technique to draw causal inferences from simple recursive models. They have exploited the clear distinction which exists in the United States between party identification and voting. As we have seen party identification was conceived as an enduring part of the individual's character, while attitudes to issues and candidates were considered relatively transient. Since party identification had existed before the advent of current issues and current candidates, it was regarded as *causally prior* to them even if *measured at the same time* as attitudes towards candidates and issues. These recursive models have suggested that party identification has a greater direct effect upon the vote than issue attitudes. They also show that party identification has at least as much influence on issue attitudes as issue attitudes have on the vote. In short, issue attitudes are more determined by partisanship than vice versa (Schulman and Pomper, 1975; Declercq, Hurley and Luttberg, 1976).

4. *Use other enduring characteristics as prior causes.* Of course, any other enduring characteristics with a strong influence over political attitudes and partisanship might be used in the same way. Thus some European studies have used general ideology, religion or social class as prior variables in a recursive causal model (Robertson, 1976a).

5. *Distinguish retrospective and prospective orientations.* One problem with such models is that party identification is *not* as enduring and invariant as we used to assume. Party identification is itself affected by people's attitudes towards current issues and candidates. This led Fiorina (1981) to propose a model in which *retrospective judgements about the performance of governments* in the past influence *current party identification* which in turn affects *prospective judgements about how parties will perform* in the future. This gives a nice causal sequence – past, present, future – even though all the factors are measured by questions in a single survey. Applying this model, Fiorina shows that there are substantial effects in both directions between partisanship and issue attitudes with partisanship still perhaps the more important factor. But at the end we are still left with a nagging doubt about whether attitudes with different time references can really be measured by questions asked in a single survey.

With all their technical problems, these analyses do suggest that party identification strongly conditions voters' attitudes towards political issues, even though there are also substantial flows in the other direction. The weight of evidence from United States studies – where party loyalties are notoriously weak – suggests that partisanship predominates.

Non-recursive causal models

Non-recursive causal models accept that causation is two-way. And the statistical techniques involved are not very difficult to apply. So why doesn't every competent researcher use them? Why do we not know, definitely, whether issues or partisanship predominate?

The problem is one of data, not technique. To estimate the flows of influence between two variables that directly influence each other we need to find some other factors (called *exogenous variables*) which directly affect one and only one of the two that are locked in mutual causation. Without this way into the relationship, we would find ourselves going round in circles, saying that A depends on B, but that B depends on A – and so on indefinitely. Unfortunately, it is very difficult to find exogenous variables which directly affect partisanship but not issue attitudes (or vice versa). None the less, a few researchers have tried, though their results must be treated with caution. We list four such studies.

1. Jackson. Jackson (1975a) was one of the first to apply a non-recursive model to the question of issue voting. Jackson assumed that some social background variables (race and occupation) influence issue attitudes but not party identification; while others (city versus suburban residence) affect party identification but not issue attitudes. These social background variables were his exogenous variables. On the basis of these somewhat unconvincing assumptions Jackson showed that at the 1964 presidential election 'party identifications are highly influenced by people's evaluations of what policies each party advocates while party affiliations have little direct influence on the voting decision except for people who see little or no difference in the parties'. So here was an early hint that party identification was not a constant but was coloured by policy evaluations. In another article, Jackson (1975b) found, plausibly, that current ratings of parties and candidates were particularly important in shaping the party identification of younger voters. Together Jackson's studies strongly suggested that party identification is not unresponsive to current politics. People might well get their initial party identification through socialisation processes in the family, but thereafter political forces influence the development of party loyalties.

Two more recent papers, by Page and Jones (1979) and Markus and Converse (1979), have presented ambitious attempts at dealing with two-way causation. These are important examples of the way issue-voting must be studied in the future but they do not allow a final judgement as yet.

2. *Page and Jones.* Let us take the Page and Jones study first. They looked at the 1972 and 1976 presidential elections and found an even smaller role for party identification than had Jackson's studies of earlier elections. Dramatically, Page and Jones found that party identification had *no effect at all* on policy evaluations. Thus party loyalty neither influenced people's policy attitudes (i.e. no persuasion effect) nor even their perceptions of the candidates' policy positions (i.e. no projection effect). In 1976, but not in 1972, they did find some effect of policy evaluations on party identification.

Furthermore, candidate evaluations, in both years, appeared to influence party identification but party identification only influenced candidate evaluations in 1976. Thus, far from being the fundamental influence on political attitudes and behaviour, Page and Jones' analysis indicated that party identification had little connection with other political variables and, in so far as it was linked to issue and candidate attitudes, party identification was consequence rather than cause.

But this failure of the Michigan approach did not mean that the rational choice concept could be slotted in as a replacement. Page and Jones' analysis showed a very close link between policy and candidate evaluations but it was a *two-way* link. Candidate evaluations had more influence on policy evaluations than policy evaluations had on candidate evaluations. So while persuasion or projection or policy rationalisations were still very much in evidence *candidates rather than parties* were the driving force.

In order to reach these conclusions Page and Jones had to assume (somewhat implausibly) that certain exogenous variables influenced one or two, but not all three, of party identification, policy evaluation and candidate evaluation. Furthermore, policy evaluations and candidate evaluations were so closely related that there were considerable problems in distinguishing statistically between them. All of this means that Page and Jones' findings cannot be regarded as conclusive. They form a competent attempt to deal with a difficult problem but we need many similar studies before we will know just how sensitive the findings are to the assumptions made.

3. *Markus and Converse.* Markus and Converse also used non-recursive techniques to look at the question of issue voting. In several respects their model was more ambitious even than Page and Jones'. They used a 1972–76 panel survey and explicitly included influences from past issue attitudes and past party identification on present attitudes. Markus and Converse found that party identification influenced the voters' *perceptions* of candidates' personalities. Candidate *evaluations* were also influenced directly by party identification. Final vote choice closely followed candidate evaluations, though party identification had a tie-breaking role when candidate evaluations were evenly balanced. So the impact of party identification on voting behaviour was largely indirect, routed through evaluations of the candidates.

In some respects Markus and Converse's findings confirm those of Page and Jones. For example, both studies stress the central role of candidate evaluations in influencing other attitudes as well as in determining the final vote. However, the structure of Markus and Converse's model depends much more on prior assumptions than does Page and Jones'. *By assumption* they permit no influence from issue attitudes to party identification. *By assumption* they preserve party identification's traditional role as a causal, rather than dependent, variable. Conversely, their analysis cannot disprove Page and Jones' conclusion that party identification is a dependent variable because that conclusion is ruled out by the assumptions which underlay the whole Markus and Converse analysis.

4. Franklin. It is a pity, perhaps, that these new methods of non-recursive causal modelling have been applied to United States presidential elections because their findings seem so uniquely American or even uniquely presidential. Clearly, candidate evaluations are enormously important in US presidential elections but we must doubt how far that finding can be generalised to parliamentary elections in Britain, Europe or the Commonwealth. The only comparable non-recursive study of issue voting in Britain omits candidate evaluations of the party leaders altogether. This study finds that party identification has much more influence than policy attitudes on the vote; and party identification has much more influence on policy attitudes than vice versa (Franklin, 1985).

Conclusion

So which is the cause and which is the effect? As yet there is no clear consensus as to whether policy predominates over partisanship or vice versa. Some studies, particularly those that apply recursive models, suggest that partisanship is more influential than policy attitudes. Other studies using non-recursive techniques suggest that partisanship is not important at all and that candidate evaluations are more influential than policy evaluations – which is however the old party identification model transformed into a candidate identification model.

If we must abstract some interim conclusions from these and other findings, we would say:

1. Political loyalty may be focused on party or, especially in American elections, it may be focused on the candidates.
2. On some gut issues feelings are so intense that persuasion effects will not operate and even projection effects may be weak. These are the issues which most influence electoral choice.
3. Parties and candidates may encourage projection by avoiding clear policy stances, or by making different policy appeals to different groups and regions.
4. While there is every reason to suppose that the relative influence of issues and party loyalties will depend upon political conditions, many of the apparent changes reflect new ways of collecting or analysing

data. Issues may have become somewhat more significant since the 1950s, but we now realise that their importance in the 1950s was underestimated by over-simple research techniques.

5. Even though recent work suggests that issues are more important than in the 1950s there is no case for a restoration of the classic rational voter model. Issue preferences for parties or candidates often depend upon emotional partisanship or generalised warmth towards the candidates. And many other influences than issue preferences affect evaluations of parties and candidates. Issues fail to determine electoral choices to more than a limited degree, and they are themselves influenced by such choices.

References

ABRAMSON, P. R. (1983) *Political Attitudes in America* (San Francisco: Freeman).

ANDERSEN, K. (1979) *The Creation of a Democratic Majority 1928–1936* (Chicago: Chicago University Press).

BARRY, B. (1970) *Sociologists, Economists and Democracy* (Chicago: Chicago University Press).

BECK, P. (1976) 'A Socialisation Theory of Partisan Realignment', in R. Niemi and H. Weisberg (eds), *Controversies in American Voting Behaviour* (San Francisco: Freeman).

BERELSON, B., LAZARSFELD, P. and MCPHEE, W. (1954) *Voting* (Chicago: Chicago University Press).

BORRE, O. (1984) 'Critical Electoral Change in Scandinavia' in R. Dalton, S. Flanagan and P. Beck (eds), *Electoral Change in Advanced Industrial Societies* (Princeton: Princeton University Press).

BUDGE, I., CREWE, I. and FARLIE, D. (eds) (1976) *Party Identification and Beyond* (London: Wiley).

BUDGE, I. and FARLIE, D. (1977) *Voting and Party Competition* (London: Wiley).

BUDGE, I. and FARLIE, D. (1983) *Explaining and Predicting Elections* (London: Allen & Unwin).

BUTLER, D. and STOKES, D. (1974) *Political Change in Britain* (London: Macmillan).

CAIN, B. and FEREJOHN, I. (1981) 'Party Identification in the United States and Great Britain', *Comparative Political Studies*, vol. 14, pp. 31–48.

CAMPBELL, A., CONVERSE, P., MILLER, W. E. and STOKES, D. (1960) *The American Voter* (New York: Wiley).

CAMPBELL, A., CONVERSE, P., MILLER, W. E. and STOKES, D. (1966) *Elections and the Political Order* (New York: Wiley).

CARMINES, E. G. and STIMSON, J. A. (1980) 'The Two Faces of Issue Voting', *American Political Science Review*, vol. 74, pp. 78–91.

CLARKE, H. D. and CZUDNOWSKI, M. M. (eds) (1987) *Political Elites in Anglo-American Democracies* (DeKalb: Northern Illinois University Press).

CONVERSE, P. (1969) 'Of Time and Partisan Stability', *Comparative Political Studies*, vol. 2, pp. 139–71.

CREWE, I. (1976) 'Party Identification Theory and Political Change in Britain', in I. Budge, I. Crewe and D. Farlie (eds), *Party Identification and Beyond* (London: Wiley).

CREWE, I. (1984) 'The Electorate' in H. Berrington (ed.), *Change in British Politics* (London: Cass).

CREWE, I. (1985) 'Introduction', in I. Crewe and D. Denver (eds), *Electoral Change in Western Democracies* (Beckenham: Croom Helm).

CREWE, I. and DENVER, D. (eds) (1985) *Electoral Change in Western Democracies* (Beckenham: Croom Helm).

DALTON, R., FLANAGAN, S. and BECK, P. (eds) (1984) *Electoral Change in Advanced Industrial Societies* (Princeton: Princeton University Press).

DECLERCQ, E., HURLEY, T. L. and LUTTBERG, N. R. (1976) 'Voting in American Presidential Elections', in S. A. Kirkpatrick (ed.), *American Electoral Behaviour* (Beverly Hills: Sage).

DOWNS, A. (1957) *An Economic Theory of Democracy* (New York: Harper & Row).

DUNLEAVY, P. and HUSBANDS, C. (1985) *British Democracy at the Crossroads* (London: Allen & Unwin).

ENELOW, J. and HINICH, M. (1984) *The Spatial Theory of Voting: an Introduction* (Cambridge: Cambridge University Press).

FIORINA, M. (1977) 'An Outline of a Model of Party Choice', *American Journal of Political Science*, vol. 21, pp. 601–25.

FIORINA, M. (1981) *Retrospective Voting in American National Elections* (New Haven: Yale University Press).

FRANKLIN, M. N. (1985) *The Decline of Class Voting* (Oxford: University Press).

HARTWIG, F., JENKINS, W. R. and TEMCHIN, E. M. (1980) 'Variability in Electoral Behaviour', *American Journal of Political Science*, vol. 24, pp. 553–8.

HILL, D. B. and LUTTBEG, N. R. (1983) *Trends in American Electoral Behaviour*, 2nd edn (New York: Peacock).

HIMMELWEIT, H. T., HUMPHREYS, P. and JAEGER, M. (1981, 1985) *How Voters Decide* (Milton Keynes: Open University Press).

JACKSON, J. E. (1975a) 'Issues, Party Choices and Presidential Votes', *American Journal of Political Science*, vol. 19, pp. 161–86.

JACKSON, J. E. (1975b) 'Issues and Party Alignment', in L. Maisel and P. M. Sacks (eds), *The Future of Political Parties* (Beverly Hills: Sage).

JENNINGS, M. and NIEMI, R. (1974) *The Political Character of Adolescence* (Princeton: Princeton University Press).

KEY, V. (1966) *The Responsible Electorate* (New York: Vintage).

LAZARSFELD, P., BERELSON, B. and GAUDET, H. (1944) *The People's Choice* (New York: Columbia University Press).

LE DUC, L. and CLARKE, H. (1984) 'Partisan Instability in Canada: Evidence from a New Panel Study', *American Political Science Review*, vol. 78, pp. 470–84.

LIPSET, S. M. (1985) 'The Elections, the Economy and Public Opinion: 1984', *Political Studies*, vol. 18, pp. 28–38.

LIPSET, S. M. and ROKKAN, S. (eds) (1967) *Party Systems and Voter Alignments* (New York: Free Press).

MCDONOUGH, P. and PINU, A. (1984) 'Continuity and Change in Spanish Politics', in R. Dalton, S. Flanagan and P. Beck (eds) *Electoral Change in Advanced Industrial Societies* (Princeton: Princeton University Press).

McLEAN, I. (1982) *Dealing in Votes* (Oxford: Martin Robertson).

MARKUS, G. and CONVERSE, P. (1979) 'A dynamic simultaneous equation model of electoral choice', *American Political Science Review*, vol. 73, pp. 1055–70.

MARKUS, G. (1982) 'Political Attitudes during an Election Year: a Report on the 1980 NES Panel Study', *American Political Science Review*, vol. 76, pp. 538–60.

MEEHL, P. (1977) 'The Selfish Voter Paradox and the Thrown-Away Vote Argument', *American Political Science Review*, vol. 71, pp. 11–30.

MILLER, W. L. (1980) 'What was the Profit in Following the Crowd? The Effectiveness of Party Strategies on Immigration and Devolution', *British Journal of Political Science*, vol. 10, pp. 15–38.

MILLER, W. L. (1983) 'The Denationalization of British Politics: the Reemergence of the Periphery', in H. Berrington (ed.), *Change in British Politics* (London: Cass).

MILLER, W. L. (1987) 'Dealignment at the Top: The Nature, Origins and Consequences of Labour's Crisis', in H. D. Clarke and M. M. Czudnowski (eds), *Political Elites in Anglo-American Democracies* (DeKalb: Northern Illinois University Press).

NIE, N. S., VERBA, S. and PETROCIK, J. (1976, 1979) *The Changing American Voter* (Cambridge, Mass.: Harvard University Press).

NIEMI, R. and WEISBERG, H. (eds) (1976, 1984) *Controversies in Voting Behaviour* (Washington, DC: Congressional Quarterly).

NORPOTH, H. (1978) 'Party Identification in West Germany', *Comparative Political Studies*, vol. 11, pp. 36–61.

NORPETH, H. and RUSK, J. (1982) 'Partisan Dealignment in the American Electorate: Itemising the Deductions since 1964', *American Political Science Review*, vol. 76, pp. 522–37.

PAGE, B. I. and JONES, C. C. (1979) 'Reciprocal Effects of Policy Preferences, Party Loyalties and the Vote', *American Political Science Review*, vol. 73, pp. 1071–89.

PETROCIK, J. (1980) 'Contextual Sources of Voting Behaviour: The Changeable American Voter', in J. Pierce and J. Sullivan (eds), *The Electorate Reconsidered* (Beverly Hills: Sage).

ROBERTSON, D. (1976a) 'Surrogates for Party Identification in the Rational Choice Framework', in I. Budge, I. Crewe and D. Farlie (eds), *Party Identification and Beyond* (London: Wiley).

ROBERTSON, D. (1976b) *A Theory of Party Competition* (London: Wiley).

SARLVIK, B. and CREWE, I. (1983) *Decade of Dealignment* (Cambridge: Cambridge University Press).

SCHULMAN, M. A. and POMPER, G. M. (1975) 'Variability in Electoral Behaviour: Longitudinal Perspectives from Causal Modelling', *American Journal of Political Science*, vol. 19, pp. 1–18.

STOKES, D. (1963) 'Spatial Models of Party Competition', *American Political Science Review*, vol. 57, pp. 368–77.

VERBA, S. and NIE, N. H. (1972) *Participation in America: Political Democracy and Social Equality* (New York: Harper & Row).

WEISBERG, H. (1983) 'A Multidimensional Conceptualisation of Party Identification', *Political Behaviour*, vol. 2, pp. 33–60.

7

The Social Bases of Voting Behaviour

A cross on the ballot is an implicit statement of social identity. Elections are a measure of social divisions. They provide information on the extent to which society is organised and divided by such factors as religion, class and ethnicity.

This chapter examines in turn the electoral implications of four major waves of change which have swept through Western societies (see Table 7.1). The first and oldest of these is the *national revolution*. This refers to the often violent ways in which centralising elites imposed their authority on groups accustomed to greater autonomy. For a modern nation state to develop, these nation builders had to establish their dominance over peripheral areas and over privileged organisations such as the Catholic church. In many places this centralising process stimulated the formation of parties designed to defend the interest of the periphery or the church against the centralising elite.

The *industrial revolution* is the second wave of change. This sharpened existing divisions between town and country and created new conflicts between employers and workers. Throughout Europe, left-wing parties were formed to press workers' interests. But material influences on voting only predominated in countries such as Britain and Sweden where the national revolution was resolved early and with relative ease.

These two revolutions, the national and the industrial, created social cleavages which were reflected in the party systems that emerged in Western democracies around the time when the suffrage was extended to the masses. New voters were available voters, relatively unrestricted by old party loyalties, and wiiling to

Table 7.1 *Some social bases of voting behaviour*

Wave 1 *The national revolution*	*Wave 2* *The industrial revolution*	*Wave 3* *The growth of the state*	*Wave 4* *Post-industrial influences*
Centre/ periphery	Class	Private/ public sector	Education
National and linguistic divisions	Trade unions	Housing tenure	Affluence
Religion	Social mobility	State-dependence	Post-materialism

align themselves with whatever parties served their current interests. Since then party systems have shown a remarkable degree of stability. In a famous analysis, Lipset and Rokkan (1967) referred to the *freezing* of party systems. They argued that 'the party systems of the 1960s reflect, with few but significant exceptions, the cleavage structures of the 1920s'. Such continuity came from the capacity of parties, once established, to retain their hold on sections of the electorate. In a sense, it is parties rather than voters which are anchored in the social structure – and in the social structure of the 1920s rather than of the present day: old social cleavages created a party system which thereafter structured electoral choice by itself.

Two decades have passed since that analysis and the picture is now less clear. Major parties of the 1960s have lost some ground and faced significant challenges from new parties. But these new parties have found it difficult to establish themselves because they face a mobilised electorate which still has fairly strong commitments to the old parties – even if those commitments are now somewhat less firm than they once were. Thus the more recent waves of social change have had less overt effect on party systems than the divisions of the national and industrial revolutions.

The third wave of social change that we shall discuss is the *growth of the state* since 1945. The expansion of the public sector is itself a product of the success of left-wing parties in achieving power. As the right has regained strength in several democracies in the 1980s, it has promised a drastic reduction in the role of the state, and has at least stabilised the levels of state employment and expenditure (Rose, 1985). None the less, post-war expansion of state activities has supposedly led to growing political divisions: (1) between those who work for the state and those who work for private sector firms, (2) between those who live in state-owned housing and those who are owner-occupiers, and (3) between those who are directly dependent on the state for financial support and those who are not.

The importance of the state in society and the electoral significance of public versus private sectoral divisions, varies from nation to nation. In Sweden, the Social Democrats are successfully shifting their social base from manual workers to public employees; by contrast, sectoral divisions are much less significant in the United States where the public sector remains relatively small.

Post-industrial influences are the fourth and most recent wave of social change. As affluence spreads, as educational standards rise, as white-collar professional jobs expand and blue-collar manufacturing jobs decline, there is some evidence of a shift in Western democracies from class politics to value politics – to a politics which emphasises the quality of life rather than just material well-being. This transition increases middle-class support for left-wing parties and so changes the ideological emphases of such parties.

After reviewing each of these waves, we shall turn in the final section of this chapter to a miscellany of other social influences on voting – age, generation, gender and social environment. Some of these are very important, though they do not fit into our scheme of waves of change.

Cleavage Structures of the National Revolution

Centre versus periphery

Centre and periphery are social and political concepts, not just geographical ones. The centre contains the seat of governmental authority; it is the location for major economic as well as political decisions; it dominates the flow of communication through society; and it is usually located near resource-rich areas. By contrast, peripheries generally control few resources, are often isolated from other regions and contribute little to the national flow of communication (Rokkan and Urwin, 1983, p. 14). The extent to which society is dominated by a single centre is itself a variable; highly centralised states like Britain and France contrast with polycentric countries like Switzerland, West Germany and the United States where power, wealth and influence are more dispersed. Star-shaped road and rail networks usually indicate a single powerful centre.

Conflict between centre and periphery is a fundamental part of nation building and nation maintenance. Reflecting historic struggles as well as current conflicts, contemporary peripheries are most politicised when national identities and distinct languages are involved. Many French-Canadians are more French than Canadian; some Scots and Welsh people (and most of those who are bilingual) would not take kindly to a British label. In all these examples, peripheral culture witnessed a temporary resurgence of electoral expression in the 1970s. In Canada Rene Levesque was elected Premier of Quebec in 1976 on a separatist programme. Yet four years later Quebec separatists were defeated in a referendum (within Quebec!) on whether to negotiate political sovereignty from Canada. In Scotland the share of the vote obtained by the Scottish National Party increased from 5 per cent in 1966 to 30 per cent in October 1974 but had dropped back to 11 per cent by 1983. In Wales the surge was less pronounced. The party Plaid Cymru reached 12 per cent of Welsh votes in 1970 yet fell back to 8 per cent by 1983. To a substantial extent, electoral support for peripheral parties represented a protest vote against the governing party as much as a deep-seated affirmation of national identity. Where primordial loyalties and inflexible political nationalism enter the political arena, they operate through violence more often than voting. Witness, for example, the activities of the IRA in Northern Ireland and ETA in the Basque region of Spain. Even the success of Welsh nationalists in establishing Welsh language and culture in public institutions owes more to direct action than to electoral behaviour.

The economic distinctiveness of the periphery also strengthens the electoral base of peripheral parties. The centre is often weighted towards the services sector while the periphery can be predominantly rural (north Wales and the Scottish highlands) or industrial (South Wales and the industrial belt in Scotland).

Scandinavia provides the clearest example of parties based on *agricultural* peripheries. Agrarian parties were formed to resist cultural as well as economic penetration by the cities. Aided by proportional representation and repackaged in a Centre Party label, these parties have survived the sharp fall in the size of the agricultural sector. North-East England, on the other hand, is a typical *industrial* periphery. A highly unionised work-force in heavy industry has protected the Labour party from the sharp decline it has suffered in suburban and southern Britain where the expansion of the services sector has been more marked. In addition the recession of the 1970s and 1980s widened long-standing differences in living standards between Northern and Southern England. But because these economic concerns do not coincide with divisions over language or national identity they lack the explosive character of peripheral movements elsewhere. Instead, regional interests are pursued through administrative machinery rather than the ballot box or direct action. The people try to cope with government rather than resist it.

Religion

Religion is the second cleavage associated with the national revolution. Much psephological blood has been spilt on the question of whether religion or class is the most important influence on voting in contemporary democracies. Lipset (1960) commenced the battle with his observation that 'on a world scale the principal generalisation which can be made is that parties are primarily based on either the lower classes or the middle and upper classes'. Rose and Urwin (1969) dissented. Analysing party support in seventeen democracies, they found that 'contrary to Lipset's assertion, religion, not class, is the main social base of parties in the world today'. More recent studies have examined the issue at the level of the elector (does religion or class explain more votes?) rather than the party (how many parties are based on votes from members of a particular religion or class?). For example, Lijphart (1979) considers the relative power of class, religion and language to determine votes in four countries where all these cleavages are present – Belgium, Canada, Switzerland and South Africa. Religion wins in the first three; language in the fourth. Lijphart's general conclusion (1982) offers a judicious compromise: 'social class is important in virtually all industrial democracies and religion is frequently not important at all; however, when both factors play a role, religion tends to have a stronger influence on party choice'.

The role of religion in electoral politics is greatest in Catholic countries and least significant in Protestant societies. Religiously-mixed countries fall between these poles. We will consider each of these categories separately before discussing the impact of secularisation on religious voting.

The Catholic world. In all the main democracies in this group except for Eire, there is a striking relation between religion and votes. Eire is just so completely and enthusiastically Catholic that there is no significant anti-clerical element there. So Catholicism in Eire has been a force which binds rather than divides, though voting in the abortion referendum of 1983 indicates a growing religious/secular divide (Girvin, 1986). Elsewhere – in Austria, Belgium, Italy, Malta and France – the conflict between church and state, clerical and anti-clerical forces, the village priest and the local school teacher, remains important in political life. In Austria, Belgium and Italy, explicitly Catholic parties compete for dominance with the secular left. In interwar Austria conflict between Catholics and socialists produced civil war. In Belgium, support for right-wing parties is almost total among the small minority who go to church more than once a week. And in Italy about two-thirds of Christian Democrats attend church regularly (Sani, 1977, reporting a 1975 survey).

These examples show that the critical variable in Catholic countries is *religiosity*, usually measured by frequency of church attendance. This indicator picks up involvement in that broad network of Catholic social organisations which has long underpinned the Catholic vote. Attendance at Mass often betokens a conservative and traditional attitude to life, as much as a strictly religious one. This is particularly true of older women, who are the most regular church-goers in Catholic countries and the firmest supporters of Catholic parties.

French Catholicism lacks a party vehicle but has long been identified with conservative forces. This is illustrated by the failure of France's *Mouvement Republicain Populaire* (MRP), an attempt to create a centre-left Catholic party in the post-war years. The left-wing politics of some Catholic shepherds was no match for the traditional right-wing politics of the flock. Even pro-clericalism does not mean deference to clerics. When thinking of religious groups in politics do *not* think of the altar or the pulpit: think of the pew.

Religious influences on voting are still marked in France. In the presidential election of 1981, Francois Mitterrand, the candidate of the left, received the support of 88 per cent of the non-religious, 61 per cent of those who no longer attended church, 40 per cent of those who went to church occasionally and only 20 per cent of regular church-goers.

Malta provides an extreme example of the relationship between religion and politics in Catholic countries. Before the 1930 election, the Catholic hierarchy issued a pastoral letter which stated: 'You may not, without committing a grave sin, vote for Lord Strickland [then prime minister] and his candidates, or for all those, even of other parties, who in the past have helped and supported him.'

Religiously-mixed countries. In Europe, these countries include the Netherlands, Switzerland and West Germany. Though not a separate state, Northern Ireland must also be included here. With the dramatic exception of Northern Ireland, religion in these countries no longer provides a major focus of policy differences. In the long run, this peaceful coexistence of Catholics and protestants will no doubt be reflected in a weakened association between religious affiliation and the vote. This has long been visible in the Netherlands where declining support for denominational parties led to the emergence of a single Christian Democratic Appeal in 1977. In West Germany, too, the steady growth of the social democratic SPD is widely attributed to the decline of traditionally conservative catholic milieu (Kuchler, 1978). Yet parties with a religious base still exist in all these countries; the capacity of the religious factor to outlast the issues which gave rise to it should never be underestimated. Change is across generations rather than within individuals.

In the Anglo-American world, protestant countries with marked Catholic minorities include Australia (where Catholics form 25 per cent of the population), Canada (43 per cent but about 88 per cent in Quebec), and the United States (25 per cent). In contrast to their European counterparts, which can generally trace the religious cleavage back to the Reformation, these countries lack parties with an explicitly religious rationale, and religious cleavages may not be *about* religion. Indeed, in contrast to the pattern in continental Europe where Catholics support right-wing parties, Catholics in Canada, Australia, the USA and Britain tend to support left-wing parties partly for social and ethnic reasons, though, at least in Britain, this may also be partly because the left is associated with opposition to the established Protestant church. None the less, the influence of religion on voting is clear enough. In Australia, denomination and church attendance come second, albeit a poor second, to class in accounting for electoral choice (Aitkin, 1974). In Canada, although the general relationship between social structure and electoral choice is much weaker than in other democracies, a majority of Catholics support the Liberal Party. In the United States the electoral significance of denomination has suffered a long-term decline apart from a short-term surge in 1960 when John Kennedy became the first Catholic President. But the association of Protestants with the Republicans, and Catholics with the Democrats, persists. This is not just a consequence of Catholic concentration among lower-class groups. More generally, moral and religious values still suffuse American political culture and despite the formal separation of church and state America comes close to having protestant non-conformity as its established religion. These values were expertly exploited by Ronald Reagan in the presidential elections of 1980 and 1984.

Protestant countries. Religion no longer commands much influence over voting behaviour in the protestant countries of Britain and Scandinavia. The evolution of electoral choice in twentieth-century Britain has been a story of the replacement of religion by class as the principal cleavage. At the start of the century, the equations linking non-conformity with the Liberals, and the Anglicans with the Conservatives, still worked well; 'the Church of England', it was said, 'is the Conservative Party at prayer'. As late as the 1960s, Butler and Stokes found a strong legacy of this religious tradition among older voters. However, political differences by religion and religiosity had virtually disappeared among younger cohorts. Catholics, non-conformists, Jews, Hindus, Muslims and atheists remain, for a mixed bag of reasons, more pro-Labour than one would expect from their class composition; but these patterns lack the electoral punch which religion carried earlier in the century. Active state discrimination against non-Anglicans continued until the late nineteenth century, and was followed by positive discrimination in favour of Anglican schools, but the controversies provoked by these issues died away in the early decades of this century.

In Scandinavia, where national Lutheran churches were established in the Reformation, religion has long been even more marginal than in Britain. In 1977, 68 per cent of Swedes aged 18–25 said they had no religious beliefs; this compared with 14 per cent among a comparable group of Britons. (But note that British interviewers have been known to classify agnostics under Church of England!) Such electoral influence as religion has had in Scandinavia comes from protestant fundamentalists asserting the traditional values of the family, respect for authority and temperance. In Norway these values provide a base for a significant Christian People's Party but attempts to emulate this party of cultural protest have met with little success elsewhere in Scandinavia.

Secularisation. By this we mean a change in the balance between the religious and the irreligious; a decline in the 'space' occupied by religion whether in society at large or in individual belief systems. Either religiosity itself, or simply its political relevance, may decline as secularisation proceeds.

Secularisation has been an important trend in Catholic Europe since 1945. It has taken the form of declining observance rather than declining adherence to religious belief. In Italy weekly church attendance fell from 69 per cent in 1956 to 35 per cent in the 1980s. Over a similar period the membership of Catholic Action, a leading Catholic organisation, dropped by three-quarters. In France the proportion of practising Catholics declined from 36 per cent in 1952 to 26 per cent in 1968 and then fell further to 12–15 per cent in 1983. In both countries generational turnover and the movement of people from the rural communities to urban areas have been crucial factors in this process of secularisation.

Secularisation might be expected to strengthen parties of the left as the Catholic working-class becomes more susceptible to left-wing overtures. There is some indirect evidence for this. In Italy the Communists scored uninterrupted electoral gains between 1946–76. In France, secularisation was one key which opened the gates of the Elysée Palace to François Mitterrand in 1981. But too simple a view should not be taken of the electoral impact of declining religious observance. Declining class loyalties have hindered left-wing parties as much as secularisation has helped them. Moreover, Catholic parties have not stood still: they have transformed themselves into broad catch-all parties of the centre-right. This transformation has been helped by the church's growing reluctance to enter the political arena openly and explicitly. So the most important consequence of secularisation has probably just been to make centre-right politicians work harder for their votes, and campaign directly on broadly right-wing rather than specifically religious themes.

Secularisation generates its own tensions and counter-movements. American history is littered with extreme right-wing movements, such as the Know-Nothings and the Ku Klux Klan, which have attempted to reassert traditional moral values against the 'threat' from atheists, city dwellers, Jews, immigrants and catholics. Right-wing protestantism is one element in these movements of cultural reaction (Lipset and Raab, 1971). The most recent revival of the Christian right in the United States is indicated by the fact that white 'born-again' Protestants made up 17 per cent of the electorate in 1980. Politically, this renaissance was spearheaded by Moral Majority Inc., an organisation which issued a Family Issues Voting Index (known to critics as the 'moral hit-list') summarising the voting behaviour of American congressmen on relevant moral issues. The religious revival contributed to the defeat of several liberal senators in the 1980 elections. Elsewhere in the democratic world, the 1980s saw signs of a religious renaissance among the 'post-secular', young, well-educated middle-classes. Even when not couched in religious terms the re-emergence of traditional moral views on issues such as abortion and censorship may prove to be electorally significant. A secular society is not necessarily a permissive society.

Cleavage Structures of the Industrial Revolution

Class

There is no agreement among sociologists and political scientists about the meaning of the term 'class'. Different writers use the term for different purposes and define it in different ways. Provided their definitions are clearly stated and their conclusions follow from those definitions no harm is done. Indeed, different perspectives can add a variety of useful insights. What is important is that we treat the term as an analytical tool and do not set out on a foolish quest for the 'real' meaning of class: it does not exist.

None the less some famous definitions are widely used. According to Max Weber, the influential German sociologist, a social class consists of a number of people who share similar life chances as a result of their position in the labour market (Weber, 1948, p. 181). This definition does not so much identify the classes of a particular society as provide a test by which they can be identified. So Weberian sociologists can all accept Weber's definition while disagreeing over what classes actually exist in a particular society at a particular time.

In more concrete terms, defining classes directly and unambiguously, the most influential categorisation of classes has been provided by Karl Marx. In capitalist society, he distinguished between the bourgeoisie, who own the means of production, and the proletariat, who must sell their labour to make a living. Marx's definition is still useful since the bourgeoisie has proved to be strongly conservative in its voting behaviour – and the 'petty bourgeoisie' (small employers and the self-employed) even more so. But additional differentiation is needed within Marx's proletariat: after all, porters, postmen and professors all sell their labour. For purposes of electoral analysis, we suggest three 'class' divisions are particularly useful:

1. *Between manual and white-collar employees*. This is the simplest and most common way of classifying occupations. It still has some validity in that white-collar employees usually have higher incomes, better conditions of work and more promotion opportunities. But the rapid growth of routine non-manual jobs (for example clerks and typists) has created a predominantly female 'white-collar proletariat' whose class position is similar to, and sometimes worse than, many manual workers.
2. *Between those employees who exercise authority in the workplace and those who do not*. The work situation of the department head clearly differs from that of his secretary – as does the foreman's from that of the shop-floor worker. Some sociol-

ogists argue that the exercise of authority is now the fundamental division in the work-place (Dahrendorf, 1959); it is at the very least an important one.

3. *Between employees whose jobs are based on technical expertise and those whose jobs are not* (Bell, 1973). This separates the professional from the manager and the skilled from the unskilled worker. As we will see, the voting behaviour of professional people whose main task is to apply specialist knowledge is less right-wing than that of managers whose main job is to control the labour of others.

The market researcher's 'social grade' scheme and the British government's own 'social class' scheme are based on factors such as occupational prestige, income and life-style rather than on a Weberian or Marxist concept of class interest. They resemble the American approach of bundling together income, occupational prestige and education in a single basket called *socio-economic status*. For this reason, some British sociologists have developed their own measurement schemes: one used in a major study of the 1983 general election is shown in Table 7.2. It is more theoretically sophisticated but as yet less common than the market researcher's classification. It is not intended to provide a single multi-purpose ranking of occupations – the salariat are the richest group, for example, but not the most politically right-wing.

Given some such scheme for assigning individuals to classes, the index developed by Alford (1963) is frequently used to measure the extent of class voting. This index is obtained by taking the percentage of the working-class voting for the left-wing party and subtracting from this the percentage of the middle-class who vote for the party of the left. (If there are more than two classes in a class scheme, all but two must be ignored, or the classes must be grouped into one broad middle-class and one broad manual-class.) For example, in the British election of 1983, 36 per cent of manual workers voted Labour compared to 16 per cent of white-collar workers, yielding an Alford index of 20. In 1955, the percentages were 62 per cent and 23 per cent respectively, giving a score of 39 – almost twice as high as in 1983.

Alford's index is undoubtedly crude. It is usually based solely on the blue-collar/white-collar distinction; it cannot distinguish a fall in class voting from a change in the nature of class voting; it

Table 7.2 *Classifying occupations in Great Britain*

Designation	*Description*	*Distribution of population %*
Market research: social grade (Monk, 1978)		
A	Higher managerial or professional	3
B	Lower managerial or administrative	13
C1A	Skilled or supervisory non-manual	23
C1B	Lower non-manual	
C2	Skilled manual	31
D	Semi-skilled and unskilled manual	19
(E)	(Residual, on pension or other state benefit)	(11)
Registrar general: social class (OPCS, 1980)		%
I	Professional, etc.	6
II	Intermediate	25
III(N)	Skilled non-manual	12
III(M)	Skilled manual	35
IV	Partly skilled	16
V	Unskilled	6
Heath, Jowell and Curtice (1985): class scheme		%
Salariat	Managers, administrators, professionals, supervisors of non-manuals	27
Routine non-manual	Rank and file white-collar employees	24
Petty bourgeoisie	Farmers, small proprietors, own-account workers	8
Foremen and technicians	Supervisors of manuals; or those with discretion at work	7
Working class	Rank and file manual employees	34

NOTE: Distributions are based on allocating household members to the head of household's job except for the Heath, Jowell and Curtice scheme which is based on the respondent's own occupation. Figures are based on the early 1980s.

ignores changes in the relative sizes of classes; and it focuses only on the major left-wing party, ignoring what is happening to right-wing parties. None the less it is still a useful starting-point for making cross-national comparisons or documenting time-trends.

The scale gives a significant positive reading on class voting in nearly all democracies. In his original study of voting in the mid 1950s, Alford gave scores of 41 for Britain, 34 for Australia, but much lower figures for the United States (16) and Canada (8). In continental Europe, class voting is much less prevalent than in Britain: West Germany, Holland and Italy all score much lower than Britain on the Alford index. However, in Scandinavia class voting exceeds even the British level: the average Alford index for Denmark, Norway and Sweden was around 55 in the mid-1950s though this had fallen to 35 by 1980 (Borre, 1984). In short, class voting is high though declining in Britain and Scandinavia; generally much lower in continental Europe; while former British dominions show a mixed pattern.

The explanation for this variation is, crudely, that class matters electorally in Britain and Scandinavia since other cleavages, especially religious cleavages, are relatively weak. It is the absence of other divisions, rather than the intensity of class conflict, which makes the class alignment so conspicuous in British and Scandinavian elections.

Surveys of class consciousness confirm this picture, for although class awareness is common in industrial democracies belief in (still less support for) class conflict is unusual. In Britain most people will describe themselves in class terms, given some encouragement by an interviewer, but only a minority believe that class is a central determinant of life-chances or that class barriers are strong (Robertson, 1984, ch. 4). In the United States, as one would expect, individualistic values are even more predominant: most white working-class Americans account for their lowly position in terms of their *own* rather than *society's* failings (Hochschild, 1981). Only France and Italy have even a large minority of the working-class who subscribe to a general critique of society, and this no doubt is partly a consequence as well as a cause of the strong communist parties in these countries (Lash, 1984).

Were class the only influence on voting, middle-class parties would never have survived the transition to universal suffrage, though they might do well now that the middle class has expanded.

To be successful, bourgeois parties, for over half a century, have had to attract a higher proportion of cross-class support than parties of the left. Britain is the most striking example here. In 1983, 78 per cent of Labour's vote came from manual workers – but so too did 50 per cent of Conservative support. In a comparative context this represents a remarkable achievement by the British right. The Conservative Party has retained its position as the principal political expression of the bourgeoisie, thus avoiding the splits which long proved costly to the right in Scandinavia. Yet it has maintained and recently strengthened its appeal to the working class, despite the disintegration of the religious cleavage and despite the historic moderation of the Labour Party. No wonder working-class Conservatism has been such a prominent theme in British electoral analysis (Crewe, 1984).

Is class voting in decline in liberal democracies? Until the 1960s, it appeared that the class alignment was strengthening rather than weakening. Writing in 1968, Allardt noted that in Scandinavia 'class explains more of the variation in voting behaviour and particularly more of the working-class vote than some decades ago. As equality has increased, working-class voters have been more apt to vote for workers' parties.' In the United States, too, class voting peaked in 1948 as the New Deal generation matured. But these inferences must now be sharply modified. As Figure 7.1 shows, the Alford index has fallen sharply in several democracies over the past two or three decades. Furthermore, class voting is generally lower among the young than the old. If this reflects generational rather than life-cycle effects, class voting is likely to continue its decline as older generations die off (Inglehart, 1984, p. 30).

Some of the apparent decline represents a change in the *nature* of class voting rather than a true decline in class voting itself. For example, the modest fall in Conservative support among routine white-collar employees in Britain contributes to a drop in the Alford index even though such employees may actually be concluding that their class interest rests with the workers rather than the managers. Marx's apocalyptic vision of a simple political dichotomy between workers and capitalists would show up as a *decline* in class divisions on the standard Alford index calculated on the political differences between manual and non-manual employees. Yet even among manual workers, voting seems to have

Figure 7.1 *Alford index of class voting, 1948–84*

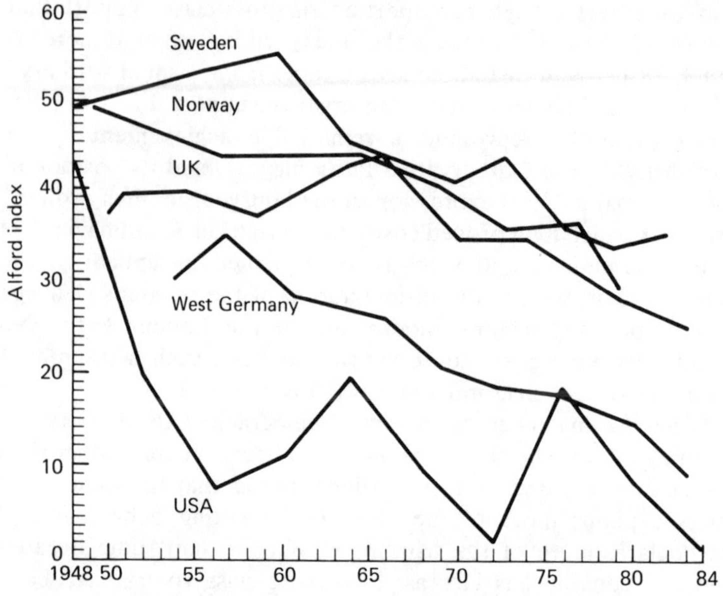

SOURCES: Inglehart (1984), Sandberg and Bergland (1985)

become less communal and more privatised, less traditional and more instrumental, less automatic and more contingent. The factors underlying this change include the decline of traditional working-class communities, increasing geographical and social mobility, the privatisation of social life, the growth of home ownership and rising education standards.

These changes have led to a declining proportion of workers fitting the traditional class stereotype – minimum education, living in rented housing, working in heavy industry and surrounded by friends and relations who themselves possess these attributes. Such 'stereotypical' workers have in fact remained relatively loyal to parties of the left; the point is that there are fewer of them about. As one British commentator put it: 'Labour's traditional supporters are disappearing into service jobs and their own homes.'

Even if left-wing parties retain their *share* of the working-class vote, they are threatened by this decline in the *size* of the working-class. Over the last twenty years, many democracies have become white-collar societies. By 1974 the number of white-collar workers in West Germany exceeded the number of blue-collar workers. In Britain rank-and-file manual employees made up only a third of the work-force by 1983, according to Heath's stringent definition of the working-class (see Table 7.2). Changes in the relative size of the classes between 1964 and 1983 could by themselves have cut Labour's share of the vote by 7 per cent (Heath *et al*., 1985, pp. 35–39). These effects of changes in class size are not picked up by Alford-style analyses which focus on differences in voting behaviour between classes.

As the natural class constituency of left-wing parties decays, and electoral volatility grows, parties become increasingly subject to the slings and arrows of political fortune. Political events in Europe in the 1970s were generally unfavourable to the left. The recession posed particular problems for parties committed to a large public sector; the ecology movement creamed off some support from traditional parties of the left; and popular reaction against the tax 'burden' of the welfare state also hindered the left, especially in Scandinavia. These problems continued into the 1980s, with the success of stridently right-wing politicians such as Margaret Thatcher in Britain and Ronald Reagan in the United States. In this difficult environment, left-wing parties must earn their votes through attractive policies and presentation. They are in the same position as European right-wing parties that can no longer rely on automatic support from religious groups – no better, no worse.

Trade unions

A second consequence of the industrial revolution, intimately linked with class, is the growth of trade unions. As the industrial wing of the working-class movement, trade unions could be expected to increase electoral support for the left. And in nearly all democracies left-wing voting is more common among trade unionists than the non-unionised. In Britain, Labour is still the leading party among union members though their support for Labour fell from 55 per cent in February 1974 to 39 per cent in 1983, partly as a consequence of the Alliance surge. In West Germany, union ties are also a major influence on party preference even though the unions were reorganised into an officially non-partisan federation – the *Deutscher Gewerkschafsbund* (DGB) – after 1945. While the electoral contrast between members and non-members is sharper in some countries than others, it is discernible almost everywhere.

The electoral impact of unions depends on their penetration into the work-force and on how they are organised. Membership figures range from about 40 per cent of the work-force in West Germany to 85 per cent in Sweden, with most countries registering a small decline in union penetration during the recent recession. But organisation is at least as important as penetration. Where trade unions are themselves divided on political and/or religious lines, their main effect is to reinforce rather than change voting intentions. In much of Europe, Catholic unions have long been an important part of the church's organisational network, often in competition with communist-dominated unions as in France and Italy. Membership of a Catholic or communist union reflects and conserves rather than causes the relevant socio-political identity. Insufficient attention to this process of self-selection has led some observers to exaggerate the impact of union propaganda on members' voting behaviour (Gallie, 1983). The main effect of trade union communication activities – shop-floor canvassing, journals, meetings, education – is *reinforcement* not change.

Even where the unions are not split on political or religious lines, their electoral impact can be exaggerated. Despite the growth of white-collar unions, the typical trade unionist is still a male manual-worker working in a large, often publicly-owned manufacturing plant. Such people would be predisposed to the left even if they were not union members. Indeed, among this group party preference and union membership form part of a general configuration of pro-worker attitudes. Butler and Stokes (1969, p. 167) show that in Britain about a third of the difference in Labour support between members and non-members is simply due to the contrast in the class composition of the two groups. Furthermore, even in Britain, partisanship is one factor in the decision to join a union (at least for those workers who have a choice): union members are more left-wing than non-members *even at the time of joining*. So even among British manual workers trade unions probably reinforce an existing partisanship more often than they create a new one. Among the growing band of white-collar unionists, however, trade-union membership exerts an influence which cuts across class and in the long run this may well prove to be the arena in which unions have most electoral impact.

The role of trade unions in industry and politics can itself become a political issue which influences the votes of members and non-members alike. For decades a majority of Britons (including a majority of trade unionists) have expressed reservations in opinion surveys about the power of the unions and about their close links with the Labour Party – though many of these voters also feel that the Labour Party is particularly well equipped to deal with industrial relations problems, precisely because of these much-criticised ties (Crewe, 1984).

The similarity between members' and non-members' views on trade-union issues is a powerful tribute to the *unimportance* of trade union communication networks in shaping political ideas. Clearly, left-wing voting among union members can coexist alongside a critical perspective on the role of trade unions in national politics.

Social mobility

The industrial revolution created societies with considerable occupational mobility. In particular, the steady expansion of white-collar jobs in industrial society has increased the proportion of the electorate whose current class is higher than that in which they were brought up. By the 1970s about one in five British electors had crossed the increasingly open boundary from the manual to the white-collar classes; only one in ten had made the reverse journey.

Inter-generational mobility is thus matched by considerable *intra*-generational mobility. For example, in Australia in 1967, one in two white-collar male breadwinners had begun their *own* occupational careers in manual jobs (Aitkin, 1982). Much of this mobility is forced by the general shift to non-manual work; it indexes changing industrial requirements rather than personal achievements; the career prospects of a child from a working-class family have not improved relative to those of a middle-class child. None the less, even forced mobility, deportation of workers to exile in the middle-class as it were, gives added point to an investigation of the electoral consequences of social mobility.

Hypotheses abound. Undoubtedly the most popular is that the

'ups' will rapidly acquire the political colouring of their new habitat while the 'downs' will desperately hang on to the remaining vestiges of their middle-class identity. If this is true, right-wing parties will be the main beneficiaries of social mobility. It has also been suggested that the socially mobile provide a rich vein of support for the extreme right. The 'ups' may resent their lack of acceptance by their new classmates while the 'downs' may allay the pangs of status strain through the simplistic explanations offered by extreme ideologies for their plight.

The truth is less grand. Most people cope with mobility in a perfectly straightforward way; often, they do not even define their change in terms of vertical class movement at all. The consistent finding of nearly all surveys of mobility and voting is that the mobile occupy an *intermediate* electoral position between the class of origin and the class of destination (Thompson, 1971). The first-generation middle-class give more support to the left than the stable middle-class but less than the stable working-class. Thus, early socialisation has a continuing but less than totally dominant effect on adult electoral behaviour.

There is some evidence that the 'ups' are more likely than the 'downs' to change their votes. The 'ups' move right while the 'downs' sit tight. But the situation is complicated by the tendency for the upwardly mobile to be drawn from right-wing, working-class backgrounds in the first place. In Britain the rate of movement from the working-class into the middle-class is twice as high among children from Conservative as from Labour homes (Butler and Stokes, 1974, p. 98). Many of these blue-collar Conservative families belong to the sunken middle-class.

Social mobility is a powerful explanation of cross-class voting. In 1963, the downwardly mobile provided one in five of Britain's working-class Conservatives while the upwardly mobile made up a remarkable 70 per cent of middle-class Labour supporters. A decade later, white-collar workers with blue-collar family origins still accounted for most Labour voting among middle-class men (Heath, 1981, p. 242). Thus some of the apparent decline in class voting is undoubtedly due to forced class mobility caused by the growth of white-collar jobs. While the radical chic of the third-generation middle-class may be the most appealing explanation of white-collar socialism, the manual backgrounds of the first-generation middle-class are statistically more important.

The Impact of the State

As the echoes of the national and industrial revolutions fade, some authors have argued that a new fault line has emerged around the role now played by the state in production and consumption. The growth of the public sector is the third wave of social change identified at the start of this chapter. Dunleavy and Husbands (1985) argue that the growth of the state since 1945 has led to several new divisions in society:

1. Between *employees* in the public and private sectors – a production sector effect.
2. Between those who *use public services* (principally in housing and transport) and those who use private services (home owners and car owners) – a consumption sector effect.
3. Between those who are *supported by the state* (pensioners, the unemployed and claimants of supplementary benefit but *not*, of course, those who get huge amounts of tax relief on their mortgages, or huge investment subsidies!) and those who are not – a so-called state-dependence effect.

These divisions cut across the vertical division of social class which is why they are termed *sectoral* cleavages. Many working-class people who own a car, have a mortgage and work for a private firm find themselves on the conservative side of these divisions. Such voters, it is claimed, are less likely to vote on a class basis, are more responsive to the mass media and become more volatile in their electoral behaviour.

Here then is an elegant explanation for class dealignment in general and the problems confronting left-wing parties in particular. The question is: does the explanation work both in the sense of explaining voting patterns and in the more rigorous sense of being the *only* explanation for the observed voting patterns? This we consider in the three sub-sections which follow. Our answer is that in several countries employment sector does indeed correlate with voting patterns, but largely within the ranks of the middle class. Housing tenure is important in Britain, less so in other countries, but several factors are involved in this correlation even in Britain. Overall, we do not believe that sectoral divisions can explain partisan weakening and class dealignment, both of which spring more from changes in the class structure itself.

Private and public sector employment

Public sector employment in Western democracies grew substantially in the 1960s and early 1970s. In Sweden it doubled between 1960 and 1975. In Britain, jobs in the public *corporations* (such as gas and electricity) have remained fairly stable but employment in the public *services* (such as health and education) rose from 14 per cent of the work-force in 1961 to 23 per cent in 1982. By 1980, the United States was the only major Western nation in which public employment was less than a fifth of the labour force (Rose, 1984, p. 131; 1985, p. 6).

The British case suggests that employment sector affects the votes of white-collar employees more than manual workers. Blue-collar workers in the public sector are more likely to vote Labour than their private sector counterparts but this is partly because of their heavy concentration in the nationalised heavy industries. Among the middle classes sectoral effects are more significant. There is of course a long tradition of white-collar public-sector radicalism. Even in the 1960s, CND supporters were concentrated heavily 'in the employment of state and local authorities' (Parkin, 1968). But since then, as government employment has expanded especially in the caring professions, the number of left-wing public-sector graduates has increased, though they remain a small section of the total electorate. Growing unionisation among this group has helped sustain their non-Conservative values. The Liberal/SDP Alliance proved particularly attractive to them in the 1983 election. But are these 'silk-stocking socialists' attracted to the public sector *because* of their radicalism? Perhaps public sector employment only strengthens liberal values which originate elsewhere – in family background, higher education or a post-materialist ideology. In Britain the growth of state employment has been only one contributory factor towards middle-class radicalism.

Even among the middle-classes, the electoral significance of employment sector varies with its salience as an issue in contemporary politics. There is some evidence that sectoral influences on voting sharpened at the 1983 British election in response to the emphasis placed on the private sector by the 1979–83 Conservative administration. In Denmark, too, employment sector emerged as a major influence on middle-class voting behaviour in the late

1970s largely in response to heated debate about the future of the public sector (Andersen, 1983). Support for Danish socialist parties among public sector professionals was especially marked when the military and police were excluded from the analysis – which suggests that sectoral divisions are more complex than the simple public/private dichotomy and that the details of current political debate define the politically relevant sectors (Dunleavy, 1986). It remains to be seen whether this new cleavage will continue to be important in Danish voting behaviour. In Sweden, however, the large and heavily unionised public sector has become a cornerstone of support for the successful Social Democrats.

Housing tenure

In the list of public/private services, housing stands alone as an electoral influence. There is little evidence that people who use other private services, whether in education, transport or health care, are propelled in a right-wing direction (many are already there anyway). But housing tenure is undoubtedly a strong influence on electoral choice in Britain, almost equalling class in its ability to predict votes. Within each social class, Conservative voting in Britain is highest among those who own or are buying their home and weakest among council tenants. Private tenants form an intermediate group. Among the middle-class, ownership is the dominant tenure and thus merely reinforces Conservative pre-eminence. Among the working-class, there is more variation in tenure; large sections of the working class own their own homes and this cuts across traditional Labour loyalties.

Some portion of the relationship between housing tenure and voting merely reflects the concentration of council tenants among younger and less affluent workers in Northern industrial areas. But there is little doubt that there is also a genuine housing effect at work. Between 1963 and 1970, Butler and Stokes (1974, p. 112) found that Labour support fell more among council tenants who moved to privately-rented or owner-occupied accommodation than among those who stayed on the council estates. And 'housing mobility' is very common: a majority of people whose parental home was a council house now own their own home.

But *why* does housing tenure influence electoral choice? For advocates of the sectoral approach, the crucial factor is the economic interest of the various tenure groups as reflected in political debate and presented in the media. There must surely be something in this. After all, home ownership is a form of property which allows capital accumulation, a fact which has led some sociologists to write of *housing classes* rather than tenure groups (Saunders, 1979). But advocates of the party identification model of voting point out that attitudes to housing policy do not vary much by housing tenure and do not influence voting behaviour (Harrop, 1981). These authors suggest that the important factor is the *social composition of the elector's neighbourhood*. Council estates in particular bring together large numbers of working-class people in a way that helps to sustain the predominance of Labour loyalties among them. The owner-occupier is only marginally less likely to be surrounded by others with the same tenure, thus reinforcing Conservative sympathies. In Sweden, part of the recent fall in class voting has been attributed to declining residential segregation by social class. This in turn results partly from deliberate public policy (Stephens, 1981). 'Contextual' or neighbourhood effects of this kind are tricky to verify but almost certainly important. (We discuss them in more detail later in this chapter.)

Voting differences by housing tenure are well-established in Britain. They have not increased since the early 1960s (Heath, Jowell and Curtice, 1985, p. 57). What has changed is the *size* of the various tenure-groups. Owner occupation has become the predominant tenure as the private rented sector has gone into decline. But as yet this has not really helped the Conservatives. Heath, Jowell and Curtice point out that on a strict definition of the 'working-class', working-class home owners formed the same proportion of the electorate in 1983 as in 1964. The expansion of home ownership among manual workers was offset by the contraction of the working class itself: *the new home owners were also the new middle class*. These authors believe the Conservatives have so far benefited far more from occupational trends than from housing trends. They argue that the proportion of the electorate whose housing tenure cuts across their class has not increased substantially. Thus housing is a continuing source of division rather than a new cleavage capable of explaining trends towards electoral volatility and partisan dealignment.

Housing policy is highly politicised in Britain. Whereas in Britain 'council housing' is still a major form of tenure, in the United States and Australia 'housing projects' and 'housing commission areas' cater for a small part of the under-class. Outside Britain, housing policy is based on subsidies to house builders rather than direct involvement in construction. In consequence, privately rented accommodation is now much less common in Britain than elsewhere. Britain is, then, a society in which any 'housing effects' on voting are likely to be particularly strong; and strong results obtained from detailed studies of housing and voting in Britain have limited applicability to other countries. For example, there is not a strong relationship between housing tenure and voting among the Scandinavian working class (Worre, 1980), at least when contextual effects are taken into account.

State dependence

Through a mixture of pensions schemes, unemployment pay and social security benefits most democracies now provide a financial safety net for their citizens. But is state dependence associated with support for left-wing parties, as the sectoral account of voting predicts? In Britain state dependence does not appear to be a major direct influence on electoral choice though the most telling comparisons have still to be made (see Dunleavy and Husbands, 1985, ch. 6). For example, although old people living on *state pensions* are a strongly Conservative group (which runs counter to the hypothesis) it remains possible that old people with *private pensions* are even more solidly Conservative. However, unemployed people are no more inclined to vote Labour than unskilled workers from whose ranks they are largely drawn. State dependence effects may none the less exist, waiting to be teased out by more detailed analysis, but the major result of state dependence may prove to be apathy, abstention and withdrawal from the political system rather than left-wing voting. The pioneering study of unemployment in the Austrian village of Marienthal (Jahoda, Lazarsfeld and Zeisel, 1933), like recent studies of the current wave of unemployment (Schlozman and Verba, 1979), showed that the major effect of dependence may be apathy and loss of self-esteem rather than left-wing activism – however depressing that conclusion may be to the revolutionary or moralist.

Post-industrial Influences

Where sectoral theorists see the growth of the state as the crucial new influence on electoral behaviour, other authors have stressed the importance of post-industrialism in reshaping voting patterns. Post-industrialism denotes a science-based, professional, white-collar, service-oriented society in which *knowledge* rather than *capital* is the key political resource and *education* rather than *class* is the major source of political values (Bell, 1973; Kumar, 1978). Reared during the post-war era of affluence and peace, younger generations are believed to have turned away from a concern with safety and security towards new political goals. In this section, we examine some crucial themes in this post-industrial framework: education, affluence and post-materialism.

Education

The vast expansion of further and higher education since 1945 increases the importance of understanding the link between education and voting. Between 1950 and 1982, the number of students in tertiary education grew from fifteen to fifty-five per 1000 population in the United States and from three to fifteen in Great Britain (and the proportion of the population which has had such education is of course many times greater than the number currently receiving it). Higher education is still the preserve of a minority – but it is a vocal minority and one which will continue to grow as older, poorly-educated generations die off.

A comparison between the top and the tail of an educational distribution – between, let us say, graduates and those with minimum education – reveals marked differences in political attitudes and behaviour. The top category tends to be better informed and more interested in politics. The well-educated are also more active in politics, particularly in the local community. In addition, the well-educated are much more liberal on social issues; they are more tolerant of new ideas, groups and people; they are less religious; they take a more optimistic view of human nature and they are less attracted to political extremes, whether of the left or the right (Astin, 1977, ch. 2). These education effects appear to be greatest for students who study arts and especially social sciences at degree level but there may well be an element of self-selection involved here. It is also plausible to suppose (but not easy to prove) that education increases the autonomy of *ideas* for an individual, reducing the impact of economic *self-interest* on electoral choice. By contrast, limited education has been associated with support for politicians who offer simple solutions to complex problems – the National Front in Britain and George Wallace in the United States, for example.

These contrasts help to account for a persistent finding of election surveys. This is the tendency for the best-educated section of the middle class to offer *less* support to conservative parties than middle-class people with more limited education (Aitkin, 1974; Rose, 1974). Since an extended education often leads to a high income, this finding is a powerful tribute to the radicalising role which higher education can play. In Denmark in 1979, 54 per cent of 20–29 year olds with higher education supported parties to the *left* of the Social Democrats (Andersen, 1983). In Britain in 1983, Alliance support was almost twice as strong among middle-class people with degrees as among middle-class people with no O-levels (Heath, Jowell and Curtice, 1985, p. 67). No country has enough left-wing graduates to vote a radical party into office – but there are enough to form a powerful bloc within existing parties, such as Britain's Labour Party, and to cause a fracas when they defect to the SDP. Fragmentary evidence suggests that a high proportion of these middle-class, left-of-centre activists are directly employed in education, mainly as teachers. Thus, the educated elite structures the alternatives presented to the mass electorate in a way which belies its numerical size.

Graduates are heavily employed in the public sector, especially in services such as education. Thus public sector employment, and the associated high levels of trade union membership provide a possible explanation of the link between high education and left-wing voting. But we think there is a genuine 'education effect' at work. Higher education probably inculcates political values which in turn produce a preference for working for the state.

Affluence and post-materialism

From the late 1940s to the early 1970s, the Western world witnessed a period of unprecedented economic growth. Living standards rose, ownership of consumer durables increased and the memory of mass unemployment receded. 'You've never had it so good' became a cliché which summarised the experience of a generation. This led to two theories about the electoral effects of affluence. The first was the *embourgeoisement* theory, focused on the working class, which was popular in the 1950s. The second was the theory of *post-materialism*, focused on the middle class, which was popular in the 1970s. Although the oil-fired recession of the 1970s now gives a slightly dated ring to both theories, they remain important in shaping our understanding of how economic developments produce social changes which in turn affect electoral behaviour.

Embourgeoisement. The embourgeoisement thesis maintained that as manual workers and their families became more affluent, they assumed a more middle-class way of life and became assimilated into middle-class society (Goldthorpe *et al*., 1968, p. 1). This in turn increased the likelihood of their voting for parties of the right. The thesis was frequently invoked in Britain to explain Conservative pre-eminence in the 1950s; it also gained currency in France. Yet as Britain's Labour Party recovered in the 1960s, the theory came to be seen as based on an over-simple view of the relationship beeen material possessions and party loyalties. As Goldthorpe *et al*. pointed out, 'a washing machine is a washing machine is a washing machine'; it is not a badge of middle-class (let along Conservative) identity. To be useful, embourgeoisement must be understood in a broader sense, denoting the shift from community-centred to family-centred life among sections of the working class, with the result that electoral choice becomes a matter of individual calculation rather than community reflex. But even this change only makes a fall in left-wing voting among the working class possible rather than inevitable.

Post-materialism. Just as the embourgeoisement thesis was used to explain Labour's decline among the working class, so the idea of post-materialism has been invoked to account for the left's growing penetration of the middle class. In a dramatic metaphor, Inglehart (1971, 1977) referred to 'a silent revolution' in Western democracies. He argued that the post-war period of economic growth and relative international peace had produced a new generation of young post-materialists – people who took their material and physical well-being for granted and who had become more concerned with post-material values. These included life-style issues such as ecology, nuclear disarmament and feminism as well as enhanced opportunities for individual participation in social and political organisations. From a survey of nine European democracies, Inglehart observed that post-materialists were most common among young well-educated people in the most affluent European countries; however, post-materialists were much more likely to define themselves as left-wing in all of the societies he examined. In the United States, Miller and Levitin (1976, p. 107) found a similar concentration of 'new liberals' among 'yuppies' – young, 'upwardly mobile' urban professionals, especially those in the far West.

Inglehart's theory of post-materialism has been heavily criticised, especially in Europe. It is argued that like the embourgeoisement theory before it, post-materialism takes too simple a view of the effect of affluence on political values. Middle-class radicalism is as old as politics itself; it is not wholly a product of the post-war economic boom. Some scholars argue that the flowering of alternative politics in the 1960s was caused by social change (especially the expansion of higher education) and by political developments (especially Vietnam), not by value change induced by economic growth (Marsh, 1977). Other critics focus on Inglehart's methodology, pointing out that his original (but not most recent) measure of post-materialism was based too narrowly on a single survey question which asked people to prioritise four goals: maintaining order, fighting rising prices (two 'materialist' goals), protecting free speech, and extending political participation (two 'post-materialist' objectives). These criticisms notwithstanding, we feel 'post-materialism' is a useful label for a particular style of politics even though the analysis must go beyond Inglehart's own interpretation.

Even in its 1960s heyday, post-materialism was a minority interest. Inglehart's own survey, carried out in 1972/3, showed that post-materialists formed between 7 and 14 per cent of the national populations he studied. Even in the United States, post-materialists were heavily out-numbered by the silent majority, as George McGovern discovered when he went down to a crushing defeat by arch-materialist Richard Nixon in 1972. Because post-materialists are still a minority, Green Parties and new radical groupings find it difficult to achieve more than a toe-hold of parliamentary representation. But post-materialists are relatively active in protests and demonstrations, and active too in party politics. There are sufficient post-materialists to become a potent force *within* established parties of the left, as the British and Dutch Labour Parties and the French Socialists have discovered. Post-materialism influences *party politics* directly, but *electoral politics* only indirectly.

There are conflicting views on whether the recession has put a stop to post-materialism. One view is that post-materialism was merely a fragile flower of 'sunshine politics'. As Inglehart (1981) himself points out, by the end of the 1970s 15–24 year olds (such as the readers of this book) were much less post-materialist than their counterparts (such as the authors) had been a decade earlier. According to this interpretation, post-materialism is only of real significance to the 1960s generation which, even as it moves into positions of power, remains both more politicised and more radical than the generations which preceded and followed it.

A second view is that the recession has slowed the growth of post-materialism in the Western world but has not stopped it. Inglehart (1984, pp. 28–9) again:

> Despite economic difficulties, post-materialist issues continue to play a major role. Throughout the Western world, the most massive political demonstrations of recent years have not been directed against unemployment – on the contrary, the longest and most intense ones have been aimed at preventing the construction of nuclear power plants and other projects that might reduce unemployment.

Although Inglehart is again referring to activists rather than voters, we are sympathetic to his view. Since post-war affluence did *not* create post-materialism, it is unlikely that the end of affluence will mean the end of middle-class radicalism.

Other Influences

This final section of the chapter examines some social bases of voting which do not fit neatly into our categorisation according to waves of social change. They are, however, important none the less. These remaining influences are age and generation, gender, and the social environment in which people live.

Age and generation

Young voters are a particularly interesting section of the electorate. Social and political trends usually begin earliest and cut deepest among the young, often presaging long-term electoral change as older generations die off. Inglehart's concept of post-materialism, for example, leans heavily on the concept of political generations. Yet sometimes the distinctive electoral behaviour of the young merely reflects the stage they have reached in the life-cycle, in which case there may be no long-term implications at all. These problems notwithstanding, there are four main findings about the relationship between age and electoral behaviour.

1. The young are more left-wing than the old. This is true of most democracies but not all and it is in any case far from clear whether age itself is the causal factor. Britain is one country with persistent age effects; Conservative voting has long been more common among the elderly even when the skew among old people towards women and the middle class is taken into account (Abrams and O'Brien, 1981). In other countries, age differences in voting reflect the experience of a specific generation rather than the life-cycle itself. For example, in the United States the Republican lead among older voters has been attributed to the party's strength in pre-Depression years. It is also worth noting that left-wing parties are of more recent vintage and also more secular than parties of the right; these factors undoubtedly help to explain the attractiveness to younger voters of such parties as Holland's *Democrats '66* and Canada's NDP (New Democratic Party). Christian Democracy, by contrast, finds its natural home among older, more religious cohorts.

2. The young are more attracted than the old to political extremes. Although numerous surveys have shown that the young are more liberal on social issues than the old, there is equally clear evidence of a link between youth and support for extreme right parties such as the George Wallace movement in the United States and the

National Front in Britain. There is a similar link on the extreme left, though here the relationship is stronger with radical, anti-establishment parties than with the more orthodox Communist left. Older voters have a long-established tradition of support for the major parties. Young voters lack this history of party voting and so are more open to the appeals of all kinds of parties, including small extremist parties.

3. *The young are more attracted than the old to new parties.* In tandem with other newly-enfranchised groups, the young are the major means through which electoral realignment (and dealignment) takes place. The explanation is straightforward: 'with the ageing of the voter, the relatively plastic attitudes of youth tend to harden and the acquired habits of the early voting years begin to become more deeply fixed' (Butler and Stokes, 1974, p. 58). For a long time political scientists believed that it was length of attachment to a particular party rather than chronological age which provided this immunity from the appeal of new parties. If this historic tie were broken among older voters, they were expected to be equally available for mobilisation by new political forces. However, recent studies suggest that young people may be intrinsically more open to the appeal of new parties after all.

4. *The young respond more to events than the old.* The malleability of first-time voters means that political events around the time of their entry to the electorate can leave a permanent mark on the voting habits of a generation. We note the pro-Democratic bias of the New Deal generation in the United States, the high Labour support among the 1945 generation in Britain and the continuing liberal sympathies of the 1960s generation in many Western countries (defining political generations by the date at which they enter the electorate). The voting behaviour of new voters is generally an intensified reflection of current trends in the electorate as a whole. Even in countries where the young are normally sympathetic to the left, first-time voters have been known to offer even more support to conservative parties than their elders when the political winds were blowing to the right.

Gender

As a 'minority' group (albeit one which happens to be in a numerical majority) it is surprising that women have proved to be more conservative in their electoral behaviour than men. At least until the 1970s women were more likely than men to support the major party of the right than of the left. Although the differences were often small, this finding applied to every country for which information was available (Randall, 1982, p. 50). But this contrast cannot be laid at the door of any deep-seated differences between men and women; there are two obvious intervening factors. First, on average women live longer than men – about one general election longer in Britain. As we have seen, older voters are often heavily Conservative. Secondly, women (especially older women) are much more regular church-goers than men, a factor associated with Christian Democratic support in Catholic countries where gender differences in voting patterns have always been most evident.

As the role of women in society changes, so too does their electoral behaviour. In most countries, gender differences in voting are declining. Indeed in the United States and Britain (Figure 7.2) there are signs that women may now be less conservative than men, fuelling speculation about a reverse gender gap. By a margin of 7 percentage points, women were *less* likely than men to support Ronald Reagan in the 1984 presidential election (Norris, 1986). The most obvious reason for this is the massive emergence of women onto the paid labour market, especially in routine white-collar jobs. This has increased trade union membership among women and in other ways has marked a break with traditional roles.

In any case female support for Conservative and Catholic parties never reflected a truly right-wing ideological stance among women. It is men, not women, who dominate the extreme right and almost monopolise the violent right; female conservatism comes closer to simple adherence to the traditional order than to a right-wing ideology as such (Randall, 1982, p. 52). Thus women are also less prominent than men on the communist and ultra-left. But on issues of war and peace, and other life-threatening questions, women are far more dovish than men. American women were more likely to oppose their government's intervention in Korea and Vietnam; British women were far less enamoured of the Falklands episode. These contrasts in attitudes dwarf the small gender differences in electoral behaviour itself.

In most democracies women form a majority of electors but a minority of voters. Yet as with party choice, gender differences in

Figure 7.2 *Conservative vote by gender, USA and Britain, 1945–84*

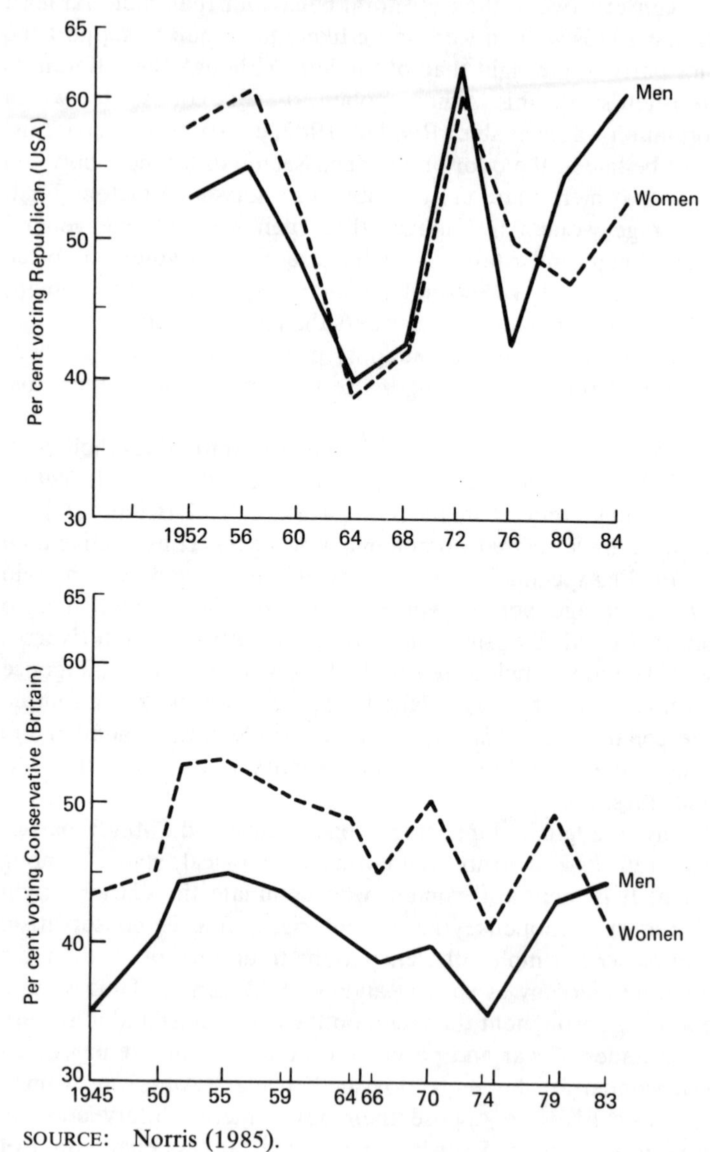

SOURCE: Norris (1985).

turn-out are small, declining and largely attributable to the greater longevity and more limited formal education of women. In Sweden and Canada, women now vote at the same rate as men; in Finland, a male lead of 11 per cent in turn-out in 1911 had disappeared altogether by the 1970s. Turn-out among younger women often equals that of men.

The first generation of women voters must have disappointed the suffragettes. As is normal among newly-enfranchised groups, turn-out was low. In addition, women's electoral choices were strongly influenced by their husbands'. Such independence as women showed strengthened traditional conservative parties. Despite the agitation and the violence associated with campaigns for female suffrage, despite the fears of those who opposed it, the actual introduction of female suffrage hardly caused a ripple on the political waters (Figure 7.3). Younger women have 'caught up' with patterns of electoral behaviour among men. Whether women will now 'forge ahead', as implied by the notion of a reverse gender gap, is more doubtful. Although gender is fundamental to the division of social and occupational labour, it has not so far proved to be a major political issue for the mass electorate.

The social environment

How people vote depends on how people around them vote – on their families, neighbours, friends and work-mates. These are 'context effects' on voting though the terms 'area' 'milieu' or 'neighbourhood' effects are also used. They differ in kind from the other influences considered in this chapter. The social environment *amplifies* the electoral impact of factors which structure social interaction, such as class and religion. It works *in conjunction* with these other factors, exaggerating and often outlasting them, but ultimately remaining dependent on them – a secondary process of behavioural adjustment rather than a primary cause.

In Britain, an important example of the context effect is the tendency for individuals to adopt the dominant partisanship of the area in which they live. A middle-class person living in a retirement resort on the South Coast is far more likely to vote Conservative than the same type of person living in a Northern industrial town. Indeed, how people vote in Britain now depends more on *where they live* than on *what they do* (Miller, 1977, 1978). Further-

Figure 7.3 *Achievement of women's suffrage in national elections*

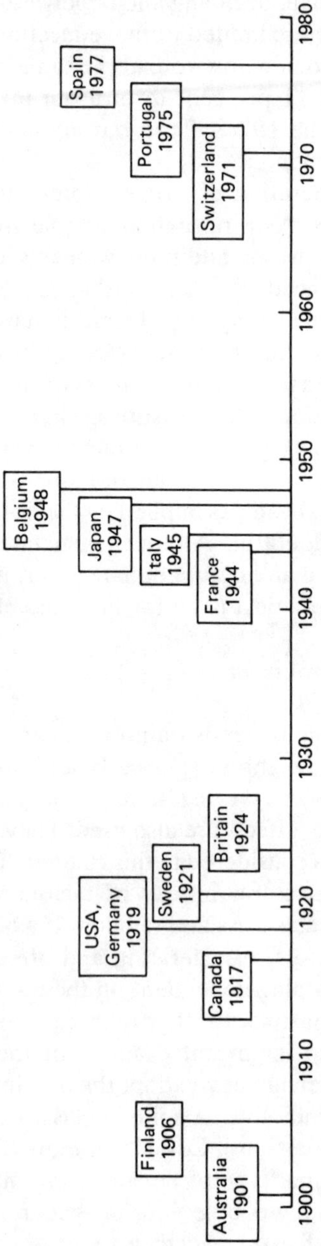

more, these context effects on voting are increasing in Britain, leading to a decline in the number of marginal seats and in the ability of the electoral system to delivery majority governments (Butler and Kavanagh, 1984, Appendix 2). This apparent anomaly – increasing context effects on voting in an era of considerable mobility and privatisation in life-styles – may be explained by class and partisan dealignment which has freed electors to respond more sensitively to the cues of their social environment. But partisan dealignment is found in many democracies where there is no evidence of a growth in context effects. There is still a mystery here waiting for a solution.

Four factors have been invoked in explanation of context effects. The first and most common is *contagion*. According to this theory, partisanship, like infections, spreads through social contact; those who talk together, vote together. The home, the neighbourhood, the school, clubs and organisations, even the work-place tend to bring people more into contact with those who live close by. People may not indulge in long philosophical discussions about politics, but they do give many cues to their political feelings in their conversations and in their life-styles. There is a pervasive, if seldom explicit, pressure towards the locally dominant party choice. The contagion idea fits neatly into the party identification model of voting.

The weakness of the contagion theory is that few studies have captured the mechanism of personal influence at work. Dunleavy (1979) is particularly critical; he claims that advocates of the contagion theory 'simply assume that political alignments brush off on people by rubbing shoulders in the street'. More research is certainly needed into who says what to whom with what electoral effects. But some evidence already exists. Fitton (1973) reports one pioneering study in which he interviewed every resident in a neighbourhood, to find out who talked regularly to whom. More recently, Eulau and Rothenberg (1986), working with national United States surveys show that although the neighbourhood is not *in itself* perceived by voters as an important political environment, *particular neighbours* who are personally linked to a voter do form a social network which independently affects partisan attitudes.

Dunleavy (1979) himself supports a second, *sectoral* theory of context effects. According to this account, context effects merely reflect the tendency for people who live together to have a similar sectoral position. It is this shared sectoral position, rather than contagion, which produces so-called context effects. In solidly working-class areas, manual workers are more likely to live in council houses, to be unemployed or to work in the public sector than working-class people living in more middle-class areas. (For a similar claim that what matters is *who lives where*, rather than *where people live* as such, see Kelly and McAllister, 1986.)

However Garrahan (1977) has shown that even among people with a similar sectoral position in the housing market (council tenants) there is a marked tendency for individuals to support the locally dominant party. Moreover, council tenancy and owner occupation may themselves depend for their partisan effects more upon the class composition they imply than upon the economic interests of different tenure arrangements themselves. The Thatcher government in Britain has helped to resolve this research problem by encouraging sales of council houses to sitting tenants. When a council tenant buys his house he changes tenure but does not change his neighbours. Some survey evidence suggests that council house sales to sitting tenants did *not* change their partisanship: those who bought council houses were somewhat more Conservative than other council tenants *before* they made their purchase, and no more so *afterwards* (Heath, Jowell and Curtice, 1985, p. 49; but see also Butler and Stokes, 1974, p. 112).

A third possibility is *self-selection* of residential areas. The miner's son who qualifies as a school teacher and then returns to his home area to teach is a clear example. He lives in a Labour constituency because he votes Labour, not *vice versa*. Such self-selection undoubtedly occurs but there is no evidence that it has occurred on a sufficient scale to explain the context effect. In fact the context effect is greatest among the working class who are not highly mobile (Heath, Jowell and Curtice, 1985, ch. 6).

Explicitly *political factors* are the fourth possibility. Once a particular party is established as the local majority it gains media attention, can perform numerous personal favours for local citizens, and may even become symbolically identified with the locality. Personal as well as party incumbency is certainly an important advantage in securing re-election to the United States Congress, and there are signs that personal incumbency is becoming more important in Britain. Again, however, this cannot explain the sheer magnitude of the context effect.

Another political explanation is that the minority party supporters are too *demoralised* to go to the polls – but the context effect operates in Australia where voting is compulsory as well as in Britain and the US where it is not.

Overall, therefore, the weight of evidence favours the contagion idea that the context effect is due primarily to social interaction within a spatial context. However, the evidence of contagion is still mainly indirect, derived more from social psychological studies of opinion formation than from direct studies of interpersonal influences on electoral behaviour.

Conclusion

The social characteristics reviewed in this chapter can be combined in innumerable ways among the electorate, and the overall configuration can itself affect voting behaviour. This point is developed in the concept of *status inconsistency*, which refers to a situation in which a person stands on a higher rung on some ladders of stratification than on others. Examples include unemployed graduates, or millionaire members of low-status ethnic groups. It was once fashionable to argue that status inconsistencies generated psychological strains which were then expressed in distinctive electoral behaviour – support for political extremes, say, or alternatively complete withdrawal from politics. This theme has rather gone out of fashion, perhaps because such 'inconsistencies' are increasingly common and presumably decreasingly stressful. (In fact, we suspect they were always more troublesome to the analysts than the electors.) But at least the concept of status inconsistency did focus on the oft-neglected question of how social characteristics combine together.

Similarly for societies: it is the *configuration* and *intensity* of social divisions, as much as their nature, which determines the flavour of electoral behaviour. Where cleavages such as class and religion run deep and reinforce each other, so as to give sharply-etched sub-cultures, voting choice merely reflects communal loyalties. But where divisions are cross-cutting or simply less intense, voting becomes a genuinely political act, shaped but not dominated by an elector's social identity. The most important electoral trend of the post-war period has been the decline in the power of the entire set of social factors to determine the voter's choice. Social *dealignment*, though not *realignment*, is the watchword. It makes the dangers of sociological determinism, always very real in electoral studies, even more acute. In concluding a chapter on the social base of elections, it is well to remember that politics also matters.

Further Reading

Lipset and Rokkan (1967) provided the major account of the historical development of party systems in Western Europe though their thesis of the freezing of party systems now needs supplementing with a more recent source such as Maguire (1983) or Dalton, Flanagan and Beck (1984). On centre/periphery contrasts, Rokkan and Urwin (1982, 1983) are comprehensive guides. There is no single source on religion and voting though Whyte (1981) examines Catholic political behaviour. As with many other social influences on voting, Rose's (1974) large compendium contains a useful account of religion and electoral behaviour in twelve democracies.

Discussions of class voting are dogged by either too little or too much concern with the *concept* of class. Still, a tour through the sociological classics of Marx (McLellan, 1980), Weber (1948), Dahrendorf (1959), Bell (1973) and Parkin (1983) remains worthwhile. But be warned – many will not survive the journey.

Empirical studies on class and voting begin with Alford (1963), whose figures are dated but whose index lives on, and Lipset (1981, ch. 7). More recent material includes Borre (1984), Robertson (1984), Heath, Jowell and Curtice (1985) and Crewe (1984). On trade unions, see Gallie (1983) on France; Butler and Stokes (1969, ch. 7) on Britain; and, again, the relevant sections of Rose (1974). Heath (1981) is a clear introduction to social mobility and contains some information on mobility and British voting; Thompson (1971) is more comparative. Dunleavy and Husbands (1985) argue powerfully for the electoral importance of the growth of the state; see also Dunleavy (1986) and Rose (1985).

For age and generation, Abramson (1975) is an accessible American study; Converse (1976) is more technical; Crewe, Sarlvick and Alt (1977) and Crewe (1984) are good sources on Britain. On education, Jennings and Niemi (1974) is a careful

American study; Astin (1977, ch. 2) reviews the American literature on the effects of a college education. Randall (1982) is a useful text on women and politics; Lovenduski and Hills (1981) is a comparative study of women's political participation.

On embourgeoisement, see Goldthorpe *et al*. (1968); on post-materialism, see Inglehart (1981, 1984), Marsh (1977, chs. 7 and 8), Barnes, Kaase *et al*. (1979, Pt 2) and, for a much-neglected study, Parkin (1968).

References

ABRAMS, M. and O'BRIEN, J. (1981) *Political Attitudes and Ageing in Britain* (Mitcham: Age Concern).

ABRAMSON, P. (1975) *Generational Change in American Politics* (Lexington, Mass.: Heath).

AITKIN, D. (1974) 'Australia: Class Politics in the New World', in R. Rose (ed.), *Electoral Behaviour: a Comparative Handbook* (New York: Free Press).

AITKIN, D. (1982) *Stability and Change in Australian Politics* (Canberra: Australian National University Press).

ALFORD, R. (1963) *Party and Society* (New York: Rand McNally).

ALLARDT, E. (1968) 'Traditional and Emerging Radicalism', mimeographed paper cited in S. M. Lipset, *Revolution and Counter-Revolution* (London: Heinemann).

ANDERSEN, J. (1983) *Class Voting in Disguise: the Concept of Social Class, the Political Role of Women and the Decline of Class Voting in Denmark* (Aarhus: Aarhus University Press).

ASTIN, A. (1977) *Four Critical Years: Effects of College on Beliefs, Attitudes and Knowledge* (San Francisco: Jossey-Bass).

BARNES, S., KAASE, M. *et al*. (1979) *Political Action: Mass Participation in Five Western Democracies* (Beverly Hills: Sage).

BELL, D. (1973) *The Coming of Post-Industrial Society* (New York: Basic Books).

BORRE, O. (1984) 'Critical Electoral Change in Scandinavia', in R. Dalton, S. Flanagan and P. Beck (eds), *Electoral Change in Advanced Industrial Societies* (Princeton: Princeton University Press).

BUTLER, D. and KAVANAGH, D. (1984) *The British General Election of 1983* (London: Macmillan).

BUTLER, D. and STOKES, D. (1969, 1974) *Political Change in Britain* (London: Macmillan).

CONVERSE, P. (1976) *The Dynamics of Party Support* (London: Sage).

CREWE, I., SARLVIK, B. and ALT, J. (1977) 'Partisan Dealignment in Britain 1964–1974', *British Journal of Political Science*, vol. 7, pp. 129–90.

CREWE, I. (1984) 'The Electorate: Partisan Dealignment Ten Years On' in H. Berrington (ed.), *Change in British Politics* (London: Cass).

DAHRENDORF, R. (1959) *Class and Class Conflict in Industrial Society* (London: Routledge & Kegan Paul).

DALTON, R., FLANAGAN, S. and BECK, P. (1984) *Electoral Change in Advanced Industrial Societies* (Princeton: Princeton University Press).

DUNLEAVY, P. (1979) 'The Urban Basis of Political Alignment: Social Class, Domestic Property Ownership and State Intervention in Consumption Processes', *British Journal of Political Science*, vol. 9, pp. 409–44.

DUNLEAVY, P. (1986) 'The Growth of Sectoral Cleavages and the Stabilization of State Expenditures', *Society and Space*, vol. 4, pp. 129–44.

DUNLEAVY, P. and HUSBANDS, C. (1985) *British Democracy at the Crossroads* (London: Allen & Unwin).

EULAU, H. and ROTHENBERG, L. (1986) 'Life Space and Social Networks as Political Contexts', *Political Behaviour*, vol. 8, pp. 130–57.

FITTON, M. (1973) 'Neighbourhood and Voting: a Sociometric Examination', *British Journal of Political Science*, vol. 3, pp. 445–72.

GALLIE, D. (1983) *Social Inequality and Class Radicalism in France and Britain* (Cambridge: Cambridge University Press).

GARRAHAN, P. (1977) 'Housing, the Class Milieu and Middle-class Conservatism', *British Journal of Political Science*, vol. 7, pp. 126–7.

GIRVIN, B. (1986) 'Social Change and Moral Politics: the Irish Constitutional Referendum 1983', *Political Studies*, vol. 34, pp. 61–81.

GOLDTHORPE, J., LOCKWOOD, D., BECHHOFER, F. and PLATT, J. (1968) *The Affluent Worker: Political Attitudes and Behaviour* (Cambridge: Cambridge University Press).

HARROP, M. (1981) 'The Urban Basis of Political Alignment: A Comment', *British Journal of Political Science*, vol. 11, pp. 388–98.

HEATH, A. (1981) *Social Mobility* (London: Fontana).

HEATH, A., JOWELL, R. and CURTICE, J. (1985) *How Britain Votes* (Oxford: Pergamon).

HOCHSCHILD, J. (1981) *What's Fair?: American Beliefs about Distributive Justice* (Cambridge, Mass.: Harvard University Press).

INGLEHART, R. (1971) 'The Silent Revolution in Europe', *American Political Science Review*, vol. 65, pp. 991–1017.

INGLEHART, R. (1977) *The Silent Revolution: Changing Values and Political Styles among Western Publics* (Princeton: Princeton University Press).

INGLEHART, R. (1981) 'Post-Materialism in an Environment of Insecurity', *American Political Science Review*, vol. 75, pp. 880–99.

INGLEHART, R. (1984) 'The Changing Structures of Political Cleavages in Western Society', in R. Dalton, S. Flanagan and P. Beck (eds), *Electoral Change in Advanced Industrial Democracies* (Princeton: Princeton University Press).

JAHODA, M., LAZARSFELD, P. and ZEISEL, H. (1933, 1971) *Marienthal* (Chicago: Aldine-Atherton).

JENNINGS, M. and NIEMI, R. (1974) *The Political Character of Adolescence* (Princeton: Princeton University Press).
KELLY, J. and MCALLISTER, I. (1985) 'Social Context and Electoral Behaviour in Britain', *American Journal of Political Science*, vol. 29, pp. 564–86.
KUCHLER, M. (1978) 'What Has Electoral Sociology in West Germany Achieved? A Critical Review', in M. Kaase and K. von Beyme (eds), *Elections and Parties* (London: Sage).
KUMAR, K. (1978) *Prophecy and Progress: The Sociology of Industrial and Post-Industrial Society* (London: Allen Lane).
LASH, S. (1984) *The Militant Worker: Class and Radicalism in France and America* (Aldershot, Hants: Gower).
LIJPHART, A. (1979) 'Religious *vs* Linguistic *vs* Class Voting: the Crucial Experiment of Comparing Belgium, Canada, South Africa and Switzerland', *American Political Science Review*, vol. 73, pp. 442–58.
LIJPHART, A. (1982) 'The Relative Salience of the Socio-Economic and Religious Issue Dimensions: Coalition Formation in Ten Western Democracies 1919–1979', *European Journal of Political Research*, vol. 10, pp. 201–11.
LIPSET, S. (1960, 1981) *Political Man* (Baltimore: Johns Hopkins University Press).
LIPSET, S. and RAAB, E. (1971) *The Politics of Unreason: Right-wing Extremism in the United States 1790–1970* (London: Heinemann).
LIPSET, S. and ROKKAN, S. (1967) 'Cleavage Structures, Party Systems and Voter Alignments', in S. Lipset and S. Rokkan (eds), *Party Systems and Voter Alignments* (New York: Free Press).
LOVENDUSKI, J. and HILLS, J. (1981) *The Politics of the Second Electorate* (London: Routledge & Kegan Paul).
McLELLAN, D. (1980) *The Thought of Karl Marx* (London: Macmillan).
MAGUIRE, M. (1983) 'Is There Still Persistence? Electoral Change in Western Europe, 1948–79' in H. Daalder and P. Mair (eds), *Western European Party Systems* (London: Sage).
MARSH, A. (1977) *Protest and Political Consciousness* (London: Sage).
MILLER, W. E. and LEVITIN, T. (1976) *Leadership and Change: the New Politics and the American Electorate* (Cambridge, Mass.: Winthrop).
MILLER, W. L. (1977) *Electoral Dynamics in Britain Since 1918* (London: Macmillan).
MILLER, W. L. (1978) 'Social Class and Party Choice in England', *British Journal of Political Science*, vol. 8, pp. 257–84.
MONK, D. (1978) *Social Grading on the National Readership Survey* (London: JICNARS).
NORRIS, P. (1985) 'The Gender Gap: America and Britain', *Parliamentary Affairs*, vol. 38, pp. 192–201.
NORRIS, P. (1986) 'Conservative Attitudes in Recent British Elections: An Emerging Gender Gap', *Political Studies*, vol. 34, pp. 120–8.

OFFICE OF POPULATION CENSUSES AND SURVEYS (1980) *Classification of Occupations and Coding Index* (London: HMSO).

PARKIN, F. (1968) *Middle-Class Radicalism: The Social Bases of the British Campaign for Nuclear Disarmament* (Manchester: Manchester University Press).

PARKIN, F. (1983) *Marxism and Class Theory: A Bourgeois Critique* (Cambridge: Cambridge University Press).

RANDALL, V. (1982) *Women and Politics* (London: Macmillan).

ROBERTSON, D. (1984) *Class and the British Electorate* (Oxford: Blackwell).

ROKKAN, S. and URWIN, D. (eds) (1982) *The Politics of Territorial Identity* (London: Sage).

ROKKAN, S. and URWIN, D. (1983) *Economy Territory Identity: Politics of West European Peripheries* (London: Sage).

ROSE, R. and URWIN, D. (1969) 'Social Cohesion, Political Parties and Strains in Regimes', *Comparative Political Studies*, vol. 2, pp. 7–67.

ROSE, R. (ed.) (1974) *Electoral Behaviour: a Comparative Handbook* (New York: Free Press).

ROSE, R. (1974) 'Britain: Simple Abstractions and Complex Realities', in R. Rose (ed.), *Electoral Behaviour: A Comparative Handbook* (New York: Free Press).

ROSE, R. (1984) *Understanding Big Government: The Programme Approach* (London: Sage).

ROSE, R. (1985) *Public Employment in Western Nations* (Cambridge: Cambridge University Press).

SANDBERG, J. and BERGLAND, S. (1985) 'Reflections on Scandinavian Party Systems', paper delivered to the International Political Science Association World Congress, Paris.

SANI, G. (1977) 'The Italian Electorate in the Mid-1970s: Beyond Tradition?', in H. Penniman (ed.), *Italy at the Polls: The Parliamentary Elections of 1976* (Washington, DC.: American Enterprise Institute).

SAUNDERS, P. (1979) *Urban Politics: a Sociological Approach* (London: Hutchinson).

SCHLOZMAN, K. L. and VERBA, S. (1979) *Injury to Insult: Unemployment, Class and Political Response* (Cambridge, Mass.: Harvard University Press).

STEPHENS, J. (1981) 'The Changing Swedish Electorate', *Comparative Political Studies*, vol. 14, pp. 163–204.

THOMPSON, K. (1971) 'A Cross-National Analysis of Inter-Generational Social Mobility and Political Orientation', *Comparative Political Studies*, vol. 4, pp. 3–20.

WEBER, M. (1948) *Essays in Sociology*, H. Gerth and C. Wright Mills (trans and eds), (London: Routledge & Kegan Paul).

WORRE, T. (1980) 'Class Parties and Class Voting in the Scandinavian Countries', *Scandinavian Political Studies*, vol. 3, pp. 299–320.

WHYTE, J. (1981) *Catholics in Western Democracies: a Study in Political Behaviour* (Dublin: Gill & Macmillan).

8

The Responsive Voter: Short-term Influences on Voting Behaviour

Voting is a political act. A simple point but one that can easily disappear in the welter of analyses linking electoral choice to social causes. Further, the influence of purely political factors such as party leaders and political debate is increasing as traditional class and party loyalties weaken and more votes come up for grabs. While the social structure influences levels of party support, a number of other factors produce increasing variations around these levels. These other factors are the subject of this chapter. We begin with three factors which are important between elections as well as at election time – the economy, the media and the politicians. We then turn to influences which peak at election time: these are the impact of the campaign itself and the role played by canvassing, money and opinion polls.

The Economy

In October 1972, the Department of Health, Education and Welfare in the United States wrote to 24,760,000 welfare recipients, announcing that: 'Your social security payment has been increased by 20 per cent, starting with this month's cheque, by a new statute enacted by the Congress and signed into law by President Richard Nixon.' One month later, President Nixon was re-elected. He had clearly learnt the lesson adumbrated by Lord Brougham in 1814: 'A government is not supported a hundredth part so much by the constant, uniform, quiet prosperity of the country as by those damned spurts which Pitt used to have just in the nick of time.' Edward Tufte (1978, p. 65) uses such examples to illustrate his 'basic principle': 'When you think economics, think elections. When you think elections, think economics.'

Considerable research effort has now gone into specifying precisely how the economy influences elections – and vice versa. These studies have used statistical techniques to examine the relationship between government popularity, as measured in regular opinion polls, and assorted economic indicators. In reviews covering research in numerous countries, Paldam (1981) and Schneider (1984) concluded that:

1. Economic variables normally explain between 20 and 40 per cent of the variation in government popularity. (Whether this means the glass is a third full or two-thirds empty is a matter of opinion.)
2. The relative importance of economic factors varies between countries and over time. Unemployment, real disposable income and inflation are the most consistent influences; a country's trade balance is generally *not* significant.
3. Economic factors are more successful at explaining opinion poll ratings of the government's performance than voting intentions – and more successful in explaining voting intentions than in explaining voting behaviour. This is probably because voting in a polling booth is a more robust phenomenon than transient verbal responses to doorstep interviewers.
4. Electorates are myopic, weighting their judgement of the government towards the performance of the economy in the recent past. 'What have you done for me lately?' means in the last twelve months!

This last point raises the disturbing possibility of a *political business cycle* in which governments create a pre-election boom but delay the inflationary cost until after the election – and their own re-election. Indeed, Tufte goes so far as to claim that democracies in which the election date is decided by the government are now synchronising with the fixed, four-year election cycle in the United States. This, he argues, is because pre-election booms in the US stimulate the whole international economy and encourage politicians elsewhere to call an election in the brief 'window' before boom turns into bust. (For a sceptical comment, see Alt and Chrystal, 1983, pp. 118–22.) It is ironic that in responding to the electorate's preoccupation with pocket-book issues politicans may in the long run harm the performance of the economy on which their popularity substantially depends. Yet as long as voters discount all but the recent past, and politicians discount all but the near future, it is difficult to see how this unforeseen and undesirable consequence of elections can be avoided. Indeed pre-election booms will continue as long as politicians *believe* reflation may increase their popularity, even if their belief has no basis in fact.

Governing parties do not have it all their own way. After the OPEC oil crises of the 1970s, elected governments lost ground throughout the Western world as ruthless electorates punished governing parties for having the misfortune to preside over the recession. In the 1984 elections to the European Parliament most parties holding office in their own country lost seats even though blame for the world's difficult economic state could hardly be pinned on the Assembly's door. This suggests that electorates blame elected representatives for economic ills, however caused, and that voters take any available electoral opportunity to express this opinion.

An important spin-off from these studies of the economy and elections has been the identification of a 'base-line' cycle of government popularity – that is, the sequence which can be expected even before the state of the economy is brought into play. In the United States, there is a gradual depreciation in presidential popularity as the voters who floated into the winning candidate's camp during the campaign begin to drift away once the president is forced to take the hard decisions of office. For Britain, Goodhart and Bhansali (1970) suggest a U-shaped curve in which a post-election honeymoon for the winning party is followed by mid-term blues; and this is in turn supplanted by a swing back to the governing party before the next election (see also Miller and Mackie, 1973). Most studies now incorporate a base-line cycle of surge and decline into their analyses, together with estimates of the often dramatic effects of such one-off events as the Falklands war or the Watergate crisis. (A good example of these more sophisticated studies is Clarke, Stewart and Zuk, 1986.)

All this research is pitched at a high level of aggregation, far removed from the psychology of the individual voter. Much remains to be uncovered concerning the mechanisms linking the economy with government popularity. Three questions suggest themselves. First, what standards do electors use in judging government performance? People may respond just to economic changes which are particularly large or which diverge from what they have grown accustomed to (Alt and Chrystal, 1983, p. 168). Clearly the electoral impact of a 1 per cent rise in unemployment during the 1980s was much less than in the 1950s when total unemployment was far lower. But *how much* less, and *why*? Secondly, where do electors obtain their information about the economy? The evidence suggests, perhaps surprisingly, that media reports of the national economy are more important than the elector's own economic position. People do *not* vote their own pocketbooks but that of the nation as a whole (Feldman, 1984). Kinder (1983) notes: 'As a basis for political belief, primitive self-interest seems to have been drastically over-promoted.' And media coverage of economic issues such as jobs and prices does not accurately reflect trends in official statistics; the priorities of journalists are more important (Glasgow University Media Group, 1980; Westerstahl and Johannson, 1985). The third question is whether social groups differ in their demands of and response to the economy. Manual workers do seem to be more sensitive to unemployment, the middle classes more concerned with inflation. Yet so far these differences between groups have proved to be remarkably small.

The Mass Media

In the 1950s and early 1960s, an academic consensus emerged about the impact (or lack of it) of the mass media on voting behaviour. Summarised in the slogan *reinforcement not change*, this orthodoxy maintained that voters used the media in a selective way so as to sustain existing party loyalties (Klapper, 1960). Thus, left-wing voters would be unlikely to watch party political broadcasts by right-wing parties, would probably discount such programmes even if they did watch, and might well forget the broadcast arguments even if they were convinced at the time. Newspaper readers, too, read papers which confirmed rather than challenged their political views. These mechanisms of selective exposure, interpretation and recall were regarded as firm barriers against media influence.

Times change and academic interpretations change with them. For four main reasons, the media must now be considered full members of the family of influences on voting behaviour:

1. The media are more important when party loyalties are weak – and party loyalties have diminished in the Western world since the 1960s.
2. The media are more important when there are new subjects to cover – and Western politics has seen major developments since the 1960s.
3. The media are more important when coverage is credible – and the arrival of television with direct visual evidence, and often a self-proclaimed political neutrality, has strengthened the credibility of the media.
4. The media are more important when people rarely discuss politics – and television has not only supplanted conversation as a major channel of political communication, it also now provides an agenda for discussion, particularly among those least involved with politics.

Although most political scientists now acknowledge the significance of the media, no new consensus has replaced the old orthodoxies. As a reaction to the rather mechanical approach of these early studies, the *uses and gratifications* model gained well-deserved ground in the 1960s and 1970s. Here the question was not 'what do the media do to voters?' but 'what do voters do with the media?' To what use do voters put information obtained from the media? For example, Blumler and McQuail (1968) carried out a survey in Leeds during the 1964 election on why people watched party political broadcasts. Four main reasons were identified. In order of importance, these were (1) general surveillance of the political environment; (2) reinforcement of voting decisions; (3) vote guidance and (4) the excitement motive – politics as spectacle. Theoretically, one would expect the effect of a party political broadcast, or media coverage of politics generally, to depend on the reasons for the initial exposure. In practice, only a few interactions of this kind have been found. None the less the assumption of an audience which is active rather than passive, which sees *through* rather than *with* the eye, is undoubtedly a strength of the uses and gratifications approach.

More recently, radical political scientists have accused the media of distorting the flow of political communication. According to Dunleavy and Husbands (1985) television and the press define what are to count as acceptable political views, influence citizens into similar modes of thinking and also create a stream of messages favourable to particular parties. Such blatant assertions of media bias and omnipotence are no more helpful than the blunt generalisations of the reinforcement view. But the thesis of the *agenda setting* function of the mass media does deserve serious attention.

According to this view, the media influence *what people think about* if not *what they think*. Newspaper and television editors make judgements of news priorities; the judgements of one editor influence the views of others; and the result is a media consensus which affects the public's sense of the importance of various issues. In the USA the impact of the media on the public agenda appears to be cumulative over a period of about four months (Eyal, 1981). So ironically the effect of mass communication is sharpest in the area of topic-selection, where editorial decisions are most subjective.

Television is far and away the most important medium of electoral communication in nearly all democracies (Table 8.1). Television reaches an overwhelming majority of the electorate with an authority unmatched by the less regulated and more partisan press. It is a foolhardy politician who ignores or even misjudges the demands of television – for strict deadlines, frequent interviews, good visuals and a forgiving attitude to what is still, compared to print, an inflexible technology. Many campaign events are now what Boorstin (1961) called pseudo-events, designed exclusively for television. Prime ministers, to take just one example, only shop in the local market when the cameras are present. In short, television no longer *covers* elections; television has *become* the election.

With its high pictorial content, television necessarily emphasises slogans, symbols and personalities rather than complex arguments. Above all, television conveys *images rather than issues*. Even when it tries to do otherwise it fails. The Carter–Reagan debates in 1980 illustrate the nature of political television. They *were* long enough

Table 8.1 *The mass media in liberal democracies*

	Papers/1000		*TV/1000*			*Party political broadcasts*	
	1965	*1982*	*1965*	*1982*	*TV-Year*	*Paid*	*Free*
Australia	372	337	172	428	1958	yes	yes
Austria	249	320	—	306*	1956	no	yes
Belgium	284	224	162*	304*	—	no	yes
Canada	217	226	270	460	1953	yes	yes
Denmark	347	356	228*	366*	—	no	yes
Finland	—	515	160*	415	—	no	yes
France	247	191	133*	369	1962	no	yes
West Germany	326	408	193*	354*	1961	no	yes
Ireland	244	229	114	241	1965	no	yes
Italy	112	82	116*	405	—	no	yes
Japan	450	575	183*	560	—	yes	yes
Netherlands	291	322	171*	305*	—	no	yes
Norway	384	483	132*	315*	1961	no	no
Sweden	505	524	270*	387*	—	no	yes
Switzerland	377	381	106*	370	1959	no	yes
United Kingdom	479	421	248*	457	1951	no	yes
United States	311	269	362	646	1952	yes	no

NOTES:
(1) Papers/1000 – daily newspaper circulation per 1000 inhabitants: TV/1000 – television sets per 1000 inhabitants: TV-year – first election in which TV played a major role: Paid party political broadcasts – paid party political broadcasts (i.e. advertisements) on TV: Free party political broadcasts – free TV time for political parties.
(2) * based on licenses issued (always lower than sets in use).
(3) — not ascertained.
(4) Occasionally figures are from closest year for which information is available.

SOURCES: Smith (1981) and UNESCO *Statistical Yearbook 1984*.

to deal with issues, and expert observers agreed that Carter demonstrated his superior command of the facts. But polling evidence shows that Reagan 'won' the debates because he appeared genial, reasonable, relaxed. Viewers were receptive to the images, not the issues.

In Western democracies there are three pure models of television election coverage. These are (1) unregulated (2) state-regulated and (3) party-dominated. In the *unregulated* model, politicians compete for coverage by journalists who are not subject to special campaign rules. The election is simply one story among many. There is no free air-time made available to parties though paid political advertising may be permitted. Historically, the United States has provided the closest approximation to this pattern. In the *state-regulated* model, election coverage is governed by special regulations hammered out between broadcasters and the state. These rules ensure rough parity of coverage for the contending parties but also impose some restrictions on journalistic freedom. The parties are allocated political broadcasts but paid advertising is not permitted. Britain is the classic example here. In the *party-dominated* model, state intervention takes the more direct form of substantial control over broadcasting by the party in power. This pattern was characteristic of the early years of television in many European countries with a strong state and publicly-owned broadcasting authorities. France and Italy were notable examples. In both countries, political control over key broadcasting appointments produced a bureaucratic style of election coverage – cautious, unimaginative and wholly tedious. However, recent reforms have moved both countries towards the state-regulated model. Though cable and satellite television may soon upset the balance yet again, the state-regulated form is currently the dominant model of television election coverage in liberal democracies.

Does the television medium shape the electoral message? What, in other words, have been the consequences of television's rise to pre-eminence among the mass media? First, television contributed to but did not create the nationalisation of electoral politics. The same television news is now watched by people from all social groups and geographical areas. Television 'nationalises' socially as well as geographically. (By the same token, television cannot by itself account for growing regional diversity in British voting behaviour. However, regional news and current affairs programmes mean that, in Britain, it may be a more powerful homogeniser socially than geographically.) Secondly, television has probably contributed to the growth of electoral volatility. Where partisan newspapers reinforced party loyalties, television exposes a mass audience to both sides of an issue, thus eroding strong party identification (Smith, 1981, p. 178). It does this, furthermore, in the home, away from countervailing social pressures such as the work-place. Thirdly, television has led to more emphasis on party leaders. Issues and policies are covered more successfully in the quality press, which remains an important medium for the minority of electors who follow politics in a newspaper of record. Television's emphasis on leaders has in turn weakened party organisation in local areas. Finally, television has changed the kind of politician who rises to the top of the greasy pole – or, at least, who stays there. Ranney (1984, p. 103) puts the point well:

> The auditorium situation calls for a commanding presence, a strong voice projected at a high volume, large gestures, and dramatic punch lines with plenty of pauses for cheers. The TV-room situation calls for a pleasant and friendly presence, a moderate tone of voice, small and natural gestures, and a general conversational manner.

Yet despite all this, it should always be remembered that television acts primarily as a filter for information which originates elsewhere. Television is the main election battleground but it does not determine which party has the biggest guns.

The Politicians

Although electoral choice may ostensibly be between policies or parties, much of the voters' thinking is about leaders. This is not just a characteristic of presidential systems. In Britain during the 1960s, Butler and Stokes (1974, p. 353) measured the number of spontaneous comments about parties (when respondents were asked about parties) and leaders (when respondents were asked about leaders). They found almost as much comment about leaders as parties. Clarke *et al.*'s study (1979) of the Canadian electorate shows that those without strong partisan commitments and with relatively low interest in politics are especially prone to see politics in terms of political leaders. By contrast, those with higher levels of interest tend to give rather more weight to issues.

Because leaders change more often than the parties they lead, attitudes to leaders can be important explanations of electoral change. Stokes (1966) estimated that in American presidential elections between 1952 and 1964 the net effect of the candidates varied between an 8 per cent advantage for the Republicans and a 5 per cent advantage for the Democrats. The largest effect in this period was in 1956 when General Eisenhower ('I like Ike') was re-elected. Some recent work (Markus and Converse, 1979) suggests that assessments of candidates are now the major *direct* influence on how people vote. But even in the United States leadership evaluations are still strongly coloured by the elector's pre-existing party loyalty. Thus a favourable image expensively projected through television certainly does not guarantee success at the polls.

The electoral impact of leaders varies with the nature of the political system. First, leaders are more important in presidential than parliamentary systems. Even in the Chancellor-led parliamentary system of West Germany, leaders are less important than in the presidential United States (Klingemann and Taylor, 1978). Secondly, leaders are more significant when parties are relatively weak. In the United States, where they are notoriously weak, incumbency is a major and growing advantage because Senators and Congressmen can exploit their office to build up a personal relationship with their electors. Conversely, candidates for a party's nomination often impose themselves on it more than they are selected by it. In Britain by contrast, parties are still relatively strong. So a Member of Parliament knows that his survival depends mainly on his party's popularity though there is now a small incumbency effect there too. Thirdly, candidates (if not top party leaders) are more important when the electoral system allows voters to choose between candidates for the same party, as with the single transferable vote and many party list systems (see Chapter 3). In Finland, whose list system of proportional representation allows voters great flexibility, media personalities and sports stars often receive a disproportionate share of their party's vote. The same thing can also happen in majoritarian systems, though more rarely. Until 1982, 100 members of the Upper House of the Japanese parliament were elected in a single national constituency: those with the highest votes were elected. Thus Japanese voters had an effective intra-party choice, and television personalities once again did very well as candidates.

What gives a candidate voter appeal? This is *not just* a matter of a pleasing manner in a television studio; it is also a question of overall fitness for the job. Competence was a key element in the evaluations of American presidential candidates in 1972 (when Nixon defeated McGovern) and along with integrity, competence was again a principal dimension in 1980 (when Reagan defeated Carter) (see Markus, 1982).

Studying presidential elections from 1956 to 1980, Davidson (1982) distinguished three components in attitudes to candidates – experience, qualifications and image. Significantly, only experience and qualifications, the elements most strongly related to competence, predicted electoral choice. Of course, television is the main source of information about a candidate's likely effectiveness in office and has strengthened the importance of leaders relative to party organisation. Still, it would be naive to conclude that fitness for the job is a quality which can be administered like make-up just before a television interview. To be attractive to the voters, a candidate must appear competent – and the best way to *seem* competent is to *be* competent.

The Campaign

'The election' wrote Labour politician Richard Crossman, 'is the end of a long process'. Even in an era of electoral volatility, voters are swayed not so much by the frenetic electioneering of the campaign as by the overall record of the governing party. Indeed, election campaigns are in large measure debates about the performance of the government. Was the Conservative Party responsible for the rise in unemployment between 1979 and 1983? Should President Carter have done more to get the American hostages out of Iran in 1980? These are the kinds of questions which dominate campaigns. They show that campaigns are not so much separate from the pre-election period as intensive reviews of it, during which the government's record is picked over. *Retrospective voting* is the term used to describe electors who cast their ballot on the basis of government performance; it is a phrase which explains much about the character of election campaigns (see Chapter 6).

The distinction between the campaign and the pre-campaign phase is in any case largely formal. Legally, the difference is sharp; special rules about advertising, finances and broadcasting usually come into play when the official whistle is blown. The length of the 'hot' campaign varies considerably – legally at least three weeks in

Britain though now, by convention, four; roughly six weeks in West Germany; and about eight weeks in Canada. But the political reality is that the next campaign begins as soon as the last one is over, with a steady build-up in intensity as polling day approaches. As David Truman (1951) observed, 'elections are not likely to be understood until they are studied as a continuous process in which the campaign and balloting are at most climaxes.'

On the whole, election campaigns do not determine election results. They are more like end-games at chess, putting the final touches on a predictable outcome. For the United States, Mann (1979, p. 79) has argued that 'the outcomes of most congressional elections are determined well before the onset of active campaigning'. Similarly, in ten of the last twelve general elections in Britain, the party in the lead at the start of the campaign was still ahead on polling day and the average net change wrought by the campaign was about 4 per cent. Of course, this net figure ignores the ebb and flow within the campaign and the mutually cancelling movements towards and away from a particular party at any one time. In the 1983 campaign in Britain, opinion polls indicate that 17 per cent of the electorate showed signs of vacillation. But this *gross* change tends to cancel itself out, leaving a much smaller degree of *net* change. This distinction between gross and net change helps to explain why the net impact of the campaign on election results has not increased as dramatically as overall volatility during the past twenty years. The surface waters can remain undisturbed even though there is more and more churning in the deep.

Of course, examples can be found of decisive campaigns. The triumph of Willy Brandt and his coalition partners in the West German election of 1972 is widely attributed to their head start in advertising. Superior campaign strategy has also been invoked to explain Pierre Trudeau's Liberal victory in Canada in 1974. And Britain's Labour Party demonstrated in 1983 that campaigns can be lost if not won. But as Stokes (1981, p. 279) has remarked, 'it is all too easy after the fact to attribute to strategy and organisation the shifts of party strength that are due to broader conditions prevailing in the country'.

Campaigns are more significant in elections fought under proportional representation. A small change in the number of seats obtained by a party under PR can dramatically alter its bargaining position in post-election negotiations about a coalition government. This is most obvious with small parties such as Italy's Republican Party and Israel's religious Poalei Agudat party. Both have been government members in recent years despite receiving little more than 2 per cent of the vote and a handful of seats (Penniman, 1981, p. 124). In Britain, under the first-past-the-post system, small parties such as the National Front and the Communist Party have little choice but to regard elections as an opportunity for publicity rather than for achieving a share in power, or even a share in representation.

Under proportional representation, the campaign strategy adopted by individual candidates depends heavily on whether voters can choose between the names on a party list. Where this is possible, candidates face the additional complication of a competition with colleagues from their own party. In the Irish election of 1977, thirteen of the thirty-two defeated deputies lost their seats to party colleagues. In Greek elections in the same year, the actress Melina Mercouri of *Never on Sunday* fame fought a vigorous campaign which gave her many more preference votes than any other Socialist candidate, despite only being placed second on her party's list (Penniman, 1981, p. 120). Japan's electoral system which only allows voters to express a single preference despite multi-member constituencies has a similar effect. At the other extreme, party ballots in Israel do not even list individual candidates, producing centralised campaigns dominated entirely by the parties.

Whatever the electoral system, the central feature of party campaigns is that they are always teetering on the brink of chaos. In the cut-and-thrust of debate, strategy invariably takes a back seat to tactics. Party officials may formulate a plan before the campaign, and have been known to remember what the plan was afterwards, but in the middle of the game the object is not so much to score as to avoid own goals. No one has time to think about such abstract concepts as maximising the party's vote even if anyone were given the specific responsibility of doing so. Rather, the questions are: How can we respond to our opponent's attack on our economic policy? Who's going to appear on the television discussion programme tonight? And what are we going to do with these leaflets? 'The trouble with political scientists', said a Massachusetts politician, 'is that they attribute a reasoned working out of things which are not worked out reasonably' (Rose, 1967). All models of campaign decision making which assume perfect information and perfect rationality are perfectly wrong.

Because most campaigns are a political revision class for the nation, the main task confronting established parties is to mobilise existing resources rather than to create new ones. The government's record, the party's image, the electorate's party allegiances – all are relatively fixed quantities which must be exploited to the full so that the party pulls its weight on election day. Yet how this is achieved does vary considerably. To the extent that it exists at all, party strategy in campaigns depends on three main factors: (1) whether the party is in or out of office; (2) whether the party is ahead or behind in the opinion polls; and (3) whether the party is new or established.

Ins and outs

Especially for the governing party the real work is over by the start of the campaign. A government's chance of re-election depends on how successfully it manipulates the resources of office. These resources include (1) the aura of government, (2) control over economic policy (3) manipulation of the electoral system and (4) choice of election timing in almost all parliamentary democracies.

American presidents are particularly adept at using the legitimacy of their office to help their re-election prospects. From Andrew Jackson in 1928 to Ronald Reagan in 1984, incumbents have campaigned on the theme that they are too busy shouldering their awesome responsibilities to have time for campaigning. 'Re-elect the President' was Richard Nixon's slogan in 1972, a phrase based on the correct assumption that the office was more reputable than the man.

Government parties are crucially dependent on their record since they can only offer more of the same in the future. By contrast, opposition parties can propose a change of direction, a fresh start, innovative ideas and new people. 'It's time for a change' is undoubtedly the most common and successful theme available to oppositions. But whether the voters accept that it is time for a change depends again on government performance – thus, the strategic task of the ins is to create opportunities before the campaign; that of the outs is to exploit opportunities during the campaign. As the old maxim puts it: 'Oppositions don't win elections, governments lose them.'

Ahead or behind?

Avoiding mistakes is a key objective in all campaigns. For the leading party, it is the only principle which matters. This does not mean shutting up shop altogether. Harold Wilson learned to his cost in 1970 that some activity is desirable even if talk is dangerous. By 1983, the Conservatives had learned this lesson. They despatched Margaret Thatcher on a series of high-visibility, low-risk visits to new technology factories. For the trailing parties, the object is to seize the initiative and engage the enemy, thus obtaining that most powerful but often most fleeting of election resources – momentum.

New or established?

For new or little-known parties, the first task is to establish an awareness and identity among the voters. In the United States, first-time Congressional candidates must develop a high 'recognition factor' as a base from which to build a distinctive image. Many political consultants are at hand to proffer advice on the marketing of the candidate; none offers a money-back guarantee if the campaign fails! (Incidentally, one basic rule on which all consultants seem to agree is to keep the candidate out of campaign decision making.) In Europe, where there are fewer elections and those that do take place are still strongly influenced by party loyalties, there is less room for a candidate to develop a specific image. But even in Britain, new parties such as the Social Democratic Party (SDP) have to regard their first few elections as an opportunity to lay down resources which can be transformed into votes later. This is a crucial phase since a 'brand image' is not easily changed once it has been created.

Canvassing

'The canvass' looms large in the thinking of local activists everywhere. Innumerable campaign hours are spent discussing, planning, conducting and analysing the canvass, often without any real thought as to its effectiveness. Canvassing began in the eighteenth century as a way of persuading individual voters, often with bribes, threats or a judicious combination of the two, to support a particular candidate. With the emergence of the mass media and universal suffrage, the ostensible function of the canvass shifted from persuasion to mobilisation of existing supporters. But even this purpose is pursued by a dwindling band of local activists; the proportion of British voters called on by the parties during campaigns fell dramatically between 1951 and 1974 before picking up again in the three-party contest of 1983 (Figure 8.1).

As a guide to voting intentions, canvass returns are totally and completely useless. The canvass is undertaken by biased party workers who are untrained in research techniques. The results are then interpreted by people whose job it is to look on the bright side. This leads to absurd figures such as those obtained in Chorley in 1964 when the three main parties separately canvassed the same street with widely differing results (Table 8.2). But the canvass has

Figure 8.1 *Local activity in British campaigns*

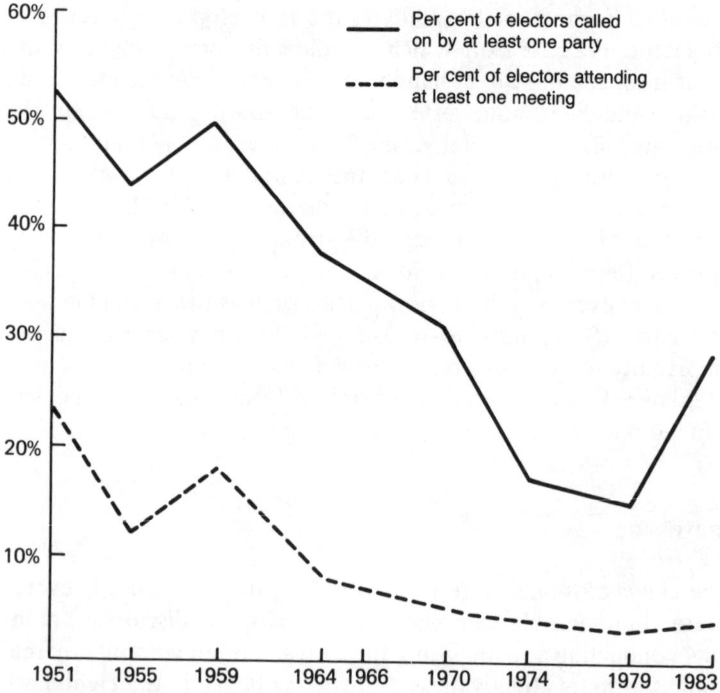

SOURCE Gallup.

Table 8.2 *Results of a canvass of the same street in Chorley, England by different local parties, 1964*

	Canvass by		
Result	*Conservative activists (May)*	*Labour activists (May)*	*Liberal activists (September)*
Conservative	95	31	10
Labour	27	159	18
Liberal	0	0	22
Doubtful	28	12	44
Not contacted	50	0	108

SOURCE: Butler and King (1965), p. 220.

other latent functions: it gives the activists something to do, acts as a test of members' commitment and provides a straw at which politicians can clutch when the opinion polls look really black.

In addition canvassing does increase turn-out at least at local elections. A classic experiment by Eldersveld and Dodge (1954) showed that Michigan electors contacted by students posing as party workers were more likely to vote than those sent communications through the mail. But turn-out among this latter group was still greater than among a control group which was not contacted at all (for the first study of this type, see Gosnell, 1927). This finding has subsequently been repeated in other countries although more recent research suggests the contact effect is greater among younger electors (Bochel and Denver, 1971; Miller *et al*., 1980). The canvass is particularly effective at stimulating turn-out at local elections when turn-out is generally low; and less effective in the high-key atmosphere of a general election. Moreover, if all the parties are mounting the same sort of operation, the net effect on the balance of party votes may be nil. Still, the canvass must go on.

Money

Does money buy votes? No, but it does enable a candidate's voice to be heard above the electoral babble. Whether voters like what they hear is a separate and more complicated question. In many democracies substantial campaign spending is still a *necessary* condition of electoral success but very rarely is money *sufficient* by itself. Nor is this surprising. Selling politicians is fundamentally different from soap-powder; brand loyalties run deeper and uncontrollable information about the 'product' appears on the news each night.

Challengers gain more from heavy spending than incumbents. In US Congressional elections, where there are no limits on campaign expenditure, 'campaign spending by non-incumbents has a substantial impact on their share of the vote; incumbent campaign expenditures have little effect. And spending by Republicans, candidates of the much weaker party, evidently has a greater impact than spending by Democrats' (Jacobson, 1980). So, like any other entrant into a market, the newcomer has greater need of advertising than the established market leader, yet at the same time the challenger finds fund-raising more difficult. The moral is to time market entry perfectly. In electoral politics, this often means waiting for the gap in the market created by an incumbent's death or retiral.

This was not always the case. Before mass suffrage, elections in many countries were a by-word for corruption. Dickens wrote in *The Pickwick Papers* of the voters of Eatanswill, up for sale to the candidate with the deepest pocket. In early nineteenth-century England, candidates were obliged to bribe voters, to fund innkeepers for refreshments on polling day, and to ingratiate themselves with the voters by finding all kinds of employment for them as cab-drivers, messengers, canvassers, clerks, agents and poll watchers (Pinto-Duschinsky, 1981, p. 16 estimates that the overall cost of standing for parliament in the nineteenth century amounted to about £20 000 a year at 1980 prices). In most Western democracies, such obvious corruption has now died out. With the broadening of the franchise, population growth, improved education, changing moral standards, and the emergence of the mass media and associated marketing techniques, the balance of campaign power has shifted from the individual candidate to party headquarters. (Though notably not so in the USA where financial contributions are still designed to help a candidate rather than a party.) The flow of money has moved in tandem, with most funds now given directly to the central party by large corporate donors, notably businesses and trade unions.

For three reasons campaign finance is still a problem in many democracies. First, the increasing cost of modern campaigns places a growing burden on political parties at a time when many are suffering a long-term decline in membership subscriptions. Equity is a second source of concern. Even though money does not buy votes, large discrepancies in expenditure can still create grievances which might ultimately threaten the legitimacy of the whole electoral process. In Britain, the Conservative Party is perceived as substantially outspending Labour, even though the difference is not that large and is in any case declining (Pinto-Duschinsky, 1981, p. 276). Thirdly, financial donations are given in the expectation of some sort of return. A voter may want a public-sector job, a firm may want a government contract, a trade union may want sympathetic labour legislation. In this sense things have not changed since the nineteenth century. In fact, the pattern of giving depends on the motives of the donor: in elections to the United States' House of Representatives, economic interest groups (which generally want specific favours) give most to likely winners whereas ideological groups (which want the maximum number of sympathetic legislators) reserve their largest contributions for close races.

A number of weapons have been used in the battle to control campaign spending (Paltiel, 1981). The lightest touch is *statutory reporting* of expenditure. In Britain, constituency candidates must report details of contributions and expenditure to the returning officer, a requirement of limited value since most money is spent centrally. In Israel, the reporting burden is placed not on candidates but parties, which must additionally provide annual returns. Most democracies require some form of disclosure of expenditure.

Limits on contributions are a more significant constraint on expenditure. In the United States, a limit of $1000 recently placed on individual contributions has stopped what amounted to the sale of prestigious ambassadorships to wealthy 'fat cats'. The United States, Argentina and some Canadian provinces have also prohibited corporate giving though this has often just led to the use of subsidiaries or 'parallel action organisations' which work for a particular candidate without formally joining the campaign organisation. In the United States, for example, the 'fat cat' has been replaced by the 'political action committee'.

Limits on expenditure are more common and more effective than regulation of contributions. The burgeoning cost of US presidential campaigns has been halted by expenditure limits placed on those candidates who choose to accept matching public funds (so far, most have). Britain is wholly anomalous. Strict limits are placed on candidates' expenses, which do not much matter, but no constraints at all are placed on national expenditure by the parties.

Finally, *public financing* offers another approach to the problem of funding election campaigns. Most democracies offer subsidies in kind, most frequently free access to postal and broadcasting services, but an increasing number also give direct financial support to parties. In 1957 Puerto Rico became the first country to adopt this system as a result of concern over how the governing Popular Democratic Party filled its coffers by 'macing' public servants of up to 2 per cent of their salary. In West Germany assorted government agencies now dole out large sums to foundations associated with each of the four main parties. Some commentators spot corporate trends in this intermingling of state and party.

What has been the effect of these various reforms? Where they are ignored none at all. It is an open secret that candidates for the Japanese Diet exceed the legal limits on campaign spending. Under the Marcos regime, Philippine law restricted a candidate's expenses to one year's salary for the office sought but the traditional custom of buying votes continued unabated. Elsewhere spending limits have been thwarted by the capacity of accountants to find legal loopholes faster than the assembly can close them. None the less, Alexander (1979, p. 7) believes that: (1) these reforms have benefited established and incumbent parties (who do after all enact the law in the first place); (2) the reforms have stimulated centralising tendencies in political parties, at least in unitary states; (3) they have improved party efficiency; and (4) they may also have lessened the dependence of parties on interest groups. At best the record is mixed.

Opinion Polls

Opinion polls are central to election campaigns in contemporary democracies. Party strategies depend on poll ratings more than anything else. Sometimes poll findings themselves become a major campaign issue as in the controversy during the British election of

1983 over whether telephone surveys were yielding inflated estimates of the Liberal/SDP Alliance's strength.

Concern about the impact of opinion polls has led to restrictions in several European countries on their publication during campaigns (Table 8.3). But do polls of voting intentions directly influence voting behaviour? Is there either a *bandwagon* effect, whereby electors flock behind the banner of the leading party, or an *underdog* effect, whereby electors turn away from the leading party? The evidence suggests that while opinion polls may have some effects on voting behaviour, these are neither large nor consistent. In Britain, for example, there is no evidence of a bandwagon effect favouring the leading party. However, poll reports of an Alliance up-swing may have led to a further increase in its support at both by-elections and general elections, suggesting that third parties in particular can exploit poll findings to create credibility and momentum. At the same time, there is some slight evidence of an underdog effect in the major party battle at British elections. Crewe (1986) notes:

> In eight of the twelve post-war elections the final forecast polls have tended to over-estimate the actual vote of the *outgoing government* (whether or not it is re-elected) and to under-estimate the actual vote of the outgoing opposition. This has led to suggestions that the polls do have underdog effects, but only

Table 8.3 *Democracies which restrict the publication of opinion polls before a general election*

	Number of days before election when restrictions apply
France	7
Luxembourg	30
Malta	2
Portugal	90
Spain	5
West Germany (informal restrictions)	7

SOURCE: Rohme (1985), citing a 1983 survey.

> on last-minute deciders; perhaps they produce a reaction against the prospect of the government obtaining too big a majority or induce complacency amongst the least committed of the government's supporters.

But this effect is small, if it exists at all.

Evidence from the United States confirms that opinion polls do *not* have a large, direct effect on whether or how people vote. Time differences mean that polling booths are still open in the west after the television networks have released projections of the presidential result based on early returns from precincts in the east (note that these forecasts are based on actual votes rather than intentions). Such projections may depress turnout in the west slightly, at least when there is a clear winner, but television predictions are certainly not a major cause of low turnout in American elections (Tanenbaum and Kostrich, 1983). And they are an even less significant influence on party shares of the vote.

In plurality electoral systems, fear of a wasted vote can lead minor party supporters to transfer their vote to the major party they dislike least. By providing current information on party standings, opinion polls are potentially important in tactical voting. If tactical voting were common, opinion polls could become the equivalent of the first round of voting in a double ballot system. But even in an era of dealignment, tactical voting is still uncommon, at least at general elections. Furthermore, those electors who do vote tactically often do not consult the opinion polls in deciding which parties are out of the running. In Britain, opinion polls themselves show that a full third of the electorate claimed not to have seen or heard any poll results during the 1983 campaign; only 3 per cent said they were influenced by what they learned from the polls (Crewe, 1986).

The influence of polls is indirect rather than direct. They alter party strategies, the morale of the activists and media expectations of the result. Broader indirect effects have also been postulated. Some observers suggest that opinion polls contribute to a 'spiral of silence' in which minority views become increasingly unpopular because people are unwilling to express views which they know are not widely shared (Noelle-Neumann, 1974). Other social scientists argue that the pollsters' choice of topic influences the political agenda and that their 'yes/no' questions lead to oversimplified discussion of complex problems (Marsh, 1982). But these broader effects are not well-established; they are remote from voting behaviour; and they presuppose a public which is more attentive to opinion polls than is actually the case.

Conclusion

This chapter has two conclusions, one positive and one negative. The positive conclusion is that trends in the national economy, as reported in the media, are a regular influence on variations around base-line levels of party support. Other political events – international and domestic crises, changes in party leadership, political scandals – may have larger and more dramatic effects on voting intentions but in contrast to such short-run influences the economy is a permanent fixture of continuing interest to nearly all electors. The negative conclusion of the chapter is that the other factors we have discussed – especially the campaign, canvassing, money and opinion polls – are less influential than is commonly supposed. Most election campaigns are over before they have begun.

Yet as party loyalties weaken, the short-term influences discussed in this chapter will become more important. So it is unfortunate that political science has not developed a theory which encompasses those factors. Because voting is a political act, there is an urgent need for a genuinely political theory of voting. The absence of such a theory is the major gap in our understanding of contemporary electoral behaviour.

Further Reading

On the economy, Tufte (1978) is an intriguing and non-technical introduction to what is generally a rather dry literature. The best overview is probably Alt and Chrystal (1983, Pt Three); Schneider (1984) is also useful. Alt (1979) is a good discussion of the British case. Goodhart and Bhansali (1970) and Kramer (1971) are classic papers in the field while Whiteley (1980) contains a typical sample of more recent studies. On the media, McQuail and Windahl (1981) is a comprehensive review of theory while Seymour-Ure (1974) is still a useful guide to politics and the media. For the media and elections specifically, see Smith (1981). The study of election campaigns, as opposed to elections, is a major gap; Penniman (1981) is one of the few general accounts while Butler (1986) briefly covers Britain. On money and elections Paltiel (1981) provides an excellent survey of murky waters while Alexander (1979) is a mixed bag of relevant essays. For Britain, Pinto-Duschinsky (1981) is definitive though not uncontroversial. For the United States, Alexander has produced numerous authoritative works while Jacobson's (1980) study is an impressive piece of research on money and votes in United States congressional elections. On opinion polls see Kavanagh (1981) and Worcester (1983).

References

ALEXANDER, H. (1979) *Political Finance* (London: Sage).

ALT, J. (1979) *The Politics of Economic Decline* (Cambridge University Press).

ALT, J. and CHRYSTAL, K. (1983) *Political Economics* (Brighton: Harvester).

BLUMLER, J. and McQUAIL, D. (1968) *Television in Politics* (London: Faber).

BOCHEL, J. and DENVER, D. (1971) 'Canvassing, Turnout and Party Support: An Experiment', *British Journal of Political Science*, vol. 1, pp. 257–69.

BOORSTIN, D. (1961) *The Image: A Guide to Pseudo Events in America* (New York: Athenaeum).

BUTLER, D. (1986) 'The Changing Nature of British Elections', in I. Crewe and M. Harrop (eds), *Political Communications: The General Election Campaign of 1983* (Cambridge: Cambridge University Press).

BUTLER, D. and KING, A. (1965) *The British General Election of 1964* (London: Macmillan).

CLARKE, H. D., JENSEN, J., LE DUC, L. and PAMMETT, J. (1979) *Political Choice in Canada* (Toronto: McGraw-Hill Ryerson).

CLARKE, H. D., STEWART, M. C. and ZUK, G. (1986) 'Politics, Economics and Party Popularity in Britain 1979–83', *Electoral Studies*, vol. 5, pp. 123–42.

CREWE, I. (1986) 'Saturation Polling, the Media and the 1983 Election', in I. Crewe and M. Harrop (eds), *Political Communications: The General Election Campaign of 1983* (Cambridge: Cambridge University Press).

DAVIDSON, D. (1982) 'Candidate Evaluation: Rational Instrument or

Affective Response', Paper to Midwest Political Science Association Convention, Chicago.

DUNLEAVY, P. and HUSBANDS, C. (1985) *British Democracy at the Crossroads* (London: Allen & Unwin).

ELDERSVELD, S. and DODGE, R. (1954) 'Personal Contact or Mail Propaganda? An Experiment in Voter Turnout and Attitude Change', in D. Katz (ed.), *Public Opinion and Propaganda* (New York: Holt, Rinehart & Winston).

EYAL, G. (1981) 'The Role of Newspapers and Television in Agenda-setting', in G. Wilhoit and H. de Bock (eds), *Mass Communications Review Yearbook: Volume II* (London: Sage).

FELDMAN, S. (1984) 'Economic Self-Interest and the Vote', *Political Behaviour*, vol. 6, pp. 229–52.

GLASGOW UNIVERSITY MEDIA GROUP (1980) *More Bad News* (London: Routledge & Kegan Paul).

GOODHART, C. and BHANSALI, R. (1970) 'Political Economy', *Political Studies*, vol. 18, pp. 43–106.

GOSNELL, H. (1927) *Getting Out the Vote: an Experiment in the Stimulation of Voting* (Chicago: Chicago University Press).

JACOBSON, G. (1980) *Money in Congressional Elections* (New Haven: Yale University Press).

KAVANAGH, D. (1981) 'Public Opinion Polls', in D. Butler, H. Penniman and A. Ranney (eds), *Democracy at the Polls* (Washington, DC.: American Enterprise Institute).

KINDER, D. (1983) 'Diversity and Complexity in American Public Opinion', in A. Finifter (ed.), *Political Science: the State of the Discipline* (Washington, DC.: American Political Science Association).

KLAPPER, J. (1960) *The Effects of Mass Communication* (New York: Free Press).

KLINGEMANN, H. D. and TAYLOR, C. L. (1978) 'Partisanship, Candidates and Issues: Attitudinal Components of the Vote in West German Federal Elections', in M. Kaase and K. von Beyme (eds), *Elections and Parties* (London: Sage).

KRAMER, G. (1971) 'Short Run Fluctuations in US Voting Behaviour 1896–1964', *American Political Science Review*, vol. 65, pp. 131–43.

McQUAIL, D. and WINDAHL, S. (1981) *Communication Models* (Harlow, Essex: Longman).

MANN, T. (1979) *Unsafe at Any Margin* (Washington, DC.: American Enterprise Institute).

MARKUS, G. (1982) 'Political Attitudes During an Election Year: A Report on the 1980 NES Panel Study', *American Political Science Review*, vol. 76, pp. 538–60.

MARKUS, G. B. and CONVERSE, P. E. (1979) 'A Dynamic Simultaneous Equation Model of Electoral Choice', *American Political Science Review*, vol. 73, pp. 1055–70.

MARSH, C. (1982) *The Survey Method: the Contribution of Surveys to Sociological Explanation* (London: Allen & Unwin).

MILLER, R., BOSITIS, D. and BAER, D. (1980) 'Stimulating Voter Turnout in a Primary', *International Political Science Review*, vol. 2, pp. 445–60.

MILLER, W. and MACKIE, M. (1973) 'The Electoral Cycle and the Asymmetry of Government and Opposition Popularity: an Alternative Model of the Relationship between Economic Conditions and Popularity', *Political Studies*, vol. 21, pp. 263–79.

NOELLE-NEUMANN, E. (1974) 'The Spiral of Silence: A Theory of Public Opinion', *Journal of Communication*, vol. 24, pp. 43–51.

PALDAM, M. (1981) 'A Preliminary Survey of the Theories and Findings on Vote and Popularity Functions', *European Journal of Political Research*, vol. 9, pp. 181–200.

PALTIEL, K. (1981) 'Campaign Finance: Contrasting Practices and Reforms', in D. Butler, H. Penniman and A. Ranney (eds), *Democracy at the Polls* (Washington, DC: American Enterprise Institute).

PENNIMAN, H. (1981) 'Campaign Styles and Methods', in D. Butler, H. Penniman and A. Ranney (eds), *Democracy at the Polls* (Washington, DC: American Enterprise Institute).

PINTO-DUSCHINSKY, M. (1981) *British Political Finance* (Washington, DC: American Enterprise Institute).

RANNEY, A. (1984) *Channels of Power: The Impact of Television on American Politics* (New York: Basic Books).

ROHME, N. (1985) 'A Worldwide Overview of National Restrictions on the Conduct and Release of Public Opinion Polls', *European Research*, vol. 13, pp. 30–7.

ROSE, R. (1967) *Influencing Voters: A Study of Campaign Rationality* (London: Faber).

SCHNEIDER, F. (1984) 'Public Attitudes towards Economic Conditions and their Impact on Government Behaviour', *Political Behaviour*, vol. 6, pp. 211–27.

SEYMOUR-URE, C. (1974) *The Political Impact of Mass Media* (London: Constable).

SMITH, A. (1981) 'Mass Communications', in D. Butler, H. Penniman and A. Ranney (eds), *Democracy at the Polls* (Washington, DC: American Enterprise Institute).

STOKES, D. (1966) 'Some Dynamic Elements of Contests for the Presidency', *American Political Science Review*, vol. 60, pp. 19–29.

STOKES, D. (1981) 'What Decides Elections?', in D. Butler, H. Penniman and A. Ranney (eds), *Democracy at the Polls* (Washington, DC: American Enterprise Institute).

TANENBAUM, P. and KOSTRICH, L. (1983) *Turned-on TV/Turned-off Voters* (London: Sage).

TRUMAN, D. (1951) 'Some Political Variables for Election Surveys', *International Journal of Opinion and Attitude Research*, vol. 5, pp. 249–50.

TUFTE, E. (1978) *Political Control of the Economy* (Princeton: Princeton University Press).

WESTERSTAHL, J. and JOHANNSON, F. (1985) *News Ideologies as Moulders of Domestic News* (University of Goteborg: mimeo).
WHITELEY, P. (ed.) (1980) *Models of Political Economy* (London: Sage).
WORCESTER, R. (1983) *Political Opinion Polling: an International Review* (London: Macmillan).

9

Conclusion: What do Elections do?

Most research asks what decides elections. We have seen how governments try to organise elections to get the result they want. We have seen how the voters respond to the record of the government and the appeals of opposition parties. Together, these constraints and responses decide the results of elections. But the question of what elections decide is equally important. Indeed, if elections make no difference, there is no point in studying them at all. So what do elections decide? What do they do? We first touched on this question when we discussed communist and Third World elections. Now we return to it at greater length, and now with a focus on the functions of free, competitive elections. These are considerably wider than the functions of those elections without choice which we discussed in Chapter 2.

There are two basic views of the functions of competitive elections. One emphasises their '*bottom-up*' functions – representation, choice of governments, popular influence on policies. Writers such as Butler, Penniman and Ranney (1981, p. 1) interpret elections as genuine wooing of voters by party suitors: 'those who seek to direct a country's public affairs must convince the voters that the policies they propose are feasible, desirable, and best carried out by those who propose them'. In this model voters consider the competing arguments and make their decision. Their votes are cast and counted, candidates elected to office, and a new government is formed. Control is exercised from below.

On the other hand, '*top-down*' theorists such as Ginsberg (1982) take a more sceptical view of the electoral process, even in a competitive electoral system. They argue that elections are in essence a device for expanding the power and authority of the governing elite. Elections, so this argument runs, incorporate potential dissenters into the political system, reduce popular participation to a mere cross on the ballot, and encourage people to obey the state without fundamentally limiting its autonomy.

Our own view of competitive elections is a combination of these approaches. They are *both* correct. Competitive elections are an *exchange of influence* between governing elites and voters. Elites gain authority in exchange for responsiveness to the voters; voters gain influence in exchange for obedience to decisions they only partly shape. Elections expand the authority of government while reducing the likelihood of that authority being misused. They strengthen the capacity of society to control its own destiny. They benefit both rulers and ruled. Politics is not necessarily a zero-sum game in which the total benefits are fixed and one group's gain is automatically another's loss – and this applies to rulers and ruled as much as to social and ethnic groups.

But this exchange model of competitive elections is only our view; the best way to read this chapter is to use it as a basis for forming *your own* opinion on whether competitive elections are essentially a 'bottom-up', 'top-down', or exchange process. We start by discussing 'bottom-up' functions like representation, then move on to 'top-down' functions like legitimation, and end with exchange functions such as the influence of elections on the internal decisions of the parties.

Provide Representation?

All elections involve representation but there are several different meanings of the word 'representation'. One school of thought stresses the idea of *resemblance*, the reproduction in parliament of a microcosm of the nation, representative in every way. Putting a left-wing socialist view, Aneurin Bevan (1952), former deputy leader of Britain's Labour Party, wrote that 'a representative person is one who will act in a given situation in much the same way as those he represents would act in that same situation. In short he must be *of their kind*'. Advocates of the resemblance view are invariably disappointed by free elections. Social inequality means that the pool of candidates with the time, interest, knowledge and ability to stand for parliament and win elections is not drawn equally from all social groups. It is easier to guarantee representation in this resemblance sense in places such as the Soviet Union where it can be imposed from above (and where the representatives do not have significant power).

But *no* selection process can really guarantee resemblance. However much elected officials resemble society on the day of their election, parliamentary and government experience changes their perspectives and interests. In Rousseau's words: 'the English are only free when they are electing members of parliament. Once the election has been completed, they revert to a condition of slavery. They are nothing'. And the more real power elected officials enjoy, the more it is likely to change their outlook. American populists echoed Rousseau's fears and sought a remedy in the techniques of the referendum and the recall (which allows an elected official to be unseated at any time if enough electors sign a petition). Even if the electoral system guarantees proportional representation for localities and parties, an elected assembly will always mirror society far less accurately than an opinion poll sample.

There are other concepts of 'representation', however. We may not want representation by 'people like us' so much as by 'people who will act effectively on our behalf'. Who wants representation in a court of law, or even at a press conference, by an advocate as dull-witted, shifty-eyed, inarticulate and ignorant as themselves? So there are several other interpretations of electoral representation, all of which involve the idea of making a choice between competing elites. (See Pitkin, 1967, or Pulzer, 1975, for good, readable discussions of representation.) The three main variants are as follows.

Constituency service

This is the idea that representatives should use their skills to advance the interests of their local constituents by finding them jobs, helping them with bureaucratic problems, or bringing grants and employment to the district. Constituency service is emphasised in countries such as the United States and Kenya (see Chapter 2) where weak parties are combined with first-past-the-post electoral systems.

The trustee model

This stresses the independent judgement of the legislator, once elected. The heyday of this strongly elitist view was in the nineteenth century before the rise of organised parties. Its classic exposition came from Edmund Burke, who told his electors in Bristol:

> you choose a member indeed; but when you have chosen him, he is *not* member of Bristol, but he is a member of parliament . . . Your representative owes you, not his industry only, but his judgement; and he betrays, instead of serving you, if he sacrifices it to your opinion.

Should you own any stock-exchange shares, your stockbroker would probably say the same. It is the standard claim of the professional.

The party model

This has largely supplanted Burkeian attitudes, especially among left-wing parties with extra-parliamentary origins. It sees the legislator as a footsoldier for the party, elected because of the party label and therefore morally bound to its broad programme. Where the electoral system only allows voters to choose parties, not candidates, this view is naturally strengthened.

Thus once the resemblance notion is rejected, we are left with a more practical, limited notion of electoral representation as a choice between competing elites, whether the choice is made on grounds of constituency service, trustee ability, or party membership (Schumpeter, 1943). Perhaps there is more to democracy then elite competition – but then there is more to democracy than competitive elections.

Offer a Choice?

Even though they do not always do so, elections can provide a mechanism for making a choice and a mechanism for implementing that choice. Elections can be used to choose a government or a policy, and however bad the choice at least a choice permits the business of government to proceed. Anarchy or indecision can be resolved by an election.

Extreme versions of democratic theory require elections to *aggregate policy preferences* – that is, to combine them into a single coherent decision package. Those who advocate this viewpoint focus on the positive, forward-looking choice of the policy preferred by society at large. More pessimistic, or perhaps more realistic, democrats have demanded much less of elections – merely the rejection of unpopular governments. They focus on negative rather than positive choices, on choice of people rather than choice of policy, on retrospective rather than forward looking judgements, on performance rather than promise.

Tom Paine, a contemporary of Rousseau's, argued that a *sequence* of elections was enough to keep government *responsible* even if not *representative*: 'their fidelity to the public will be secured by the prudent reflection of not making a rod for themselves' since they will have to face the prospect of 'returning and mixing again with the general body of electors in a few months'. Modern theorists, such as Riker, support Paine against Rousseau by using algebraic logic to show that no form of election is technically capable of aggregating policy preferences or choosing between alternative leaders when there are three or more alternatives and when each voter has not only a first preference, but second and third preferences as well – not an unreasonable scenario. But elections *can* effectively threaten the incumbent government with retribution (Riker, 1982, p. 242). Many empirical studies also support this interpretation of elections as a referendum on government performance (see Chapters 6 and 8). Fear of rejection by the electorate is the most effective control over government: it may be weak and uncertain but it is a great deal better than nothing.

But do free elections necessarily meet even Paine's low demands? Alas, freedom does not guarantee competition and without competition there can be no real electoral choice. Without a real choice, incumbents are not really threatened by electoral retribution. For many years the deep sectarian divide in Northern Ireland protected Unionist politicians from electoral defeat – however badly they governed, their Protestant voters were hardly likely to punish them by voting in a Catholic government. The only real risk was of losing to a protestant maverick (Rose, 1978). A *free choice* is *not* the same thing as a *real choice*.

Make Governments?

This, one might think, is the main point of competitive elections – to determine who shall govern. But this is too simple. In most democracies the electorate directly chooses the assembly rather than the chief executive. King (1981, p. 295) found that only seven of twenty-eight democracies allow for direct election of the executive – Colombia, the Dominican Republic, France, Sri Lanka, Venezuela and, ignoring their electoral colleges, Finland and the United States. Yet nowhere do assemblies govern: the USA, paradoxically, comes closest to assembly government despite the prominence of the president. More significantly, in many countries the party composition of the legislature does not automatically determine which party or parties form the executive. Rather, the election result provides a back-drop for hard bargaining between the parties over the distribution of executive posts and the general political line which the new government will follow. Election results *influence* but rarely *determine* the outcome of these discussions. The results produce a short-list of potential government coalitions. Such post-election deals are most common in countries where proportional representation means no single party has a parliamentary majority, such as Belgium, Denmark, Finland and Holland. There is a stronger, more consistent relationship between elections and government formation in democracies with: (1) first-past-the-post electoral systems and clear parliamentary majorities (Britain, Canada); (2) a relatively stable pattern of inter-party alliances (West Germany); or (3) strong anti-regime parties which restrict the room for manoeuvre of other parties (Italy).

No democracy changes the entire composition of the executive after an election. Politicians may change but the judges, generals and senior civil servants march on. Britain represents the extreme case of post-election immobility; apart from a couple of Ministers and a few political advisers, the personnel in each government department are the same after an election as before. On the Continent and in the United States, a change in the governing party digs deeper into the executive ranks. But nowhere do elections determine the entire composition of all those who develop and apply public policy. Elections may influence *how* these unelected officials govern but they fall short of completely determining *who* governs.

Conversely, just as elections often fail to determine who governs, so the executive often changes without an election. Figure 9.1 shows the relationship between the number of elections and the number of new governments formed in the main democracies since the Second World War. Countries *above* the diagonal line in the figure have had more governments than elections since the war; these are Belgium, Denmark, Italy and, the extreme case, Finland.

Most countries, however, fall *below* the diagonal line in the figure, indicating that they have had more elections than governments. For example, in the years 1945–76 Sweden's Social Demo-

Figure 9.1 *Number of elections and governments, 1945–77*

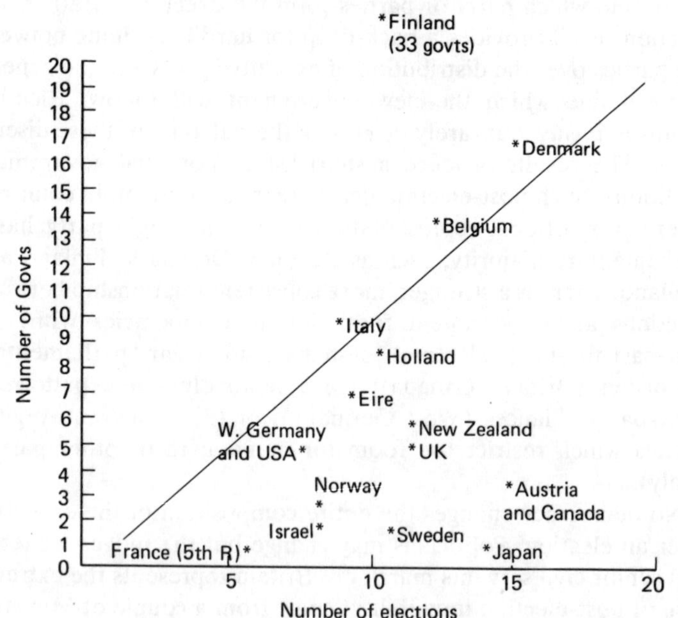

NOTE A 'new' government is one with a substantially altered partisan composition.

SOURCE King (1981, Table 12.2).

cratic Party ruled almost continuously, alone or in coalition. This was achieved by perfectly democratic means but it does indicate how elections need not produce regular changes in governing parties. In fact the most frequent pattern in post-war elections in Europe has been for the main governing party to lose votes but retain office (Rose and Mackie, 1980). Governments do not normally alter after an election. Nor do they only change then. Elections are neither a necessary nor a sufficient condition for a change of government.

Even though there is no one-to-one link between elections and governments, it is often argued that elections provide a pool of politicians from which executive offices can be filled. Recruiting people to fill political roles is essential to the character and survival of any political system so this function is certainly important. But parties rather than elections play the key role in political recruitment. This is most obvious in countries where voters cannot choose between candidates of their preferred party. Examples are first-past-the-post electoral systems, such as Britain, or party list systems where the elector must vote either for or against the whole list, as in Israel.

Most party list systems do permit voters some limited choice between candidates on a list, a procedure which widens the process of political recruitment. An alternative method of allowing electors more say in political recruitment, and a method specially suited to first-past-the-post systems, is the US primary in which a party's candidates are chosen in primary elections open to all those who declare their allegiance to a particular party. But primaries are confined to the United States and do not attract a large turn-out even there. Throughout the democratic world, political recruitment is a task handled more by activists in parties than by ordinary voters in elections.

In summary, competitive elections play an important part in government formation but the relationship is less tight, less strict than many people imagine.

Influence Policy?

As with governments, so too with policies: elections are only one influence among many. As Lindblom (1977) notes, pluralist democracies are organised so as to *limit* the capacity of the rulers to reshape society; the price of giving veto powers to many different groups is that the majority will can rarely be done even when it is clear what the majority wills. In fact there is a vigorous debate among political scientists about whether elections in democracies make any real difference to the substance of public policy.

The principal advocates of this 'politics is irrelevant' school are the convergence theorists and the Marxists. *Convergence* theorists maintain that both democratic and communist states are subject to 'a logic of industrialism in which the exigencies of modern technology and an advanced economy override political factors [including elections] and progressively shape public policies in a similar mould' (Castles, 1982, p. 6). In Western democracies, it is argued, interest groups grow in number and stature and electoral representation gives way to functional representation. (The idea is encapsulated in the title of Richardson and Jordan, 1979: *The Policy Process in a Post-Parliamentary Democracy*.) Policy results not from elections but from tripartite deals between the government, employers and unions. In responding to these problems, major parties adopt similar programmes in an effort to capture the crucial middle ground; they become catch-all parties competing on style rather than substance (Kircheimer, 1966; Wolinetz, 1979). For convergence theorists, the real contrast is between industrial and pre-industrial societies rather than between industrial societies with and without competitive elections.

At one level, the convergence thesis is quite right. What governments do depends on their resources. Countries in the Third World do not have a welfare state because they cannot afford one; in industrial societies, whether democratic or communist, such provision can be and is achieved. It is really not surprising, then, that numerous studies have shown that levels of government expenditure depend more on a country's level of economic development than on whether it has competitive elections (Wilensky, 1975).

Marxists, on the other hand, argue that the charade of conflict at election time disguises agreement over the most fundamental policy of all – that of maintaining the capitalist system (Miliband, 1969). Although elected governments are formally separate from private industry, this is to render elections more effective as devices for legitimising capitalism. Marxists agree with Veblen

(1904) that 'the chief concern of the constituted authorities in any democratic nation is a concern about the profitable business of the nation's substantial citizens'. Politicians who advocate a different system will not get elected; if they do get elected, they will change their policy; if they do not change their policy, they will be voted out of office; and if they are not voted out, the electoral system will be changed or they will be kicked out by other, less peaceful methods (Taylor, 1984). Hence capitalism cannot be eliminated by democratic means and elections are irrelevant.

Both convergence theorists and Marxists adopt an excessively Olympian perspective. Only an armchair sociologist could argue that all industrial societies are fundamentally the same, irrespective of whether they have competitive elections. Only a Marxist could argue that ownership of production is the only significant political issue and that elections which do not encompass it are a fraud. (In any case, the issue of industrial ownership and control is *not* excluded from electoral decision; indeed it has been central to many Western elections – compare for example the programme of Attlee's 1945 government with that of Thatcher's 1979 government in Britain.) In appraising the impact of elections on policy we need a less cavalier approach which is more sensitive to evidence. It is an empirical question, not a matter of theory, whether a change in a governing party produces major shifts in policy or whether it is just a case of Tweedledum and Tweedledee. Fortunately this is an area where political scientists have done considerable research recently, demonstrating in the process that elections *can* have important policy consequences.

One approach is to ask whether parties differ in their manifesto proposals and if so whether they implement their promises when elected. Despite popular and Marxist scepticism, the answer is *yes* to both queries. In a study of British elections, Rose (1984, p. 68) found that only one in seven of those subjects on which action was proposed by one major party was also scheduled for action in the other party's manifesto. In other words, priorities differed. In office, too, most pledges are redeemed. The 'redemption rate' was 85 per cent for the Conservative government of 1970–74 and 64 per cent for the less secure Labour administration which followed from 1974–79 (Rose, 1984, p. 65). Comparable figures have been obtained for the United States (Pomper, 1980, p. 163).

These statistics do not tell the whole story. Most legislation –

about 90 per cent in Britain – originates in the Civil Service or the flow of events rather than in manifestos (though much of this is non-contentious and non-political). And as a rule, governments are least successful at implementing their larger proposals. Granting bigger subsidies to Welsh hill farmers is one thing; achieving peace and prosperity for all is quite another. Yet electors vote on big issues when they vote on issues at all.

None the less, the high rate of manifesto promises fulfilled indicates that we should expect to find clear differences between those democracies where left-wing parties have dominated and those where the right has provided most governments. This is precisely what the research shows. Democracies where the left have been strong over the entire post-war period have: (1) more inflation but less unemployment; (2) higher spending on welfare and education; but (3) lower military spending; (4) a larger public sector; (5) more liberal abortion policies; and (6) a somewhat more equal distribution of income (Castles, 1982; King, 1981). Such differences only emerge after a substantial period of domination by a particular party – well beyond a single election cycle. And as Marxists are quick to point out, these contrasts *within* liberal democracies are less sharp than those *between* democracies and communist states. As we have seen, so few executive posts change hands after a Western election that governments in liberal democracies cannot be agents of social transformation. But at a more detailed level parties do make a difference – and so therefore does the electoral process which propels them in and out of office.

A final indication of how elections shape policy can be seen in Bunce's (1981) analysis of the policy cycle. This is shown in Figure 9.2. Her idea is that new governments are committed to policy innovation. They possess a 'can do' attitude carried forward from a successful election campaign. This is reinforced by the natural desire of every new leader to make a personal mark. The post-election honeymoon, when society generally accepts what it takes to be the verdict of the electorate, also provides a favourable political context within which to achieve change. These post-election bursts are often explicitly labelled: President Kennedy had his '100 Days' in 1961. As time passes, however, initial enthusiasm fades, administrative complexities intrude, and urgent new issues arise. Besides, as the new government's most original ideas are implemented, policy making becomes incremental rather

Figure 9.2 *Elections and the policy cycle*

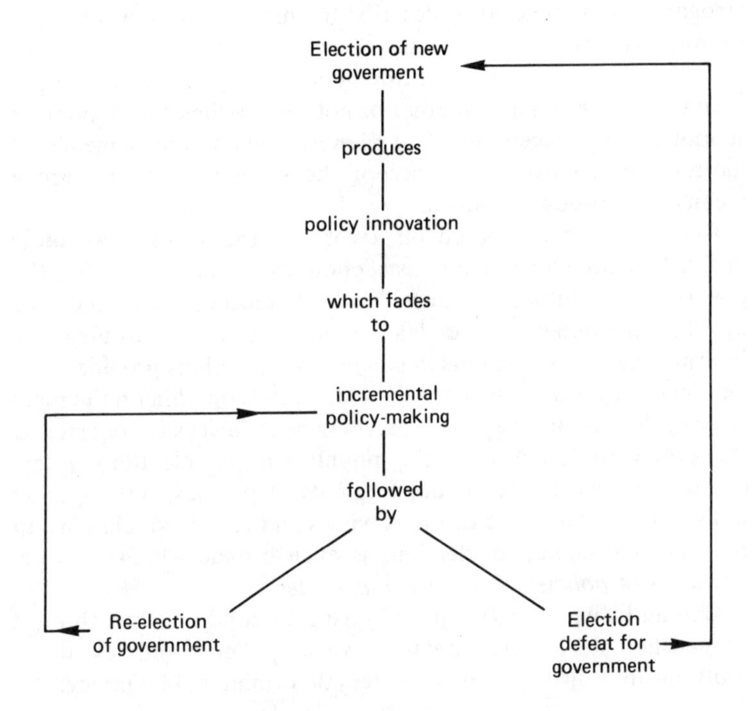

than innovative, a matter of marginal adjustments rather than major change. Things begin to drift. Re-election may provide a temporary fillip but a new cycle only begins with a different government.

Bunce suggests policy cycles can be found wherever there are new leaders, irrespective of whether they are elected or appointed. But in democracies elections ignite the spark that fires a new cycle.

Give Mandates?

A mandate is an authoritative command or order: a commission or title that justifies government action and requires compliance by the citizens. Medieval monarchs claimed a mandate from God; modern governments claim theirs from the people. Victorious parties claim a mandate from the voters to execute the proposals in their manifesto. They do so with a mixture of humility and arrogance; sometimes they describe the mandate as an instruction from the voters which they must, as good democrats, obey; sometimes they describe it as an entitlement which gives them the right to impose their policies whether or not these policies have popular support. If we accept the first view, mandates are a means of 'bottom-up' control; if we accept the second, mandates are a means of 'top-down' control.

But is their claim based on a correct reading of how voters decide? Is an election an instruction from the voters for the government to fulfil its promises? Does an election have a message for the government? (We dealt with some of the problems of interpreting election results in Chapter 4.) Elections provide some ambiguous information about the electorate's opinion on the main issue of the day but they are most inefficient devices for registering the policy preferences of the population. At elections voters choose, at best, between shopping lists of policies; only opinion polls can ascertain the customers' views on the individual items. In fact the real choice at elections is even broader: between total packages of *policies plus party plus leader*.

Dye and Ziegler (1981, p. 189) list four conditions which must be satisfied if elections are to serve as policy mandates in the 'bottom-up' sense and let the voters determine public policy:

1. Competing parties must offer clear policy alternatives.
2. Voters must be concerned with these policies, rather than with party loyalty or candidates' personalities.
3. It must be possible to ascertain the majority's policy preferences from the election result.
4. Elected officials must be bound by the positions they assumed during the campaign.

It is apparent that these conditions will rarely be met simultaneously. It is more convincing to regard elections as giving a general *mandate to govern* rather than a specific *mandate for policies*. Elections allow voters to influence who shall govern rather than exactly what they should do.

This is of course recognised by politicians themselves. In 1931, MacDonald and Baldwin sought and received a 'doctor's mandate'

– that is, the authority to do whatever their National coalition government deemed necessary to cure the financial crisis. Their manifesto read:

> as it is impossible to foresee what may arise, no one can set out a programme on which specific pledges can be given. The government must therefore be free to consider every proposal likely to help . . . the government should have a national mandate giving it freedom to use whatever means may be found necessary.

There could hardly be a more brutal statement of the doctrine of the mandate in its 'top-down' form. Yet the National government won the election by a landslide.

In France, de Gaulle came to power on a pledge to keep Algeria French. He then negotiated Algerian independence, aware that the French had become weary of the war and the methods used to fight it.

In both these cases governments claimed a mandate which went far beyond policy details. Whether this was morally justified or not, it worked.

To the extent that elections give *policy* mandates at all, they are negative rather than positive. Politicians use manifestos as a warning as well as a promise. They give due notice of the contents of their policy basket; if the basket is wholly unacceptable, it should be rejected by the voters. Elected politicians assume that the policies on which they fought the election are at least acceptable to, if not positively approved by, the electorate. And this assumption is moral rather than empirical: if the electorate is simply unaware of the new government's proposals, the politicians can claim that ignorance of the manifesto, like ignorance of the law, is no excuse.

Politicians sometimes emphasise a policy in a campaign not to *attract* voters but to *warn* them and to lay the foundations for such a mandate claim. In the United States Ronald Reagan staked out a clear ideological position in 1980. Whether or not that helped him win – and it probably did not – it certainly helped him to govern when he had won. It impressed Congress after the election even if it did not impress the voters before it.

Add Legitimacy?

Here is the heart of the matter: elections are a quest for legitimacy. This is a more fundamental perspective on elections than regarding them as primarily about choice – though when the choice offered is real, the search for legitimacy is more likely to succeed. But what is legitimacy? And legitimacy for what? And how often does the quest succeed?

The word legitimate comes from the latin *legitimare* meaning 'to declare to be lawful'. But our modern concept of legitimacy is much wider than this. By legitimate government we mean government *with justification and authority, with a right to expect obedience and respect*. Declaring something to be lawful is only one way of giving it legitimacy and not always a successful one at that. Legality is no guarantee of legitimacy in the modern sense; we are not a society of lawyers.

The lengths to which governments go to secure a high turn-out bears witness to the legitimising power of elections. Low turn-out, especially when based on deliberate abstention rather than administrative incompetence, can be extremely damaging to a regime. Elections have been boycotted in such places as Nigeria, Northern Ireland and the Philippines in an attempt to deny authority to the regimes in these places. Party voting may determine who governs but turn-out figures say much about how much authority the resulting government will have.

Elections contribute to legitimacy in several ways. First there is the *ritual* of the rallies, the leaflets, the speeches, the surfeit of media coverage. A campaign process so expensive of time and money conditions the populace to think the event significant. An election is the modern equivalent of a medieval coronation: it installs and authorises the government of the realm with a great deal of pomp and ceremony (though medieval coronations must surely have been cheaper!). The ritual distinguishes an election from an opinion poll. Secondly, there is the sense of fair play and *due process*. Although there are other acknowledged forms of due process than elections, in our populist age voting is almost universally regarded as the 'proper' way to take decisions about who should govern. Thirdly, elections contribute to legitimacy through their *representative* nature – however incomplete and approximate. Fourthly, elections confer legitimacy through *participation*: those who participate in a decision making process feel some obligation to accept the final verdict whether they like it or not.

Direct election is now the most authoritative mandate for government. It satisfies all the requirements of *ritual*, *due process*, *representation* and *participation*. It allows presidents in France and the United States to dominate their political systems with a public authority unmatched by most monarchs or indirectly elected presidents or prime ministers in parliamentary systems. In 1962 De Gaulle deliberately enhanced the authority of the French presidency by holding a referendum which made the president subject to direct election instead of being chosen indirectly by national and local government politicians. Supporters of the EEC advocated direct election to the European Assembly because they thought a parliament based on direct election (even on a low turn-out) would carry more political clout than one composed of representatives from national legislatures.

Free and fair elections provide the surest mantle of legitimacy. When elections become entangled in a web of corruption the nominal winner can soon lose authority – as witness Bhutto in Pakistan, Marcos in the Philippines, or even Nixon in the USA. But even when elections are rigged governments normally gain more authority from holding them than they lose through allegations of unfairness.

What is being legitimised?

Elections legitimise established authority. At its narrowest, that might just be the *government* of the day. But it might also be the *regime* – the established system of government. More broadly still, elections can help to establish the *political community* – the boundaries of the nation state itself. In the 1983 Northern Ireland referendum on remaining in the United Kingdom, the issue was whether the political community should be redefined. Catholics boycotted the referendum, resulting in a turn-out of only 59 per cent. Although 99 per cent of voters supported remaining in the United Kingdom, low turn-out meant that the result certainly did not strengthen the political community in Northern Ireland.

But the unique achievement of genuinely competitive elections is to legitimise *opposition*. Free elections convey the message that disagreement is not disloyalty, that there is more than one side to every political issue. In Britain, the 'outs' are given the title of 'Her Majesty's Loyal Opposition' and opposition parties represented in parliament are offered state subsidies in the form of money for research and free access to the radio and television. This model of legitimate opposition both reflects and permeates other social institutions such as schools, firms and even the family. In this way competitive elections help to sustain a diverse and tolerant society. Contradicting the thesis that elections are irrelevant to policy outcomes, some critics argue that legitimate opposition produces 'adversary politics' in which party competition generates excessive and damaging oscillations in government policy, especially on economic issues (Finer, 1980). But the benefits from forcing governments to accept the legitimacy of opposition far outweigh these costs. Finer's (1980, p. 208) criticism of the British electoral system comes dangerously (if unintentionally) close to a criticism of democracy itself:

> The system generates uncertainty. The electoral system makes the outcome of future elections highly speculative, and this generates the expectation that policies may alter very drastically.

Quite! For those who cannot cope with political uncertainty we do not recommend competitive elections.

Once the principle of competitive elections is adopted, the infra-structure follows. Competitive elections legitimise the *tools of opposition* as well as the principle. Contested elections require access to the media for all major parties, the freedom to mobilise support and a respect for due process. One technicality follows another. The Indian election of 1977, which threw Indira Gandhi out of office, illustrates this. In order to hold a competitive election, Indira Gandhi had to suspend the state of emergency, let her opponents out of jail and restore the freedom of the press. Even if she had won the election, the mere fact of the election would still have had an enormous effect on the status of the opposition.

Finally, elections legitimise *ordinary people*. When based on universal suffrage, they provide a symbol of political equality. In addition to giving people a mechanism for protecting themselves against government, elections provide a moral status which acts as a further shield. The symbol of equality is misleading, of course;

there is no absolute political equality in Western democracies, any more than there is social or economic equality. But universal suffrage places limits on the extent of inequality: the fact that we are all equal on election day limits the degree of exploitation on other days. And the right to vote is also a source of self-respect which is the most important limit on exploitation of all.

Conversely, a limited suffrage encourages the oppression of the disenfranchised. Pomper (1980) demonstrates that racial bias in both lynchings and legal executions was higher in those periods of American history when blacks could not vote. Black slaves were an exception: though denied the vote, they were too valuable to be lynched. But after the abolition of slavery, blacks were first of all enfranchised, then effectively disenfranchised, before being re-enfranchised in relatively recent years, and their treatment followed this cycle of enfranchisement. In most European countries, immigrant workers are not allowed to vote, a restriction which reinforces their low social status and makes them easy political targets in harsh economic times. In Britain, pacifists who had refused to do military service during the First World War were excluded from the franchise for some years after it, and electoral ostracism was clearly intended to encourage social ostracism.

Elections based on universal suffrage do not yield perfect political equality. This is obvious but important. What is less obvious, and therefore more important, is that denial of the suffrage strengthens political inequality. And political inequality encourages social and economic discrimination.

Legitimacy in whose eyes?

Like beauty, legitimacy is in the eye of the beholder. We have to ask not only what elections legitimise but in whose eyes they do so. Domestically, the authorities need to establish legitimacy with the *population* generally and *opposition* parties in particular. They will also need legitimacy in the eyes of the *military* if they are not to be swept away by a coup. Internationally, governments of small countries need to be seen as legitimate by *powerful neighbours* if they are to avoid invasion. Whether large or small, governments benefit from legitimacy in the eyes of the *international community*. Foreign ambassadors have an easier task if they can claim that their government was democratically elected. And as long as the claim can be made, who is going to disprove it? After all, potential critics are often standing on shaky ground themselves. Finally, nervous governments need legitimacy *in their own eyes*. Evidence of popular support in an election, whether rigged or not, offers reassurance which insecure politicians crave. (In Chapter 2 we described the classic example of Gomulka's use of the 1957 Polish election to strengthen his government's authority internally and, more critically, externally.)

Strengthen Elites?

Elections are normally analysed as channels through which voters influence leaders. But even in free democracies they can also be viewed from the top down, as institutions which expand the authority of the rulers over the ruled. For some authors such as Ginsberg (1982) this is the major function of elections – competitive elections as well as elections without choice. In the United States constitution, the president is given certain powers subject to the 'advice and consent' of the Senate. In Europe the original function of parliaments was to mobilise support for already established authority. Medieval kings sought consent, not advice, when they called a parliament. Equally with elections. 'Since the nineteenth century', notes Ginsberg, 'governments have ruled through elections even when they have sometimes been ruled by them.' Elections strengthen the political elite in three ways – by increasing the stability, effectiveness and authority of the system they control.

Stability

By giving the vote to potentially disruptive groups, elites can enhance the stability of the political system. Historically the main reason for granting extensions to the suffrage was fear of instability if nothing were done. 'Participation', says Gamson (1968, p. 141), 'is not a technique of decision but a technique of persuasion.' It is psychologically difficult for voters to rebel against choices they helped to make, even if the boundaries of the choice are drawn elsewhere. For elites, controlled participation through the ballot box is preferable to uncontrolled riots or a demand for a different type of political system.

Even more than elections, referendums turn voters into accomplices of elites. Referendums in Britain during the 1970s – on the EEC, on devolution in Scotland and Wales and on secession in Northern Ireland – were all bare-faced attempts by government to shift the *responsibility* of decision onto the electorate. That certainly did not mean that government always shifted *choice* to the electorate. On EEC membership, the government used its considerable powers of persuasion to achieve the result it wanted: It won 67.2 per cent of the vote for continued EEC membership. When British public opinion turned against the Common Market, opposition was muted by the nature of the referendum result. The people did not decide to join the EEC but they ratified a government decision against leaving it. They became accomplices after the fact. On devolution the government was more agnostic and used an indecisive referendum result as an excuse for inaction.

Elections cannot provide a complete guarantee of stability, however. The new democratic regime in Spain had all the authority of the electoral process behind it but only survived the 1981 revolt by sections of the military because it was protected (in the 1980s!) by the royal authority of King Juan Carlos. Where central authority is already weak, elections are rarely sufficient to bolster the regime, as many ex-colonies discovered after independence. But where authority is already established, as with many European countries in the nineteenth century, an extension of the suffrage reinforces authority at the centre and thus contributes to political stability.

But even in potentially revolutionary situations, and even when the government's authority is at its weakest, elections can provide a mechanism for a smooth, rather than chaotic, transfer of power. They allow the government to *exit gracefully* and in good order. The people's frustrations and discontents are eventually transferred to the new government. That, in turn, can pave the way for a return to office by the original government. For example, in the 1970s, when Bhutto in Pakistan and Gandhi in India were both being accused of high-handed behaviour in office, Bhutto contrived to win an election while Gandhi lost one. The military intervened and hanged Bhutto; Gandhi spent some time in opposition and then returned to office as support for her opponents evaporated. Less dramatically, Heath's loss of the 1974 British election defused the national crisis over the Miner's Strike, saddled his Labour opponents with responsibility for the consequent inflation (and for most of the consequent pit closures) and set the scene for a strong Conservative comeback under Thatcher. From a system viewpoint and sometimes from an incumbent government's viewpoint also, even an election defeat can be a stabilising factor. There are worse things that can happen to a politician than losing an election!

Effectiveness

Regimes are judged by results as well as by processes. In West Germany the post-war regime was first legitimised not by elections (which surveys showed were only respected by a minority) but by economic success. Only in recent decades have elections provided the basis for legitimate government in the Federal Republic. But the crucial point is that because elected governments are often legitimate, they tend also to be relatively efficient. A government based on consent need not spend time, money and credibility on ensuring the compliance of the people; instead, these resources can be used in more productive ways which enhance the legitimacy of the regime still further. Specifically, freely elected governments have relatively few difficulties in raising taxes and armies, both of which are necessary to the effective functioning of the state. Democracy is an efficient form of government, notwithstanding the complexities of democratic procedures themselves. Thus political elites are strengthened in their position by the effectiveness of the democratic system over which they preside.

Authority

Elections enhance the authority of the state over other institutions and the voters themselves. As elected bodies, governments carry weight which is denied to other bodies such as companies, churches and local interests. Election campaigns help to build or reinforce national identities and state institutions.

Elections expand elite power in addition to containing its exercise. Elections teach voters they can choose governments but not govern themselves. Elections are devices by which elites control the masses, by which the masses control elites and, crucially, by which both combine so as to achieve a capability which neither would possess alone. Elections are neither a pure confidence trick nor an exercise in pure democracy; they are a bit of both. Authors such as Ginsberg who stress the 'top-down' nature of elections grasp an important point but then exaggerate it by first assuming that there is one single political elite and then by arguing that there is a fixed quantity of authority, to be divided between rulers and ruled, rather than expanded by cooperation between them.

Educate Voters?

As with influence, so too with information. Elections are occasions for elites and electors to teach each other something about politics. And the electoral process may itself teach both rulers and ruled something about democratic ideas. For many nineteenth-century advocates of universal suffrage, this educative function of elections was fundamental. For example Thomas Hare (1873), an advocate of proportional representation, believed that elections 'cultivate the higher qualities of man's nature, foster a love of country, a regard for public duty and a just self-respect'. What non-elected governments bestow is at best 'but the attention of the kind master to his horse or his dog'. John Stuart Mill (1859) also believed that political participation would produce a more informed, cooperative and public-spirited population.

An election is an occasion for a government to place its record and its vision before the people. During a campaign, media coverage of politics expands to include more advocacy, information and analysis than normal. And there is no doubt that the electorate responds, albeit with a quality of response that would have disappointed Hare and Mill. As Schoenbach (1983, p. 299) notes,

> Many studies have shown that voters do learn from election campaigns. They get to know the goals and policies of candidates and parties better than they did before; they become aware of the major problems facing their country; and they learn some facts about the election itself – e.g. the names of the candidates, the number of seats in political institutions, and which party holds majority support in the parliament to be

elected . . . Election campaigns, for all their faults, may be the major learning experience of democratic politics.

What precisely do voters learn from campaigns? Research on British elections suggests that three main types of information are involved: first, information required to perform the act of voting, such as the party affiliation of the candidates; secondly, basic information about party policies; and thirdly, some information about the agenda of political debate – the issues that the parties deem important and the ideological framework within which these problems are located (Blumler and McQuail, 1968). The amount of learning, however, varies enormously. Voters learn more from lively campaigns; contrast general and European elections in Britain. Also, interested and informed electors generally learn more than those who start off with limited knowledge and enthusiasm. Thus campaigns increase 'knowledge gaps' between the knowledgeable and the ignorant.

Competitive elections force people to examine the alternatives. Without an election it is easy to blame the government for unemployment but come election day the voter has to ask 'could any other government do better?' If the answer is *no*, as it was in the British election of 1983, then criticisms of the government are muted. So elections can be a powerful means of reconciling the people to hard times. Politicians in democracies have often been criticised for offering more in a campaign than they can deliver in office, encouraging people to expect more of politicians than they can ever achieve. Some commentators (for instance, Brittan, 1976) argued that competitive bidding for votes by parties desperate for electoral success would eventually threaten the survival of democratic politics. We are rather more sanguine. When parties promise the earth, voters are naturally sceptical; and the 1980s have seen Western politicians competing to deflate rather than inflate expectations. Voters find claims that nothing can be done especially convincing since they seem to go against the interests of the politicians themselves. Election campaigns can be effective at educating voters to the limits of government.

Competitive elections also educate politicians. Opinion polls, canvass returns, phone-ins and doorstep conversations all provide scope for talk-back by ordinary people. Politicians never have more incentive to listen than when an election looms and all this material does give them some chance to develop a sense of the voters' concerns. Many, not all, take advantage of the opportunity. For top leaders, cocooned in television studios and ticket-only meetings, direct contact gives way to the more impersonal but also more accurate readings of the public mood offered by opinion polls. And the message of the election result itself is of course avidly digested by politicians at every level. In general, the electoral process in a liberal democracy selects and trains a different kind of politician from those produced by force, promotion or inheritance. It does wring a little humility out of politicians (who are not by nature the most humble of people) and it does develop their ability to listen.

Influence Parties?

Elections force the voters' views into the decision-making calculus of parties. Like a student confronting an impending examination, parties must face up to the election and adjust their behaviour long before the test itself. It is the *prospect* of the test, not the test itself, that contributes to education. In the same way elections not only facilitate a choice between fixed alternatives but also influence the nature of the alternatives on offer. Elections are not just incubators of new parties and burial grounds for old ones, they are also moulds which shape the character of existing parties. Elections influence parties before, during and after elections.

Before an election, electoral appeal is one factor, though rarely the only one, in the parties' choice of candidates and policies. There is plenty of evidence that parties (and governments) avoid particular policies for fear of electoral reprisals. Fear of retribution is the single most effective way in which elections allow voters to influence parties and governments. In the United States, Pomper (1980) found that parties not only tried to implement their manifesto when elected but also used their platforms to get elected; they promised a mixture of what they themselves wanted and what they thought the public wanted. In West Germany the Social Democrats made their historic switch to a reformist programme at Bad Godesburg in 1959 because their Marxist policies seemed outdated by the post-war 'economic miracle'. In 1966 they won their reward when they entered office in coalition with the Christian Democrats.

Parties retain considerable freedom in policy formation and we should not overstate the influence of elections in this regard. The electorate as a whole knows little and care less about most areas of party policy; while many rank-and-file party activists know little and care less about what the voters think. The positive influence of the electorate on policy is concentrated mainly on just two important areas: first, on defining the broad political framework within which parties must formulate policy; and secondly, on forcing parties to attend to a few key issues within that framework.

During an election campaign moribund parties are brought back to life. Enthusiasm mounts and the pulse quickens as activists discover that at last there is something specific for them to do. Organisation is consolidated and discipline is tightened as the party enters its most critical test. In an era of opinion polls, however, the popularity of the parties is visible to all who care to see long before election day and the election campaign may not always help party morale as much as in the past.

Campaigns strengthen parties in the electorate as well. In Britain, the strength of party identification rises with the approach of an election and falls again afterwards (Miller, 1983, p. 156). In the United States election of 1980, voters who had viewed politics mainly in terms of policy during the nomination campaigns, came to see it through more partisan lenses when the summer nominating conventions were over and the election campaign proper had begun (Miller and Shanks, 1982).

After an election, parties digest the lessons of the ballot box. An election defeat stimulates changes in leadership, organisation and policies; a victory encourages complacency – leaders and policies stay the same as before. When the German Christian Democrats (CDU) held power from 1949–69 they had little need of a mass membership since they used the perks of office to mobilise support at elections. But once the CDU lost power it rapidly doubled its membership (Feist, Gullner and Liepelt, 1978, p. 176). Of course, not every party is capable of learning and applying the lessons of elections. But in the long run elections tend to preserve those parties which do.

Conclusion

Competitive elections have an image problem. They only half fulfil the 'bottom-up' functions commonly associated with them while their important 'top-down' achievements are hardly appreciated at all.

An election is normally viewed as a device which (1) produces a government and then (2) attunes the government to the concerns and preferences of the voters. Competitive elections are certainly one major influence on who governs and how, but they are not the only one. They are crude instruments rather than precise tools. The ship of state has its own momentum; changes in direction can be achieved but the difficulties are great, the time-lag considerable and the destination uncertain. Just putting new officers on the bridge does not mean that a new course will be set, let alone sustained. Furthermore, elections only tell the officers that some directions are unacceptable to the crew; they rarely give specific instructions on the new course.

Despite these weaknesses, competitive elections have other virtues. They have 'top-down' as well as 'bottom-up' functions. Above all, elections contribute to the legitimacy and hence the effectiveness of governments. They exchange influence between rulers and ruled, to their mutual benefit. They expand the authority of government while reducing (not eliminating) the likelihood of this authority being misused. In the chequered history of government, that is no mean achievement.

Further Reading

King (1981) provides a very clear review of the rather technical literature on the consequences of competitive elections. The collection edited by Castles (1982) goes into more detail. On specific countries, Rose (1984) is best for Britain and Pomper (1980) is a good guide to the United States. Wilensky (1975) is one of the best representatives of the school which employs cross-national comparisons to show that economics matter more than politics. Bunce (1981) is the main source on policy cycles; see especially chs. 3 and 7. Though based purely on the United States, Schattschneider (1960, especially ch. 8) makes some similar points, snappily. For the Marxist critique of elections under capitalism, Miliband (1969) remains one of the few clear accounts. For the effects of campaigns on voters, Blumler and McQuail (1968) is an empirical study of a British election. The impact of competitive elections on legitimacy is under-studied. This aspect of elections has received more attention in the analysis of non-competitive elections: see for example Hermet, Rose and Rouquie (1978).

References

BEVAN, A. (1952) *In Place of Fear* (London: Heinemann).
BLUMLER, J. G. and MCQUAIL, D. (1968) *Television and Politics: Its Uses and Influence* (London: Faber).
BRITTAN, S. (1976) 'The Economic Contradictions of Democracy' in A. King (ed.), *Why is Britain Becoming Harder to Govern?* (London: BBC).
BUNCE, V. (1981) *Do New Leaders Make a Difference? Executive Succession and Public Policy under Capitalism and Socialism* (Princeton: Princeton University Press).
BUTLER, D., PENNIMAN, H. and RANNEY, A. (eds) (1981) *Democracy at the Polls* (Washington, DC: American Enterprise Institute).
CASTLES, F. (1982) 'Introduction: Politics and Public Policy', in F. Castles (ed.), *The Impact of Parties* (London: Sage).
DYE, T. and ZEIGLER, H. (1981) *The Irony of Democracy* (Belmont: Wadsworth).
FEIST, U., GULLNER, M. and LIEPELT, K. (1978) 'Structural Assimilation versus Ideological Polarization', in M. Kaase and K. V. Beyme (eds), *Elections and Parties* (London: Sage).
FINER, S. (1980) *The Changing British Party System 1945–1979* (Washington, DC: American Enterprise Institute).
GAMSON, W. (1968) *Power and Discontent* (Homewood, Ill.: Dorsey).
GINSBERG, B. (1982) *The Consequences of Consent* (Reading, Mass: Addison-Wesley).
HARE, T. (1873) *The Election of Representatives* (London: Longmans).
HERMET, G., ROSE, R. and ROUQUIE, A. (eds) (1978) *Elections Without Choice* (London: Macmillan).
KING, A. (1981) 'What Do Elections Decide?', in D. Butler, H. Penniman and A. Ranney (eds), *Democracy at the Polls* (Washington, DC: American Enterprise Institute).
KIRCHEIMER, O. (1966) 'The Transformation of Western European Party Systems', in J. LaPalombara and M. Weiner (eds), *Political Parties and Political Development* (Princeton: Princeton University Press).
LINDBLOM, C. (1977) *Politics and Markets* (New York: Basic Books).
MACKENZIE, W. J. M. (1958) *Free Elections* (London: Allen & Unwin).
MILIBAND, R. (1969) *The State in Capitalist Society* (London: Weidenfeld & Nicolson).
MILL, J. S. (1859, 1948) *Considerations on Representative Government*, 1948 edn, R. McCallum (ed.), (Oxford: Blackwell).
MILLER, W. E. and SHANKS, J. M. (1982) 'Policy Directions and

Presidential Leadership: Alternative Explanations of the 1980 Presidential Election', *British Journal of Political Science*, vol. 12, pp. 299–356.

MILLER, W. L. (1983) *The Survey Method in the Social and Political Sciences: Achievements, Failures, Prospects* (London: Pinter).

PITKIN, H. F. (1967) *The Concept of Representation* (Berkeley: University of California Press).

POMPER, G. (1980) *Elections in America: Control and Influence in Democratic Politics* (New York: Longman).

PULZER, P. G. J. (1975) *Political Representation and Elections in Britain* (London: Allen & Unwin).

RICHARDSON, J. J. and JORDAN, A. G. (1979) *Governing under Pressure: the Policy Process in a Post-Parliamentary Democracy* (Oxford: Martin Robertson).

RIKER, W. H. (1982) *Liberalism against Populism* (New York: Freeman).

ROSE, R. (1978) 'Is Choice Enough? Elections and Political Authority', in G. Hermet, R. Rose and A. Rouqie (eds), *Elections Without Choice* (London: Macmillan).

ROSE, R. (1984) *Do Parties Make A Difference?* (London: Macmillan).

ROSE, R. and MACKIE, T. (1980) *Incumbency in Government: Asset or Liability?* (Glasgow: Centre for the Study of Public Policy, University of Strathclyde, Study Number 79).

SCHATTSCHNEIDER, E. (1960) *The Semi-Sovereign People* (New York: Holt, Rinehart & Winston).

SCHOENBACH, K. (1983) 'What and How Voters Learned', in J. Blumler with A. Fox (eds), *Communicating to Voters: Television in the First European Parliamentary Elections* (London: Sage).

SCHUMPETER, J. (1943) *Capitalism, Socialism and Democracy* (New York: Harper & Row).

TAYLOR, P. (1984) 'Accumulation, Legitimation and the Electoral Geographies within Liberal Democracy', in P. Taylor and J. House (eds), *Political Geography: Recent Advances and Future Directions* (London: Croom Helm).

VEBLEN, T. (1904) *The Theory of Business Enterprise* (New York: Charles Scribner's Sons).

WILENSKY, H. (1975) *The Welfare State and Equality* (Berkeley: University of California Press).

WOLINETZ, S. (1979) 'The Transformation of Western European Party Systems Revisited', *West European Politics*, vol. 2, pp. 4–28.

Index

NOTE: 'r' indicates a citation in the references listed at the end of each chapter.